Congratulations on passing the first part of the National Chiropractic Examiners national boards. Now begins the work of passing parts 2 and 3. These tests are often grouped together because the content they cover is very much the same. It is the questions and the manner in which they are asked that is different.

You cannot start the review process early enough. There is a vast amount of information that you can and will be tested on. The function of your classes and required texts are to prepare you for boards. The best preparation for boards will always be attending class and reading the required texts.

In this book I have attempted to focus on the critical pieces of information that will help the test taker earn valuable points toward earning a passing grade on these sections of the national boards. You might notice that conditions or definitions are repeated in multiple sections and that their descriptions might be slightly different. In the pediatric section the most critical aspects of the term as it relates to pediatrics are emphasized while the same term may appear again with a slightly different description in the diagnostic imagine section focusing on the aspects that are most likely to be tested in that section of the board exams.

It is highly encouraged that you start using this book immediately after passing part one in conjunction with your normal class work. The function of all classes is to prepare students for boards. The purpose of boards is to ensure that you are a becoming a capable chiropractor. What information is most likely going to appear on the midterm or final of a class is also most likely going to be information that will appear on boards.

There is no way that a couple hundred pages of condensed material could ever replaced the thousands of pages of detailed information in the required texts and they should be used together with this review. When you find something particularly difficult or important add it to this review. If you find a new or better way to recall a particular piece of information, add it is the review. If you are getting lost is the sea of information and not sure where to focus your time and energy, look to this review.

This review can be a helpful tool to cram at the last moment for exam but is can be so much more if used correctly. Good luck.

Associated Clinical Sciences

Dermatology

Most skin infections are caused by Staph.

Pustule - small elevation of skin filled with lymph or pus (Staph infection)

Scar - fibers connective tissue formed in the dermis at the site of a wound, burn or sore that is healing.

Freckle - a hyper pigmented macule found in the sun exposed areas.

Dark skin - indicates increased production of melatonin; Addison's disease, pregnancy, hemochromatosis.

Light (white) skin - indicates decreased production of melatonin; albinism, vitiligo.

Red skin lesions - indicate increased blood; inflammation or vascularization.

Blueish skin lesions - indicate increased deoxygenated blood (cyanosis); shock, anemia.

Purple skin lesions - suspect Kaposi's sarcoma.

Orange skin lesions - indicate excessive Carotenoid consumption, myxedema or diabetes mellitus. Carotenoids (beta-carotene) are covered to vitamin A in the body and found in orange colored fruits and vegetables (carrots).

Yellowing of the skin indicates Jaundice that results from increased levels of bilirubin that is associated with liver disease.

Blue skin can indicate a blocked artery while red skin can indicate a blocked vein.

Raynaud's Phenomenon - sympathetic stimulation triggers a triphasic color change from normal to pale, (white) then blue and finally red.

Vesicle - small blister like elevation on the skin filled with serous fluid seen with herpes, chickenpox and more.

Bullae - large blisters or skin vesicles filled with fluid, also called blebs associated with pemphigus.

Wheal - a round elevation of skin with a white center and pale red periphery accompanied by pruritus.

Patch - a macule with some surface changes such as scaling or wrinkling.

Nodule - a small, raised lesion (node) or aggregation of cells that is firm.

Cyst - an encapsulated fluid filled mass in the dermis or subcutaneous tissue. A sac-like packet of membranous tissue that contains fluid, air or other other substance.

Wart - skin lesion cased by a human papilloma virus (HPV) that are flesh colored and firm. Common warts are often found on the fingers, plantar warts appear on the soles of the feet and genital warts which are a sexually transmitted disease.

Nevus (Mole) - a benign neoplasm of the pigment forming cells (nevus cells). Uniform brown color maybe slightly raised. A nevus that changes shape or color should be evaluated for removal.

Papule - small red elevated area of the skin, solid and circumscribed. Often precede vesicle or pustule formation. Associated with measles, syphilis, warts and more.

Macule - small (under .5 cm) discolored spots or patches on the skin, neither elevated or depressed (flat) that can be seen but not felt. Ex: vitiligo, freckles, pellagra and more.

Melasma (Chloasma) - a patchy macular hyperpigmentation (brown) on the face that is exacerbated by sunlight. Seen with pregnancy "mask of pregnancy."

Tumor - a solid mass that is greater than 1 cm in diameter and extends deep into the dermis and typically describes a new growth.

Plaque - an elevated plateau (plate) like lesion greater than .5 cm in diameter described as solid and superficial is most commonly associated with psoriasis.

Keloid - overgrowth of scar tissue due to abnormal amounts of collagen in the scar tissue. Sharply elevated, irregular shape, progressive enlargement of a scar. Most common in black folks.

Stratum Corneum - the outermost later of the epidermis consisting of corneocytes, flat dead cells with no nuclei or organelles.

Scales - thickened stratum corneum (outer layer of skin), usually dry and white (silver) in appearance that occurs when the skin fails to shed dead cells. The scales are an accumulation of dead skin cells.

Psoriasis - dry silvery scales usually on the extensor surfaces. Ex: elbows and knees. "Silver Scales and Pitted Nails" psoriasis is an inflammatory rash with sharply demarcated silvery scales. Auspitz sign is bleeding from the spot scales have been scraped off. Biopsy revels, hyperkeratosis, decreased granular later with acanthotic epidermis and inflammatory infiltrates.

Atopic Dermatitis - a skin lesion that affects the flexor surfaces (fossas) that come together and make "contact."

Crust - liquid debris (pus/serum) that has dried on the surface of the skin.

Fissure - deep cracks in the skin that can extend into the epidermis.

Erosion - loss the epidermis.

Ulcer - loss of the epidermis and part or all of the dermis.

Acrochordon (skin tag) - small, soft, benign, typically pedunculate common skin lesion (neoplasm) that is usually harmless.

Actinic Keratosis - a reddish, ill-marginated skin lesion that presents with patches 1-10 mm in diameter with rough yellow-brown scale. A precancerous neoplasm of the epidermis caused by the UV portion of sunlight.

Seborrheic Keratosis - brown or black skin lesion is one of the most common noncancerous skin growths found in older adults. Described as well marginated with a "pasted-on" appearance that can vary in size; oval to round in shape with a greasy appearance.

Seborrheic Dermatitis - dandruff

Herpes Zoster HSV 3 (Shingles)- painful vesicular lesions that follows a dermatome. Typically unilateral on the truck of the body, but not always.

Herpes Simplex Virus 1(HSV 1) - Cold core, fever blister, painful lesion around the mouth, can be found in the general region, for boards think HSV1 mouth (herpes labialis), HSV 2 genitals.

Molluscum Cantagiosum small, smooth, *dome shaped,* painless skin lesion caused by a pox virus infection of epidermal cells.

Albinism - melanocytes do not produce melanin no tissue pigment from birth.

Vitiligo - acquired idiopathic destruction of melanocytes resulting in patches of depigmentation (often having hyper-pigmented border), depigmentation of skin after development.

Tinea infections - Mycotic (fungal) skin diseases occurring on various parts of the body.

- t. barbae - beard
- t. capitis - head
- t. corporis - body, AKA ringworm
- t. cruris - groin/jock
- t. pedis - foot
- t. unguium - nails, AKA onychomycosis

Tina diagnosis is confirmed with a Wood's lamp test (UV light).

Yeast Infection - caused by candida albicans, in the mouth it is called thrush.

Tinea Versicolor - asymptomatic lesions varying color from white to brown.

Leukoplakia - white precancerous lesion of the mucous membrane.

Stasis ulceration - commonly seen lower leg and ankle region with diabetes mellitus.

Furuncle - staphylococcal infection of a hair follicle or sebaceous (oil secreting) gland.

Carbuncle(s) - multiple furuncles ("car" load)

Wen - sebaceous cyst, keratinous cysts that are lined with epithelial cells and contain epithelial debris.

Miliaria - AKA prickly heat or heat rash, a condition of blocked sweat ducts inflammation of sweat glands appears as red lumps or blisters that cause itchiness or a prickly feeling.

Urticaria - AKA hives, characterized by formation of wheals and hives caused by an allergy. Allergic reaction.

Dermatomyositis - Heliotropic rash on the eyelid.

Stasis Dermatitis - persistent inflammation of the skin in the lower extremities with a tendency toward brown pigmentation. Associated with venous incompetence. (Diabetes M.)

Contact Dermatitis - red itchy rash caused by direct contact with irritant or an allergic reaction to a substance. Diaper rash is type of contact dermatitis. It is not contagious or life threatening but it is uncomfortable.

Rubella - AKA German measles, maculopapular rash 2-3 days. Mother is vaccinated to protect their newborn.

Rubeola - AKA measles, acute contagious disease ~~ catarrhal (inflammation of mucous membranes) sym~~ colored macular eruptions. Koplik's spots - small r~~ centers on the oral mucosa that usually precede c~~

Varicella - AKA chickenpox, childhood disease ch~~ sub-dermal lesions that pass through stages of ~~ crust. Most common complication is secondary~~

Acne - papule, pustule, comedones and inflamed nodules. Inflame~~ follicle or sebaceous gland.

Acne Vulgaris - Pimples of adolescence, inflamed sebaceous glands. Most common cutaneous disorder.

Comedones - blackheads or open, white heads are closed, a clogged skin pore or hair follicle.

Erythema Nodosum - multiple non-ulcerating nodules that are tender and bilateral.

Rosacea - chronic inflammation of the nose, cheeks and forehead, MC in middle-age to older people. Characterized by papules, pustules, telangiectasia, erythema and hyperplasia of the soft tissue of the nose. AKA Acne Rosacea

Pityriasis rosea - Tan-pink skin lesion that presents with oval papule and plaques preceded by a "herald" or "mother" patch. Characterized by Christmas tree pattern of distribution on the trunk this is an acute, self limiting inflammatory skin condition with unknown etiology.

Impetigo - superficial vesiculopustular lesions with bullae (blister) formation and honey colored crusts. Most commonly found the face and the hands of children. Caused by strep or staph and is spread by scratching.

Ichthyosis - Noninflammatory lesion of increased keratinization, dry skin (xeroderma), AKA fish skin or scaly skin.

Hyperhydrosis - overactive sweat glands.

___us - pinhead sized papules that coalesce to form rough, scaly, ___ular, blue/purple lesions. Intense pruritis with lesions concentrated ___ or surfaces of arms, trunk and genitalia. Inflammatory pruritic ___ase.

Lichenification - Chronic dermatitis, constant itching resulting in patches of rough, thick skin. Epidermal thickening, visible and palpable thickening of the skin.

Induration - an increase the fibers element of tissue resulting in loss of elasticity and pliability. The skin feels thick and firm compared to normal.

Circinate - an arc shaped skin lesion; urticaria.

Annular - a ring shaped skin lesion with active borders and most often a clear center; ringworm infection.

Discoid - a disc shaped skin lesion with an elevated and active boarder.

Discoid Lupus Erythematosus - autoimmune disease that presents with red to purple papule and plaques with scaling and follicular plugging that causes depressed atrophic lesions (carpet tacking) in the sub exposed areas.

Nummular - an elevated coin shaped skin lesion; nummular eczema.

Target (Bull's Eye) - a skin lesion composed of 2-3 concentric rings; lyme disease.

Reticular - multiple skin lesions that are arranged in a net like distribution; oral lichen planus.

Confluent - multiple skin lesions that blend into adjacent lesions; tina versicolor.

Herpetiform - a group of multiple vesicles; herpes.

Morbilliform - a group of macularpapular lesions blending in the adjacent lesions; measles.

Zosteriform - a group of lesions distributed linearly along a dermatome; herpes zoster (shingles).

Serpiginous - chronic, slowing progressive condition of multiple skin lesions that form along a curved or wavy line that leaves scar tissue below and remains active above.

Photodistribution - skin lesion that are found in areas that are exposed to sunlight.

Koebner's Phenomenon - multiple skin lesions in areas of previous trauma to the skin; lichen planus.

Erysipelas - "St. Anthony's fire" is a red fiery growing lesion. Acute febrile disease, cellulitis, vesicles and bullae. Etiology: streptococcal.

Pemphigus - uncommon, potentially fatal skin condition characterized by formation of bullae or bulbous a large vesicle on the on skin and/or mucus membranes. It can be fatal and is most common associated with Jewish Men.

Dermatitis herpetiformis - chronic inflammatory disease characterized by erythematous, papular, vesicular, bullous, or pustular lesions with tendency to grouping. Intense burning and itching, primarily extensor surfaces.

Xerotic Eczema - low humidity dry skin that occurs in the winder and presents with dry, fissured skin of the trunk and extremities that primarily affects the elderly and the lower legs of all age groups.

Alopecia Areata (AA) - auto-immune disorder in which the hair falls out unpredictability in round patches. Patchy hair loss.

Alopecia Capitis Totalis - complete loss of scam (head) hair, with no change in body hair.

Alopecia universalis - hair loss over entire body.

Hirsuitism - excessive hair growth in unusual places, especially in women. Indicates increased androgen production or metabolism. Often seen with pregnancy.

Addison's disease (hypocortisolism) - decreased adrenocortical hormones resulting in bronze colored skin, irregular patches of vitiligo.

Cushing's syndrome - increased glucocorticoids resulting in edema, hair loss, skin discoloration, pink and purple striae (stretch marks).

Icterus - AKA jaundice, pigmentation of the tissues, membranes and secretions with bile pigments.

Paronychia - bacterial or fungal infection of the tissue folds around the nails of the hands and feet.

Scabies - mite that burrows under the skin, causes intense pruritus. Caused by parasitic mite.

Burrow - a linear trail produced by a parasite as it travels through the skin.

Pediculosis - Lice; called P. Pubis in the pubic region (Crabs), P. Corporis in the Body and P. Capitis on the head.

Pruritus - itching, the unpleasant sensation that provokes scratching, cutaneous hyperesthesia (pruritic)

Aphthous Stomatitis (canker sore) - small painful ulcer, pitted erythematous lesion of the mouth. (ulcer)

Intertrigo - superficial dermatitis, areas of redness in *folds of skin* that is caused by moisture, friction and sweat retention.

Nummular Eczema - discrete coin shaped lesion that coalesce to form patches that ooze and crust over. Most common in old men and young women.

Squamous Cell Carcinoma - a malignant neoplasm of keratinocytes it is the second most common form of skin cancer occurring on the unexposed areas of the body. Unlike other types of skin cancer it can spread to the nearby tissues, bones and lymph nodes.

Bowen's Disease - is squamous cell carcinoma in situ of the skin that presents with erythematous, scaling, crusting, well-marginated patch.

Basal Cell Carcinoma (BCC) - a malignant neoplasm arising from the basal cells of the epidermis is the most common human malignancy. 3 Types

Nodular BCC - the most common type of BCC that presents with a shiny blue to black papule most commonly found on the forehead or sun exposed areas.

Superficial BCC - most commonly found on the thorax presents with red, scaling, ell demarcated eczematous appearing patch.

Scletotic BCC (Scarring or morpheaform BCC) - a white atrophic, slightly eroded or crusted plaque that has a scar like appearance is the least common type of BCC.

Malignant Melanoma - a cancerous neoplasm of the pigment forming melanocytes (nevus cells) that present with irregularly shaped, colored papule or plaque. Approximately half of malignant melanoma arise for a nevus (mole).

The ABCD of Melanoma;
Asymmetry
Border irregularity
Color variation
Diameter greater than 6 mm.

Principles of Malignant Melanoma; (1) Horizontal growth phase make surgical removal a possible treatment if detected early enough. (2) The prognosis is related to the thickness of the tumor. (3) Clinical criteria allow for earl diagnosis of malignant melanoma which is critical to effective treatment.

Lentigo - benign multicolored skin lesion with well defined margin (edge) found on the sun exposed areas, especially the head and neck that maybe elevated, most common in elderly patients.

Mycosis Fungoides (Alibert-Bazin Syndrome) - the most common form of cutaneous T-Cell lymphoma that affects the skin but may progress internally over time that can produce a variety of skin lesions. This is NOT a fungal infection. That is the key piece of information.

Sexually Transmitted Diseases

<u>Catarrhal</u> – Inflammation of the mucus membrane in the body.

<u>Pelvic Inflammatory Disease</u> (PID) - any kind of serious infection of the female pelvic, such as uterus, fallopian tubes or ovaries. The infection may or may not be sexually transmitted. Most common cause is gonorrhea.

<u>Gonorrhea</u> - gram negative, Neisseria gonorrhea-diplococcus bacteria that most commonly presents with dysuria and discharge of pus from the urethra, contagious catarrhal inflammation (genital mucus membranes). The most common joint to be affected is the knee. In men Gonorrhea can cause sterility, in women it can cause Salpingitis (inflammation of the fallopian tubes). In babies it can lead to blindness, opthalmia neonatorum or neonatal conjunctivitis that is contracted when the newborn pass through the birth canal of mother infected with either Neisseria gonorrhea or Chlamydia trachomatis.

<u>Nongonococcal Urethritis</u> - Clinically resembles gonococcal urethritis, caused by Chlamydia trachomatis, obligate intracellular bacteria. Presents with copious yellow mucopurulent discharge.

<u>Chlamydia</u> – Most Common STD; causes non-gonococcal urethritis and is the, primary cause of Reiter's syndrome.

<u>Lymphogranduloma Venereum</u> - caused by any one of 3 different types (serovars) of the bacteria Chlamydia trachomatis. Note: This infection is not caused by the same bacteria that cause genital Chlamydia. Presents with ulcerations of the external genitalia with prominent involvement of the lymph nodes of the groin resulting in unilateral lymph node enlargement and can produce pelvic pain, swelling and rectal strictures. Infection detected by Frei Test, developed in 1925.

<u>Moniliasis (Candidiasis)</u> - caused by the fungus candida albicans and produces white discharge. In the mouth of a child the Candida infection is called Thrush. In women candida infection of the vagina may also be known as a yeast infection.

Trichomoniasis - common STD caused by the parasite Tichomonas vaginalis. Men typically cannot tell they are infected. Frothy greenish, yellow vaginal discharge with irritation and soreness of the vulva, perineum, and thighs with dyspareunia and dysuria. Distinct putrid odor is common.

Gardnerella vaginalis - caused by gram negative, anaerobic bacilli can occur spontaneously in the vagina or be sexually transmitted presents with characteristic malodorous (fish smelling) discharge and clue cells.

Clue Cells - vaginal epithelial cells with a distinctive stippled appearance from being covered in bacteria.

Syphilis (Lues) - caused by treponema pallidum (spirochete), a common STD spread through vaginal, anal or oral sex presents with chancers (sores) on the genitals that are usually painless but spread the infection. Contact with the sores spreads syphilis which is treated with penicillin.

Syphilis: Can be transmitted through the placenta resulting in congenital syphilis.

Congenital Syphilis:

1. Saber Shin/Saber Blade Tibia – sharp anterior bowing of tibia
2. Saddle Nose – Loss of height because of collapse bridge of the nose
3. Rhagades - fissures or cracks at the angles of the mouth and nose.
4. Interstitial Keratitis – inflammation of the cornea can lead to scarring/ blindness.
5. Hutchinson's teeth – Abnormal notched and peg shaped teeth.
6. Hutchinson's triad – deafness, Hutchinson's teeth and interstitial keratitis.

3 Stages of Syphilis;

1. <u>Primary Stage</u>: Hard Chancre is singular and painless, caused by spirochete Treponema Pallidum. This stage can last up to 8 weeks.

2. <u>Secondary Stage</u>: from 8 weeks to 2 years characterized by a widespread or diffuse maculopapular rash, a flat red area covered with confluent bumps. condylomata lata (flat warts on the vulva) and tiny brown spots on thorax, soles and palms.

3. <u>Latent Syphilis</u> - an asymptomatic state that may last for months to years, this is an infectious stage.

4. <u>Tertiary Stage</u>: After many (25) years affects the cardiovascular and central nervous systems with the potential for liver involvement. This stage is characterized by;

    a. <u>Tabes dorsalis</u> – loss of coordinated movement due to syphilitic infection of the spinal cord.

    b. <u>Gumma</u> - small soft swelling in the connective tissue of the liver, brain, testes and heart.

    c. Cannot be transmitted during this stage, non-infectious.

    d. Posterior Columns get destroyed

    e. Aortic Valve of the heart is most affected

<u>Dark Field Microscopy</u> used to test for (diagnose) <u>syphilis</u>, glows bright green. Treat with penicillin.

<u>Venereal Disease Research Laboratory (VDLR) test</u> - blood test for syphilis is positive a few days after the chancer appears.

Most Common Syphilitic Chancre is painless well defined ulcer.

Molluscum Contagiosum – caused by virus of same name. Fleshy to grey papule that become pearly white with caseous core. Viral skin infection that causes *dome shaped lesions* that are round, firm, painless and range in size. Common infection of children and adults that spreads through person to person contact or contact with an infected object.

Chancroid - caused by hemophilus ducreyi a gram neg. bacilli; presents with soft *painful* ulcerative lesions (open sores) around the genitals of men and women and suppurative inflammation in the regional lymphnodes. Rare in the USA but highly infectious.

Genital Herpes – Herpes Simplex Virus 2 (HSV-2) most common on genitals, HSV-1 most common on lips or mouth. Herpes Simplex Viruses can causes aseptic meningitis in the neonate. Herpes is a recurrent infection, the gift that keeps on giving.

Genital Warts – AKA Condylomata acuminata caused by Human Papilloma Virus (HPV) warts first appear soft, moist, pink to red and grow rapidly becoming peculated resulting in Cauliflower eruptions that becomes a painful ulcer. Cervical Cancer, Cervical Dysplasia and Vulvar Cancer can be caused by HPV infection.

AIDS - Caused by the retro virus Human Immunodeficiency Virus (HIV) that replicates in the lymphatics.

ELISA - HIV screening test – Enzyme Linked ImmunoSorbent Assay (inexpensive)

Western Blot Lab Test - is the most accurate HIV test (99.9%) (expensive)

HIV associated conditions; the most common is Pneumocystis Carinii a type of pneumonia. Giardia Lambia (diarrhea) and Kaposi Sarcoma a cancerous skin lesions.

Suppression of the immune system in HIV is directly related to the destruction of T-Helper cells.

Those at the highest risk for HIV are homosexual male IV drug users those with the least risk are drug free homosexual females.

Breast feeding is contraindicated for HIV patients.

PAP SMEAR, pap test for cervical cancer. A sample of cells are taken from the tip of the cervix and surrounding structures. Results are categorized;

I - Normal

II - Atypical Benign

III - Dysplasia, Atypical undetermined

IV - Suspected Malignancy, in situ

V - Malignancy

Chlamydia - The most common STD, causes non-gonococcal urethritis and is also the primary cause of Reiter's syndrome. Pelvic pain and swelling, rectal stricture. Causes; Lymphogranuloma venerum (chronic infection of the lymphatic system), epididymitis, proctitis, cervicitis and salpingitis.

Granuloma Inguinale (Donovanosis) - caused by Kledsiella granulomatis formally known as Calymmatobacerium granulomatis presents with large irregular genital ulcers the form keloid like scars upon healing. Much more common in underdeveloped nations.

Hepatitis B - a liver infection caused by the Hepatitis B virus (HBV) is transmitted through the blood, semen or other bodily fluids from an infected person enter the body of an uninfected person.

Geriatrics

Ageism - discrimination of the elderly.

Geriatrics - providing care for patients over 65 years of age.

Common Conditions Related to Aging;

Senile Dementia - mental deterioration in old age, loss of memory and los of control over the bodily function that can lead to cerebral failure.

Osteopenia - generalized weakness of bones that occurs when the body does not produce new bone at the same rate is reabsorbs old bone.

Spinal Stenosis - narrowing of the spinal canal that compresses the spinal cord and/or spinal nerves resulting in pain, cramping, weakness and/or numbness.

Osteoporosis - generalized decrease in density of bone (porous bone) resulting in fractures.

Falls - endogenous caused by meds or medical condition(s), exogenous caused by inability to navigate obstacles. Falls are the leading cause of fatal injury in the elderly and the most common cause of nonfatal trauma resulting in hospitalization.

Conditions Complicated by Aging;

Heart Disease (cardiovascular disease) - narrowing/blocking of blood vessels, structural wear and tear of the heart.

Diabetes - increased blood sugar levels

Stroke - disruption of blood flow to the brain causing cell death.

Depression - mood disorder with feelings of worthlessness and helplessness that is common in the elderly.

Physiological Changes of Aging:
Decreased renal function
Increased cellular mutations
Decreased function and capacity of metabolism
Decreased muscular strength with aging and inactivity

Neurological Changes of Aging:
Decreased rate and amplitude of electrical transmission
Decreased sensitivity of receptors, free nerve endings
Decreased thirst mechanism
Decreased mental (cognitive) function/ability.
Increased Peripheral Neuropathy

Cardiovascular Changes of Aging:
Decreased cardiac output
Cardiac Muscle Atrophy
Decreased sensitivity to catecholamines.
Decreased elasticity of arterial system (wall thickening).

Gastrointestinal Changes of Aging:
Decreased GI motility
Decreased acid (HCl) production

Respiratory Changes of Aging
Thickening of the Alveolar Wall
Decreased Vital Capacity
Decreased flow and diffusion rates across cell membranes.
Decreased ciliary function

Genitourinary Changes of Aging:
Decreased renal function
Decreased glomerular filtration, reabsorption and secretion.
Thickening of the glomerular membrane.
Loss of neurological and muscular activity of the urinary tact
Prostate enlargement

As age increased the risk of prostate cancer also increase to 100% at age 80.

Brain Changes of Aging;
Decreased weight of brain tissue
Decreased production of Acetylcholine
Decreased production of dopamine and other neurotransmitters

Sleep Changes of Aging;
REM sleep decreased with age
Decreased motion during sleep

Skin Changes of Aging;
Increased thickness of skin
Decreased subcutaneous fat layers
Decreased blood flow to peripheral skin
Decreased sensory input.

Geriatric patients' most common complaint is pain due to DJD that most that commonly affects the large weight bearing joints.

Tinney Gait Balance Test - have the patient stand, walk across the room quickly, turn around and return. Assess the patient's balance indicating what their risk of falling is. Also called the Performance Oriented Mobility Assessment (POMA).

Folstein's Mini Mental Exam - 30 point questionnaire that is used to determine the mental capacity or cognitive impairment of elderly patients to screen for dementia.

Claudication - pain caused by a lack of blood flow, most common in the legs but can affect the arm too.

Arterial Claudication - the pain is exacerbated by extortion and received by rest, walking starts/aggravates the pain and sitting relieves it.

Neurogenic Claudication - pain is caused by decreased nerve supply from SOL (DJD) encroaching the IVF. The pain is relived by flexion. (no pain associated with riding a bike)

Heart Disease is the leading killer of elderly patients.

Left Sided Heart Failure
- <u>Systemic Hypertension</u> - high blood pressure.
- <u>Pulmonary Edema</u> - accumulation of fluid in the lungs.
- <u>Pitting Edema</u> in the lower extremity - accumulation of fluid in the legs
- <u>Ascites</u> (fluid in the abdomen) -
- <u>Jugular Vein distention</u> - increased pressure in the superior vena cava.
- <u>Nocturnal Dyspnea</u> - shortness of breath and coughing at night.

Right Sided Heart Failure
- <u>Pitting Edema</u> - pressing with fingers will leave a depression (pitting).
- <u>Ascites</u> - more than 25 mL of fluid in the peritoneal cavity.
- <u>Cor Pulmonale</u> - RT ventricular enlargement.
- <u>Hepatomegaly</u> - enlarged liver, portal hypertension.
- <u>Jugular Vein Distention</u>
- <u>Esophageal Varices</u> - distended veins of esophagus from portal hypertension.
- <u>Hemorrhoids</u> - distended veins of the rectum.
- <u>Testicular Varicosities</u> - distended veins within the scrotum, bag of worms.

<u>Hypertension</u> - a rise in systolic and diastolic pressure is thought to be an adaptation to the increased hypo-perfusion of the brain with aging.

<u>Hip</u> - most common fracture seen in the elderly.

<u>Macular Degeneration</u> - the most common visual problem in the elderly that occurs when the central portion of the retina (macula) deteriorates and fatty deposits called druse appear under the retina. Presents with blurred or fuzzy vision that is progressive.

<u>Rodent Ulcer</u> - basal cell carcinoma, common on the nose.

<u>Cardiac hypertrophy</u> - occurs from heart pumping blood to less compliant arteries and with higher blood pressure.

<u>Orthostatic Hypotension</u> - drop in systolic bp 20 mmhg or more when changing body position, ex from a recumbent position to standing.

<u>Tonometer</u> - used to check the eyes for glaucoma.

Glaucoma - is a group of eye conditions that damage the topic nerve and causes irreversible decreased visual acuity and eventually blindness. Any loss of vision caused by glaucoma is permanent but it is possible to stop or slow the progression of vision loss with treatment.

Primary Open Angle Glaucoma - the most common type of glaucoma that develops slowly overtime (insidious) without pain due to increased intraocular pressure from clogged drainage canals resulting in progressive optic nerve damage that manifests as gradual loss of the visual field starting with the peripheral vision.

Primary Closed Angle Glaucoma - can present with sudden or insidious onset. Sudden onset is associated with sever pain, blurred vision, redness of the eye and nausea. It is believed that this type of glaucoma is caused by the iris bowing forward blocking (close) the trabecular meshwork (drainage) increasing intraocular pressure, causing (damage) to the optic nerve resulting in loss of vision. Also called Narrow Angle Glaucoma.

Normal Tension Glaucoma - the optic nerve is damaged while the intraocular pressure is within the normal range (12-22 mm/hg) with unknown cause.

Secondary Glaucoma - can result from any disease, trauma, drug or procedure that increased the intraocular pressure causing damage to the optic nerve and results in loss of vision.

Arcus senilus - gray opaque ring at the edge of the cornea. Can be caused by autonomic dysfunction from diabetes, impaired venous return, prolonged bed rest, hypoglycemia, anemia or drugs such diuretics, antihypertensives, antidepressants, sedatives.

Blood glucose and WBC count do not change with age.

Alzheimer's disease - irreversible progressive brain disorder that results in loss of memory, thinking skills and eventually the ability to perform simple tasks. Alzheimer's the most common cause of dementia in adults over 60. Diagnosis is confirmed at autopsy because there is no test or image that indicates Alzheimers.

Arterial bifurcation and facial planes are sites for normal arterial degenerative changes.

Osteoporosis - translates to porous bone, this condition is characterized as a loss of density and quality of bone making them more fragile and at greater risk of fracture. This process is silent and progressive with the first sign or symptoms bing a pathological fracture.

Senility (dementia) - normal and inevitable aspect of growing old. The preservation of long term memory with decreased short term memory. The term senility or senile dementia has been falling out of favor and no longer recommended to be used.

Mental Confusion - can be related to toxic confusion, dehydration, drug reactions, endocrine pathologies, hyper or hypothyroidism, encephalopathy, liver failure.

Multiple myeloma - Most common plasma cell dyscrasia in the elderly.

Diabetes Mellitus - most common endocrine malfunction in the elderly.

Wernicke - Korsakoff Syndrome - seen with chronic alcohol abuse.

Dizziness - a momentary light headedness or disorientation to surroundings.

Disruption of carotid baroreceptors can lead to bradycardia and hypotension, usually when rising from seated to standing position. Can result in faintness, fainting(syncope), loss of balance, and can be a symptom of aortic stenosis.

Depression is the most common example of the nonspecific and atypical presentation of illness in the elderly.

Decubitus Ulcer - bed sore, most common cause is when a bedridden patient is not turned enough.

Pick's disease - Alzheimer's disease of the frontal lobe.

Peripheral arterial disease - intermittent claudication in the elderly.

Presbyopia - hardening of the lens with age leads to loss of accommodation and hyperopia.

Presbycusis - hardening of the tympanic membrane with age leads to hearing loss initially affecting the in higher frequencies.

Cataracts - the clouding of the lens with age.

Cherry Angioma - red spot with white ring, considered normal with aging.

Iron Deficiency Anemia - most common anemia in geriatric patients.

Suicide rate is greater in older white males, up to 6 times that of the general population.

Women have slightly lower blood pressure than men in the third and fourth decades of life and slightly higher thereafter.

Incontinence - involuntary urine or fecal expulsion. A common cause of referral for institutionalization.

Acute Incontinence - rapid onset of incontinence usually resulting from illness or drugs

Persistent Incontinence - not related to illness and is persistent problem

4 types of persistent incontinence;

1. Stress - loss of urine by cough, sneeze, laugh, exertion because of pelvic wall muscle weakness, urethra hypermobility, urethral weakness. Most common in women, esp. those with natural deliveries of children, low estrogen or genitourinary surgeries. In men it is rare but usually from surgery such as transurethral prostatectomy or radiation for UTI.

2. Urge - leakage due to inability to delay after sensation of bladder fullness. Caused by detrusor m. over activity with local GU conditions like tumors, stones, diverticula, or outflow obstruction OR CNS disorders such as stroke, dementia, Parkinson's, cord injuries. These cause an "unstable bladder." (2 ways)-lower GU or neurological problem, or poorly compliant bladder where frank contraction will not occur and detrusor

pressure builds. Detected by need to void more than every two hours. Nocturia-need to void 2 or more times during sleeping hours. 40-75% of elderly have unstable bladder.

3. <u>Overflow</u> - mechanical forces from over distended bladder, urinary retention, sphincter control loss. Caused by anatomical obstruction(prostate, stricture, hydrocele, contractile bladder from Diabetes Mellitus, spinal cord injury, MS, supra-sacral cord injury.

4. <u>Functional (Pseudo-incontinence)</u> - leakage due to inability to get to toilet bc of impairment of cognitive of physical functions, psychological unwillingness, environmental barriers.(Dementia, depression, hostility)

<u>Unconscious Incontinence</u> - caused by detrusor hyper reflexia, the patient has no sense of urgency.

<u>Detrusor Hyperactivity with Impaired Contractility</u> (DHIC) 1/3 or less of bladder empties with involuntary contraction, patient do have the urge to urinate and may have to strain to complete voiding.

<u>Overflow incontinence</u>- caused by anatomical or functional overflow obstruction or hypotonic an acontractile bladder or both. Common causes: BPH, diabetic neuropathic bladder, or urethral stricture.

<u>Mixed Incontinence</u>- older women with combination of both of stress and urge incontinence.

<u>Fecal incontinence</u> - less common than urinary, 30-50% of paints with urinary incontinence have fecal incontinence. Most common causes are misuse of laxatives, neurological disorders, colorectal disorders, impacted stool (scyhbalum) that irritates rectum producing mucus and fluid that leaks.

<u>Vitamin D with Calcium</u> - reduces the risk of fracture in the elderly.

<u>Black Lung</u> - chronic exposure to coal, coal dust.

<u>Brown Lung</u> - chronic exposure to cotton.

<u>Mesotheliomoa</u> - previous exposure to asbestos (maybe many years ago).

Silicosis - emphysema from chronic exposure to silica, silica dust.

Croup - insinuatory stridor with dry laugh treated with humidifier.

Cystic Fibrosis - chronic lung disease with increased mucus secretions.

Differential Diagnosis of the geriatric patient it is important to consider multiple conditions or complaints when interpreting the signs and symptoms the patient is reporting.

Alternate Historian - if you suspect mental confusion or dementia a family member or spouse should be present.

Speak loudly and clearly using simple terms to insure the geriatric patient can hear and understand you.

Temporal Arteritis (Giant Cell Arteritis/Horton's Arteritis) - a form a vasculitis in the temporal arteries producing head and neck pain with elevated ESR and can lead to blindness if left untreated.

Toxicology

Toxicology - the study of adverse reaction by chemical substance on living tissue.

Toxicity - over extension of the therapeutic effect of a chemical substance.

Bioavailability - portion of a drug that reaches the target tissue.

Absorption - the site a drug is applied and the process of it entering the system, most commonly by passive diffusion.

Distribution - the mathematical formula that gives an indication of how widely a substance can enter body tissues. The more lipid soluble a substance is, the greater the *volume of distribution*.

Anesthetic - decreases the body's sensitivity to pain.

Analgesic - pain reliever

Synergistic - the combined effect of two or more substances is greater than the sum of their individual effects.

Pharmacodynamics - absorption, distribution, metabolism, and excretion of a drug.

Pharmacokinetics - what happens when a drug enters and moves through he body. Absorption, distribution and clearance.

Fick's Law - the rate of diffusion is equal to the concentration times the surface area times the solubility divided by the thickness of the membrane multiple by the square root of the molecular weight.

Passive Diffusion - the primary method chemicals enter the body that is defined as cross a membrane without energy input.

Active Transport - movement of ions or molecules across a cell membrane into a region of higher concentration by enzymes that require energy.

Facilitated Transport (passive mediated transport) - a process of spontaneous passive transport of ions or molecules across a membrane via transmembrane proteins.

Clearance - the means of removing a chemical from the body. Chemicals are either metabolized or excreted, make the liver and kidneys the organs of clearance.

Hypersensitivity (allergic reaction) - occurs as the result of exposure to an allergen producing anaphylactic shock.

The liver metabolizes chemicals by oxidation, reduction and/or hydroxylation to make the substance water soluble for excretion.

NSAID - Non-Steroidal Anti-Inflammatory Drug;
- Salicylates (aspirine) - can cause GI bleeding, over dose can result in tinnitus, respiratory alkalosis, vomiting
- Acetomenophen (tyenol) - a antipyretic analgesic, synergistic with alcohol, over dose can cause liver damage
- Other examples, Feldene, Ibuprofen (advil, motrin), Naproxen, Celecoxin (Celebrex)

Reye's Syndrome - a child with a virus is given aspirin that leads to neurological symptoms and may cause deafness, blindness or coma.

Expectorant - loosens stuff causing congestion to be expelled.

Antitussin - suppresses a cough

Tranquilizers - treatment fr anxiety, fear, tension,

Tyramine - found in wine and cheese, cause hypertension in PT taking MAO inhibitors.

MAO inhibitors (MAOIs) - treatment for depression, block monoamine oxidase, elevates norepinephrine, serotonin and dopamine.

Emetic - drug used to induce vomiting (syrup of epigak).

Acyclovir - treatment for herpes (viruses)

Tricyclics - treatment for depression.

Elavil - tricyclic antidepressant.

Prozac - commonly used SSRI anti-depressant.

SSRI - Selective Serotonin Re-uptake Inhibitor, used to treat depression and anxiety.

Benzodiazepines - treatment for anxiety.

Chlorpromazine - treatment for schizophrenia.

Ritalin - treatment for Attention Deficit Disorder (ADD).

Lithium - treatment for depression, can produce tremors.

Barbiturates - sleeping pills, can cause death by suppressing respiration.

Beta blockers - treatment for hypertension and arrhythmias.

Epinephrine - treatment for anaphylactic shock.

Dilantin - treatment for seizure disorders

Cholinesterase Inhibitor - an organophosphate that block the normal breakdown of acetylcholine.

Colchicine - treatment for acute gout

Alopuriral - treatment for chronic gout.

Cyanide - poison that taste of cherry seeds and smells of almonds patient presents with blue lips.

Amyl nitrate - treatment for cyanide poisoning.

Arsenic - smells of garlic.

Carbon Mondoxide poisoning - patient presents with cherry red lips, associated with blue mucus membrane.

Activated Charcoal - an adsorbent that block absorption, treatment for poisoning.

Lead Poisoning - affects the nervous system, delayed development, learning disabilities, headaches, mood disorders.

EDTA Treatment - chelation therapy, treatment for heavy metal poisoning. **Ethylene** **D**iamine **T**etra-acetic **A**cid.

Antidotes:
Chemical - combines with poison to form harmless substance.
Mechanical - prevents absorption.
Physiological - counteracts poison by causing opposite physiologic effect.

Warfarin/Heparin - Anti-coagulant medications that decrease clotting (increase clotting time), monitor patient's prothrombin time.

Cocaine - a narcotic often used as a local anesthetic (Lidocaine).

Epistemology - the investigation of the nature and origin of knowledge and the act of knowing.

Insanity - persistent mental disorder or derangement.

Psychology

<u>Mental illness</u> - the inability to cope with situations or circumstances.

<u>Mental Health</u> - stability within normal stress.

<u>Mental Status Exam (MSE)</u> - psychological (mental health) equivalent of the physical exam. An evaluation of the mental state and behaviors of the patient including objective and subjective findings.

Components of the MSE; Level of consciousness (Glasgow Coma Scale), General appearance, attitude, motor behavior, emotional state, Affect (how the patient reacts), immediate recall, verbal memory, orientation, concentration, vigilance, recent memory, remote memory, visual memory, speech, comprehension, repetition, perform calculations, naming objects, constructional ability, cognitive function, thought process.

<u>Wechsler Aduly Intelligence Scale Revised (WAIS-R)</u> - a two part test, verbal and performance that test the intelligence of adults to yield and IQ giving it the lay term IQ test.

<u>Wechsler Intelligence Scale for Children Revised (WISC-R)</u> - same as above with modification for children. IQ test for kids.

<u>Normal</u> - subjectively defined by culture. (Mathematically normal is defined as a standard deviation of +/- 1)

<u>Stress</u> - reaction to forces or a deleterious nature and various abnormal states that tend to disrupt homeostasis. The resisting force in the body that results from an externally applied force. A physical or psychological stimuli that produces strain or disequilibrium. Stress can be good or bad, as it promotes adaptation.

<u>Depression</u> - Very common, depressed mood most of the day, loss of interest most or all activities, loss of pleasure seeking, weight loss or weight gain, insomnia/hypersomnia, psychomotor agitation or retardation, fatigue or lack of energy, feeling or worthlessness, inappropriate guilt, lack of concentration, suicidal tendencies. Outward appearance of sadness and being unhappy with apathy and withdrawal.

Psychological testing:

Rorschach - Ink blot testing used to determine personality disorders using emotional singles.

WISC - Wechsler Intelligence Scale for Children, 5-16 years old. Tests verbal skills and performance of tasks. Produces and IQ.

MMPI - Minnesota Multiphasic Personality Inventory, personality testing.

Stanford Binet - MC used intelligence test for young children.

Mental Status Exam (MSE) - assess patient's orientation, attention, feelings, thought patterns and cognitive skills.

Glasgo Coma Scale - neurological scale meant to objectively measure a person's consciousness.

Bender Gastalt Test - screening for gross organic deficits.

Trail Making Test - simple test for organic impairment.

Psychological disorders:

Psychosis - severe disorganization of the personality associated with depression, delusions and hallucinations.

Hallucinations - improper perception of reality.

Phobia (phobic) - irrational fear; agoraphobia is the fear of public spaces, acrophobia is the fear of heights, astrophobia is the fear of stars.

Neurosis - a form of maladjustment in which the person is unable to cope with anxieties, leads to the use of defense mechanisms. Patient is troubled by distressing symptoms that can include anxiety, phobias, obsessions, compulsions, hysterical conversations and dissociative phenomena with the ability to distinguish fantasy from reality, "know they are crazy."

Schizophrenia - psychosis in which there is a lack of harmony between aspects of the personality.

Simple Schizophrenia - childlike delusions with periods of normal behavior.

Catatonic Schizophrenia - periods of inactivity and being withdrawn and violent behavior.

Paranoid Schizophrenia - delusional hallucinations of grandeur. The majority of schizophrenics are paranoid.

Involutional melancholia - psychotic behavior associated with the climacteric, accompanied by agitation, delusions, anxiety and paranoid reactions.

Anxiety - a neurotic disorder characterized by chronic unrealistic anxiety punctuated by panic attacks that can present like a heart attack, hyperventilation or other physical manifestations.

Hypochondria - obsession with bodily functions and constant fear of serious illness.

Compulsion - neurosis characterized by an irresistible impulse to perform an act contrary to one's better judgment or will.

Obsession - neurosis characterized by recurrent thoughts, feelings, or impulses that the subject recognizes as morbid and which he feels a strong resistance.

Obsessive Compulsive - inflexible perfectionist, caught up in the details of highly repetitive activities. 2 parts, persistent thoughts are obsessive and persistent actions are compulsive.

Post Traumatic Stress Disorder - a neurotic disorder that is produced by exposure to an overwhelming stress that is characterized by recurrent episodes of reliving the traumatic event and numbing of emotional responsiveness.

Narcissism - self love or self admiration, attention seeking.

Affective disorder - major depressive episode.

Hysterical Neurosis - wide variety of somatic and mental symptoms that result from dissociation including histrionics, theatrical gestures, attention seeking, and tend to be aggressive.

Somatization/Briquet's Syndrome - neurotic illness with multiple somatic symptoms. Conversion hysteria with multiple manifestations.

Conversion hysteria - emotional problems manifest as somatic complaints.

Schizoid - affective disorder characterized as introverted and withdrawn, emotionally cold and distant.

Rationalization - attributing one's own unacceptable desires and impulses to somebody else.

Antisocial - psychotic/sociopath, acting out their conflicts with no remorse or guilt, lack insight into consequences for their actions.

Catatonia - muscle inhibition.

Alcoholism - delirium, folate deficiency, malnutrition. Feels like bugs or worms are crawling on them.

Paranoid - suspicious attitudes leading to aggressive feelings. Unfounded thoughts/feelings that people are trying to harm them. Typically sensitive to interpersonal relationships.

Bipolar Affective disorder AKA Manic Depression - Alternating moods from mania to melancholia (depression) treated with lithium. Mood swings are a characteristic sign.

Unipolar Mood Disorder - syndrome depression, melancholia, major depressive disorder. No mood swing.

Involutional Melancholia - depression associated with the onset of menopause.

Transvestite - transgender, cross dressing.

Electra complex - libidinous fixation of daughter toward father.

Oedipus complex - libidinous fixation of son toward mother.

Jocasta complex - libidinous fixation of mother toward son.

Phaedra complex - the love and attraction between a stepparent and a stepchild.

ID - Basic instincts, survival. (Freud)

Ego - the reality testing aspect of the personality. (Freud)

Super Ego - guilt (Freud)

Personality Types; (2)

Type A - inability to relax; fast paced, polyphasic thinking, impatient, chronic sense of urgency.

Type B - more relaxed, sedated, tendency toward procrastination.

Defense mechanisms:

Reaction formation - the subject denies a disapproved motive or desire by giving strong expression to its opposite. Expresses the opposite behavior in an exaggerated form.

Repression - a guilt or anxiety producing impulse or memory is denied by its disappearance from awareness. "Bury a memory" an unconscious defense mechanism where unacceptable ideas and impulses are suppressed out of consciousness in the subconscious.

Regression - Child like behavior as an inappropriate response to stress, is a behavior characteristic of an earlier developmental stage.

Suppression - disapproved impulses or desires are not overtly revealed, or acted upon.

Sublimation - socially unacceptable motives or desires are expressed in socially acceptable forms. Changing behavior to accepted norms.

Denial - a river in Africa and/or a defense mechanism that keeps unpleasant realities out of conscious awareness. Denial is the most common defense mechanism that is also common with alcoholism.

Modeling - behavior medication by teaching the patient to imitate the desired behavior of others.

Flooding - desensitization treatment of phobias and other disorders that repeatedly exposes the patient to the distressing stimuli. Fear of spiders, keep exposing the patient to spiders.

Aversion Therapy - associate behavior with unpleasant consequences.

Shaping - provide structure in an environment of positive reinforcement

Maslow - Self Actualization, hierarchy of human needs.

Jung - collective unconscious, student of Feud that also used psychoanalysis.

James Lange - Linear Healthcare model, look for cause and effect as a direct relationship.

Freud - Father of psychoanalysis, Tripartite of the personality; id, ego, superego. Inner dynamics of the unconscious, free association.
Stages of development; Oral, Anal, Phallic.

Bender Gestalt Test - screening test for gross organic deficits.

Tail Making Test - simple test of organic impairment.

Halstead-Reitran Battery - a group of tests that together are used to compare the patient's performance from normal to brain damaged. The battery of tests include; Minnesota Multiphasic Personality Inventory, Wechester-Bellevue Intelligence Scale, Trail Making Test, Category Test, Test of Critical Flicker Frequency, Tactual Performance Test, Rhythm Test, Speech-Sound perception test, Finger Oscillation Test, Time Sense Test and Aphasia Examination.

Gynecology

Female Reproductive Organs;

2 <u>ovaries</u> that produce the ova and hormones including estrogen.

<u>Ova (plural of Ovum)</u> - female reproductive haploid cells

<u>Uterus</u> - hollow muscular organ located between the bladder and rectum. A fertilized egg will become implanted there in a normal pregnancy.

<u>Cervix</u> - cylinder shaped neck of firbomuscular tissue that connect the vagina and uterus.

<u>Labia Majorum</u> - homologous to the scrotum the outer skin folds of the external female genitalia.

<u>Labia Minora</u> - the smaller inner folds of the vulva.

<u>Clitoris</u> - homologous to the penis, located at the junction of the labia minora, lacks any reproductive function, primary source of female sexual pleasure.

<u>Introitus</u> – Entrance to a canal or hollow organ, the vaginal introits leads to the vaginal canal.

<u>Amenorrhea</u> – The absence of menstruation.

<u>Menarche</u> - first menstrual cycle.

<u>Parturition</u> - the birth process.

<u>Dyspareunia</u> - pain due to coitus

<u>Coitus</u> – sexual intercourse

<u>Atresia</u> - absence or abnormal narrowing of an opening or passage in the body.

<u>Primipara</u> - first pregnancy with viable infant.

<u>Nulliparous</u> - never given birth to a viable infant.

Multiparous - given birth to more than one viable infant.

Mastitis - localized engorgement of the breast with red streaks. Inflammation of the mammary gland

Lactation – secretion of breast milk can cause normal amenorrhea.

Meconium - newborn's first intestinal discharge; first feces

Vernix Caseosa – cheesy white covering on skin of newborn, vernix.

Colostrum - initial breast milk secreted contains IgA which is not found in mature breast milk.

Dysmenorrhea - painful menstrual cycles, menstrual cramps typically occurs around the time that menstruation begins.

Mittleschmerz – German for "middle pain", medical term for "ovulation pain"

Climacteric - cessation of menses, decline of fertility, menopause.

Pseudocyesis - false pregnancy, pseudopregnancy

Ovum – A mature female reproductive cell.

Embryonic stages; Zygote → Morula → Blastula

Zygote - a diploid cell resulting from the fusion of two haploid gametes; fertilized ovum.

Morula - a solid ball of 16 cells within the zona pellucida 3-4 days after fertilization.

Blastula - A hollow ball of cells, contains a blastocoele.

Blastocoele - fluid filled cavity found in the blastula.

Haploid - cell having unpaired chromosomes, gametes, germ cells.

Diploid - cell having two completed sets of chromosomes, one from each parent.

Ectopic - abnormal position or location.

Ectopic Pregnancy - a fertilized egg attached to a place other than inside the uterus.

Salpingitis (pyosalpinx) - infection of the fallopian tube can lead to obstruction, ectopic pregnancy and infertility.

Varices - "pregnancy tumors" involves more or more veins of the Vulva.

Follicle Stimulating Hormone (FSH) - maturation of the follicle.

Luteinizing hormone (LH) - helps stimulate ovulation.

Oxytocin - uterine contraction in labor and milk let down after.

Prolactin - milk production.

Filariasis - a parasitic roundworm infection that blocks the lymphatics causing swelling and thickening of the skin.

Delivery - the actual expulsion fo the fetus and placenta.

Parity (para) - the number of live births.

Gravidity (grava) - the total number of pregnancies including miscarriage and abortion.

Signs of Pregnancy

Goodell Sign – significant softening of the vaginal portion (tip) of the cervix due to increased vascularization.

Hegar Sign - entire cervix softens, non-sensitive sign.

Chadwick's Sign - bluish discoloration of the cervix, vagina and labia due to increased blood flow commonly seen 6-8 weeks after fertilization.

Piskacek Sign - asymmetrical enlargement of the uterus, palpable 6-8 weeks after fertilization.

Ladin Sign - softened at the midline of the uterus at the junction with the cervix. Commonly detectable after 6 weeks gestation.

McDonald's Sign - flexibility of the uterus at the uterocervical junction.

Von Ferwald's Sign - irregular softening of the fundus in the corneal area.

Ballottement Sign of Pregnancy - movement of the fetus upon pressure to cervix through vagina.

Effacement - thinning of a tissue. Cervical effacement is thinning of the cervix.

Quickening - mother's perception of fetal movement.

Lightening - descent of uterus into pelvic cavity 2-3 weeks before labor.

Engagement – sensation felt when the lowermost part of the fetus descends in the mother's pelvis. The baby's head reaches the Ischial spines.

Palpation of the fetus is possible after 22 weeks.

Physiological changes of pregnancy include; average weight gain of 27 lbs, retain 6-8 liters of water, increased resistance to insulin, increased blood volume, decreased hemoglobin and hematocrit, increased fibrinogen, increased cholesterol, phospholipids, alkaline phosphatase, SGOT, LHD, uterus hypertrophy, uterine hyperplasia, increased uterine contractibility, cervix becomes short and effaced, increased mucus production, increased glycogen in vaginal cells, breast enlargement, increased size of the anterior pituitary, elevated thyroxine, increased cortisol, and decreased FSH, increased blood volume increased cardiac output and lowers diastolic pressure, increased respiratory rate increased renin, angiotensin and aldosterone. Heart burn, nausea and constipation are common. Increased skin pigmentation.

Hydatidiform Mole: a benign trophoblastic tumor of an abnormal fertilized egg or an overgrowth of tissue from the placenta creating high levels of Human Chorionic Gonadotrophin (HCG).

3 Cardinal signs of Toxemia; **H**ypertension, **E**dema, **P**roteinuria (**HEP**)

Preeclampsia - toxemia of pregnancy after week 20 (3rd trimester)

Eclampsia - toxemia of pregnancy with seizure or convulsions before, during or after delivery.

Labor - uterine contraction initiated by hormonal changes, dilation of the cervix and expulsion of the fetus.

Vertex Presentation - baby's occiput is the presenting part.

Breach Presentation - baby's sacrum is the presenting part.

Face Presentation - baby's chin is the presenting part.

Transverse Presentation - baby's inferior shoulder is positioned to the mothers back, dangerous.

Compound Presentation - when any other body part presents with the baby's head.

3 Stages of Labor:

1st stage - from onset of true labor to full cervical dilation (10 cm), longest stage.

2nd stage - from full dilation (10 cm) to delivery of the baby (2-3 hours)

3rd stage - delivery of the placenta, shortest stage. (5-30 minutes)

Dilation - expansion/stretching of the cervix in the first stage of labor.

Puerperium - 6 weeks after delivery of the placenta during involution.

Involution a process in which organs return to their normal size and position after delivery.

Placenta Abrupta - early detachment of placenta from uterine wall dark brown bleeding.

Placenta Previa - low lying placenta, interferes with internal cervical opening resulting in c-section.

Placenta Accreta - the placenta grows deeply into the uterine wall.

Retained placenta - most common cause of post partum hemorrhage.

Uterine involution - occurs during post partum period.

Endometriosis - ectopic growth of uterine lining (endometrium) that sheds during menses and causes bleeding, lowers fertility rate.

Adenomyosis - endometrial tissue found in the myometrium (muscular layer of the uterus).

Endometrial Carcinoma - large eosinophilic, pale staining glandular cells with no vascular or lymphatic invasion.

Endometrial Polyps - any mass of tissue that projects outward. Smooth red or brown lesion with velvety texture.

Endometrial Hyperplasia - premalignant condition when the endometrium becomes abnormally thick. It is not cancer, but it can lead to cancer. Caused by and excess of estrogen without progesterone.

Leukoplakia - precancerous lesion of white patches on mucous membranes.

Leukemia - is the most common cancer in children and with Down's Syndrome.

Prolapsed cord - results in fetal suffocation

Dermoid Cyst of the Ovary - teratoma (tumor made up of several germinal layers).

Fibrocystic Disease (Mammary Dysplasia) - Common condition characterized be hyperplasia, fibrosis and cysts associated with lower progesterone and higher estrogen levels. Typically bilateral nodes (lumps) can be palpated. Cysts in the breast become tender during menses and regresses after.

Spontaneous Abortion - most common first trimester, usually attributed to chromosomal defects

Cystocele - bulging of bladder into the anterior vaginal wall.

Rectocele - bulging of anterior rectum into the posterior vaginal wall.

Enterocele - herniation of the rectouterine pouch of Douglas into the rectovaginal septum located in the posterior fornix between the uterus and the bladder.

Milia - White pinhead sized papules on the face and sometimes the trunk of a newborn, keratin filled cysts.

Tonic Neck Reflex - rotate head of supine baby and ipsilateral arm and leg extend with contralateral arm and leg flexion.

Suckling Reflex - baby will suck on finger or nipple placed in their mouth, stimulated by oxytocin.

Moro Reflex - startle reflex in newborns.

Rooting reflex - touch the cheek of a baby the head turns to that side. Primitive reflex originating in the brain stem.

Botulism - found in honey, corn syrup and molasses. Do not feed a baby botulism in the first year of life.

Milestones:

At birth - eyes open but can only visually fix on objects within about 8 inches. Time of initial bonding.

1st hour of life - nursing, breast feeding. Most babies will nurse well with the first hour(s) of life.

6 hours of life - deep sleep after a period of calm awareness.

12 hours of life - first urination and passing of meconium, first stool often tar like.

<u>7-10 days</u> - Umbilical cord falls off

<u>6 weeks</u> - gains control of head movements

<u>3 months</u> - Posterior Fontanelle closes

<u>4 months</u> - the eye is structurally complete, vision starts to improve.

<u>6 months</u> - first solid food, neonatal reflexes start to diminish. Sitting up and rolling over unassisted.

<u>6-8 months</u> - First teeth appear.

<u>9 months</u> - grasp becomes defined with index to thumb control. Able to transfer objects from one hand to the other.

<u>10-14 months</u> - Assisted walking

<u>1 year</u> - unassisted walking (12-15 months), plays games may speak a few words and follow simple instructions.

<u>18 months</u> - visual acuity is near that of an adult. Child can match shapes and colors. Starts talking with limited vocabulary.

<u>24 months</u> - motor skill start to rapidly develop, walking well, vocabulary of 200 or more words, starts to form sentences and plays along side others, not together and the anterior fontanel closes.

<u>5 years</u> - Toe and heel walking, hopping, locate sounds, potty trained.

APGAR scoring: **A**ppearance(color), **P**ulse(heart rate), **G**rimace(reflex irritability), **A**ctivity(muscle tone), **R**espiration(respiratory effort).

<u>CPR on child</u> - 80-100 chest thrusts per minute.

<u>Herpes Simplex</u> - causes aseptic meningitis in the neonate

<u>Brachial Artery</u> - best to palpate pulse on an infant.

<u>Capillary Hemangioma</u> - typically appears after birthing process on the scalp.

Caput Succadeum - benign, abnormal head shape due to swelling of the scalp the usually resolves within a few days.

Cradle Cap - yellowish, greasy, crusty, patchy skin on the scalp of new born baby that most commonly benign sever cases are rare.

Lanugo - fine fetal hair, first hair.

Enuresis - bedwetting

Nocturnal Enuresis - nighttime bedwetting.

Marasmus - general malnutrition

Kwashiorkor - protein malnutrition

Diphtheria - characteristic pseudomembrane formation, exotoxin formation can lead to myocarditis and neuritis.

The cervix is the most common site of malignancy in the female genital tract.

Turner's Syndrome - 45X, female with short stature, low posterior hairline, short webbed neck, gonadal dysgenesis.

Klinefelter's Syndrome - 47XXY, male with small testes, gynecomastia, long legs and subnormal intelligence.

Depressed fontanelles indicate dehydration.

Braxton Hicks Contractions - intermittent contractions of the uterus typically in the 2nd or 3rd trimester of pregnancy; false labor, practice contractions.

Chloasma gravidarum - mask of pregnancy; melasma, symmetrical patches of brownish pigmentation on the face

Hyperemesis gravidarum - pernicious vomiting of pregnancy, excessive or sever vomiting, nausea with possible weight loss and dehydration is more severe than morning sickness.

Dystocia - painful or difficult labor; obstructed labour, labour dystocia, most commonly caused by large or awkwardly positioned fetus.

Lochia - normal discharge from uterus after delivery.

Fibrocystic Disease (Mammary Dysplasia) - hyperplasia, fibrosis and cysts, due to a decrease of progesterone and increased estrogen. Bilateral involvement with palpable nodules. Considered benign.

Fibroadenoma - Benign palpable, moveable solitary nodules 2-4 cm usually in woman under 30 years of age.

Papilloma - pre or postmenopausal woman these growths are not aggressive and do not commonly spread throughout the body caused by HPV. Most are benign with a small chance of being malignant.

Toxic Shock Syndrome - caused by Staph aureus from a dirty tampon.

Hidradenitis - a refractory infection of the procaine sweat glands by either staph or strep.

Menorrhagia (hypermenorrhea) - Excessive bleeding for more than 8 days of more than 100 ml of blood.

Cryptomenorrhea (hypomenorrhea) - extremely light menstrual flow most commonly caused by hymenal or cervical stenosis or obstruction.

Polymenorrhea - regular but frequent menstrual cycles less than 21 days apart.

Oligomenorrhea - regular by infrequent cycle, greater than 35 days apart.

Amenorrhea - lack of normal menstrual cycle for 6 months or more.

Metrorrhagia - bleed between normal periods that can last for several days.

Menometrorrhagia - excessive irregular bleeding for more than 8 days

Dysmenorrhea - cyclic pain associated with menstrual cycle but without any demonstrable problem affecting reproduction.

Self Breast Examination - women of all ages are encouraged to perform breast self-examination at least once per month. 45% of of diagnosed breast cancers are detected by women who feel an abnormal lump.

Step 1 Visualization; stand in font of a mirror with the arms at the side and again with the arms raised above the head. Look for any changes in contour, swelling, dimpling of the skin or and changes in the nipples. Next, rest palms on the hips and press firmly flexing the chest muscles again looking for dimpling, puckering or other changes. Left and Right breasts rarely match, symmetry is not part of the inspection.

Step 2 Palpation; using the pads of the fingers start in the standing position at the outside of the breast in the armpit and moving toward the center, palpate the breast tissue using small circular motion. Check for lumps, knots and/or thickening of the skin or tissue. Take note of any changes and have any lumps evaluated by a healthcare provider. Make sure to check the entirety of both breasts and the armpits. Next lay down. This will allow the breast tissue to spread out evenly along the chest wall. Using the right arm, place a pillow under the right shoulder and once again using the pads of the fingers starting at the outside moving toward the center using small circular pattern with medium pressure to evaluate the entire breast and arm pit, then repeat on the other side. Check for discharge from the nipple, changes in texture or lumps.

Physician breast exams should be once every one to three years starting at age 20 until age 40.

Breast Cancer - fixed, immovable lump, skin changes (orange peel appearance) skin retraction (dimple), enlarged axillary lymph nodes, nipple discharge. Diagnosis confirmed with biopsy. Lab findings include increased alkaline phosphatase, hypercalcemia and increased CEA. There are 4 types of breast cancer; infiltrative, non-infiltrative, lobular and ductal.

Stages of Breast Cancer -

Stage 1 - Tumor under 2 cm with nodes present and no metastases.
Stage 2 - Tumor under 5 cm, nodules are not fixed.
Stage 3 - Tumor over 5 cm, nodules are fixed, invasions of the skin.
Stage 4 - Metastases

Ulcer of the Vulva - maybe caused by primary syphilis, chancroid, herpes or papilloma.

Vulva - the outer portion of the female genitalia.

Codylomata lata - white lesions of the vulva associated with secondary syphilis.

Benign Tumors of the Vulva;

Bartholin's Cyst - a fluid filled cyst in the Bartholin's glands.

Wolffian Duct Cyst (Mesonephric Duct Cyst, Gartner's Duct Cyst) - typically small, asymptomatic cysts along the lateral walls of the vagina arising from the vestigial remnant of the mesonephric duct.

Canal of Nuck Cyst - an abnormal patent pouch of peritoneum extended anterior to the round ligament of the uterus that can become fluid filled (a cyst).

Fibroma - a tumor of fibrous connective tissue

Condyloma Acuminata - genital warts caused by HPV.

Angioma - abnormal growth of the small blood vessels due to the aging process and do not have any known significance (besides board questions).

Hydraedenoma - adnexal tumor of the apical sweat gland.

Leiomyomas - also known as fibroids these are benign tumors of smooth muscle.

Bartholin's glands - lubricate the vagina.

Malignant Lesions of the Vulva;

Carcinoma in Situ (Bowen's Disease) - early form os skin cancer that involves the epithelium only and is easily treatable. Red, scaly patch of skin.

Paget's Carcinoma - similar to squamous cell cancer, biopsy shows large vasculated cells.

Melanoma - cancer that is derived from the melanocytes.

Vaginitis - inflammation of the vagina that typically presents with discharge, itching and pain.

Gardenella Vaginitis (Hemophilus Vaginitis) - gram variable anaerobic bacterial infection of the epithelial cells, that presents with mucopurulent discharge.

Trichomonas Vaginitis - an STD caused by a parasite, the pear shaped protozoa Trichomonas, green/yellow discharge, smell of fish, with itching or irritation.

Monilial Vaginitis - candida albican (fungal) infection, curd like discharge, white patches that can be wiped off.

Atrophic Vaginitis - prepuberty girls or post-menopausal women with dysuria, pruritus, dyspareunia.

Toxic Shock Syndrome - staph. aureus infection caused by dirty tampon.

Cervical Polyps - inter-menstrual bleeding or postcoital bleeding.

Cervicitis - maybe the most common gynecological disorder is inflammation of the cervix due to an infection.

Conditions related to the Ovaries;

Follicle Cysts - distended Graffian follicles due to atresia.

Graffian follicles - a fluid filled structure in the ovary within which an ovum develops before ovulation.

Granulosa Lutein Cysts - functional non-neoplastic enlargements of the ovary.

Theca Lutein Cysts - fluid filled cyst on the ovary.

Germinal Inclusion Cysts - invagination of germinal epithelium of the ovary.

Stein-Leventhal Syndrome (Polycystic Ovary Syndrome) - "Oyster Ovaries" are caused by a hormonal disorder that is common in woman of reproductive years. Presents with infrequent, prolonged menstrual periods. The ovaries develop numerous small collections of fluid and fail to regular release eggs.

Arrhenoblastoma - a masculinizing tumor that produces testosterone.
Conditions of Uterus;

Uterine Prolapse (procidencia) - protrusion of the uterus through the pelvic floor, firm mass in the lower vagina. There are 3 grades; I incomplete, II moderate, III complete prolapse.

Uterine Malposition - normal position is anteversion and anteflexion. Abnormal maybe described as retroversion, retroflexion, retrocession, or lateral deviation.

Pediatrics

Lanugo - fine hair covering newborns body.

Hydramnios - excess accumulations of amniotic fluid during pregnancy.

Meconium - newborn's first intestinal discharge.

Milia - distended sebaceous glands on the cheeks, chin and nose.

Telangiectatic nevi (stork bites) - deep pink areas of localized capillary dilation seen on the eyelids, upper lip, bridge of the nose or on the occiput. Usually disappear with in the first 2 years of life.

Vernix Caseosa - cheesy covering on skin of newborn.

Lochia - initial vaginal discharge after delivery contains blood (red), mucus (yellow) and uterine tissue (white). Can persist for up to 6 weeks.

Alpha fetoprotein - increased amounts indicate neural tube defect.

Embryonic stages - zygote, morula, blastula.

APGAR scoring:

Appearance (color) - Pink is normal 2 points. Some pink and some blue 1 point, all blue is bad, no points.

Pulse (heart rate) - above 100 normal 2 points, present but below 100 1 point and absent, no points.

Grimace (reflex irritability) - prompt response 2 points, mild or delayed response 1 point, no response 0 points.

Activity (muscle tone) - Active movement 2 points, arms and legs in flexion 1 point, no movement 0 points.

Respiration (respiratory effort) - Vigorous Crying 2 points, slow interrupted crying 1 point, no crying no points.

Birth weight in not a criterion in the apgar score.

Heart Rate at birth - 120 to140 beats per minute.

Respiration at birth - 40 to 60 breaths per minute.

Blood Pressure at birth, 60 to 80 systolic 40 to 50 diastolic.

Brachial Artery in the crease of elbow is the best to palpate pulse on an infant.

Dorsum of the hand is used to test body temp of a baby.

CPR on child 80-100 chest thrusts per minute.

As a child ages their Blood Pressure (BP) increases as their Pulse decreases.

Prolapsed umbilical cord - can result in fetal suffocation.

Anterior Fontanelle - depressed indicated dehydration. Often cases by 18 months of age.

Posterior Fontanelle - closes within 6 to 9 weeks.

Bulging Fontanelle - indicates increased intracranial pressure, possible the result of excessive crying.

Ductus Arteriosus - closes within the first 24 hours failure to close or remain open (patent) is called a Patent Ductus Arteriosus.

Foramen Ovale closes within a few days, Patent Foramen Ovale will have complications.

Mongolian Spots - areas of deep blue coloration seen over the back, sacrum and buttock of asian, latin or southern European babies that fade with in week and disappear by age 4.

Pupil Reflex - soft light elicit pupillary constriction.

Blink Reflex - bright light elicit squeezing the eyes shut (blinking).

Doll's Eyes Reflex - fixation of the eyes with slow head movement is normal through the 10 days after birth.

Moro Reflex - startle reflex in newborns. Elicited by releasing and allowing extension of the infant's head which causes arm to extend then clasping of the body. Present at birth until 2 months of age.

Rooting reflex - touch the cheek (corner of the mouth) of a baby the head turns to that side. Present at birth until about 4 months of age.

Suckling Reflex - present at birth elicit by placing finger or nipple in the new born's mouth.

Tonic Neck Reflex - rotate the head of baby in supine position ipsilateral arm and leg will extend with contralateral arm and leg flex. AKA Fencing Reflex. Present at birth to 5-7 months.

Righting Reflex (Labyrithine Reflex) - the correction of the body position when it is taken out of normal upright position.

Grasp Reflex - stroke the baby's palm causes the hand to close. present at birth for 5-6 months.

Stepping Reflex - baby appears to take steps when held upright with feet on a solid surface. Present from birth to 2 months.

Colostrum - the first form of mild produced by the mammary glands immediately following delivery of a newborn that contains antibodies to protect the infant against disease and is high in protein.

At birth the new born infant can smell and taste.

Down's Syndrome - trisomy 21, mental retardation, low set ears, flat nose or bridge, simian crease on palm or sole.

Turner's syndrome - 45X, female with short stature, low posterior hairline, short webbed neck, gonadal dysgenesis.

Klinefelter's Syndrome - 47XXY, male with small testes, gynecomastia, long legs and subnormal intelligence.

Herpes Simplex - causes aseptic meningitis in the neonate.

Juvenile Rheumatoid Arthritis (Still's Disease) - Inflammatory arthritis with widespread onset before the age of 16.

Marfan's Syndrome - inherited connective tissue disorder that is autosomal dominate. Results in ocular, skeletal and cardiovascular abnormalities commonly including the aorta.

Ehlers-danlos Syndrome - inherited connective tissue disorder with articular hyper mobility, hyper elasticity of the skin and wide spread tissue fragility. It is an autosomal dominate trait. Extreme flexibility with hyper-mobility.

Capillary Hemangioma - tumor that typically appears after birthing process on the scalp that is caused by a vascular anomaly.

Reye's Syndrome - Child is given aspirin with viral infection. 30-50% mortality. Early treatment is critical to PT survival. Symptoms include persistent recurrent vomiting, listlessness, irritability, confusion, convulsions, loss of consciousness. Presents with acute encephalopathy with pernicious vomiting and fatty infiltration of the viscera.

Erb' palsy - damage to upper portion of the brachial plexus, C5/C6. AKA Erb–Duchenne palsy most commonly caused by shoulder dystocia during a difficult birth.

Klumpke's palsy - damage to the lower portion of the brachial plexus, C8/T1 resulting in minus hand deformity, may result in Horner's syndrome, with ptosis, and miosis.

Bell's palsy - CN 7 disorder presents with unilateral facial paralysis.

Cerebral Palsy - broad term used to describe motor disorders from CNS damage before age 5, imparted voluntary movements. Significant number of cases also include involuntary movements of one or more body parts.

Sydenham's Chorea (Chorea Minor, Rheumatic Chorea, St. Vitus's Dance)

- CNS disease resulting in involuntary, purposeless, non-repetitive movements. Often insidious onset.

Osteopetrosis (marble bones) - genetic diseases that increase bone density and result in abnormalities of the skeleton.

Osteoscleroses - increased skeletal density with little to no disruption of the bone shape.

Craniotubular Dysplasia - abnormal skeletal modeling with very little sclerosis.

Craniotubular Hyperostoses (Van Buchem's disease) - Overgrowth of bone causing alterations of both shape and density.

Cutis Laxa - fragmented elastin results in lax skin hanging, loose skin folds.

Osteochondroses - disorder of the epiphyses during childhood. Non-infectious, non-inflammatory derangement of the normal boney growth during developmental activity.

Legg-Calve-Perth Disease - idiopathic aseptic necrosis of the femoral capital epiphysis. Most common osteochondroses

Osgood Schlatter Disease - osteochondritis of the tibial tubercle.

Scheurmann's Disease - back pain with kyphosis associated with localized changes in the vertebral bodies.

Erythema Toxicum - punk papular rash with vesicles and some purulence.

Treponema pallidum - spirochaete bacterium with subspecies that cause the diseases syphilis, bejel, and yaws that will pass from mother to child, Placenta transmission.

Phenylkeonuria (PKU) - genetic error of metabolism, absence of enzyme phenylalanine hydroxylase results in elevated plasma phenylalanine that often causes retardation.

Fructosuria - harmless excretion of fructose in the urine caused by autosomal recessive lack of the enzyme fructokinase.

Diphtheria - characteristic pseudomembrane formation, exotoxin formation can lead to myocarditis and neuritis. Corynebacterium diphtheriae is rod-shaped, Gram positive, non spore-forming bacteria.

Strabismus (cross eyes) - deviation of one eye from parallelism with the other eye.

Scurvy - Vitamin C deficiency, resulting in swollen bleeding gums, Barlow's disease, subperiosteal hemorrhage, rarely seen today.

Enuresis - bedwetting, involuntary urination.

Childhood Schizophrenia - a psychotic state with onset after age 7 similar to adult schizophrenia.

Infantile Autism (Kanner's Syndrome) - abnormal social relationships, language disorder with impaired understanding and limited speech, rituals and compulsive phenomena with uneven intellectual development.

Nocturnal eneuresis - night time bedwetting, involuntary urination at night.

Asthma - often begins in childhood, is due to an overreaction of the bronchi and bronchioles (bronchospasm) to a variety of stimuli and is characterized by a prolonged expiratory wheeze and increased eosinophils. Most common lung disease of children.

Botulism - produced naturally in honey, corn syrup and molasses, never give a baby honey before 1 year of age.

Congenital Heart Defects;

Ventricual Spetal Defect (VSD) - one or more openings in the septum of the heart that normally separates the ventricles. This condition my resolve spontaneously during infancy or may require surgical closure.

<u>Atrial Septal Defect (Ostium Secundum/Sinus Venosus)</u> - one or more openings in the septum that normally separates the atria.

<u>Patent Ductus Arteriousus (PDA)</u> - a failure of the fetal communication between the pulmonary artery and the aorta to close. ECG is usually normal.

<u>Atrioventricular Canal Defect</u> - one or more openings in the arial and/or ventricular septa at the AV valves that may includes the valve itself.

<u>Congenital Aortic Valve Stenosis</u> - typically affects the bicuspid valve and may produce sever left ventricular obstruction, leading to heart failure, abnormal ECG and poor systemic output.

<u>Coarctation of the Aorta</u> - congenital aortic narrowing most commonly in the aortic arch. Coarctation means narrowing. May present with sudden heart failure, cardiovascular collapse and sever metabolic acidosis.

<u>Tetralogy of Fallot</u> - anatomical deformity with sever right ventricular construction and ventricular septal defect allowing unoxygenated blood to bypass the lungs and enter the aorta. The 4 congenital abnormalities of the tetralogy are 1. Ventricular Septal Defect 2. Pulmonary Valve Stenosis 3. Misplaced Aorta 4. Right Ventricular Hypertrophy.

<u>Transposition of the Great Arteries</u> - congenital anatomical deformity where the aura arises directly out of the right ventricle and the pulmonary artery arises from the left ventricle producing sever systemic hypoxia.

<u>Gastrointestinal (GI) Defects</u>

<u>High Alimentary Obstruction</u> - suspect when maternal hydramnios is present. Characteristic signs in the newborn are excessive secretions, coughing and cyanosis after attempt to swallow and aspiration pneumonia. Esophageal atresia, diaphragmatic hernia, hypertrophic pyloric stenosis and duodenal obstruction are possible causes.

<u>Meconium Plug Syndrome</u> - thick inspissated, rubbery meconium with dissension and vomiting can cause complete colon obstruction.

Meconium ileus - abnormally thick meconium that is extremely tenacious and stringing creating a blockage in the ileum of the small intestine.

Hirschsprung's Disease (congenital megacolon) - failure of the Meissner's and Auerbach's plexuses to form in the bowl wall resulting in abnormal function and obstruction of the GI tract from a lack of peristalsis.

Anal Atresia - either a complete lack of an anal opening or extreme narrowing of the anus making it difficult to pass fecal matter resulting in obstruction.

Omphalocele - a protrusion of the abdominal viscera from the *midline* at the base of the umbilicus. Some portion of the infant's intestines are outside of the body

Gastroschisis - a protrusion of the abdominal viscera from an abnormal opening lateral to the umbilicus away from the midline.

Inguinal Hernia - most common in premature male newborns part of the intestine protrudes though a weakness or deformity of the inguinal canal that requires emergency surgery to repair.

Intussusception - prolapse (telescope) off one portion of the bowel into another causing an obstruction of the GI tract. It can occur in any portion of the GI tract but is most common at the junction of the small and large intestine and requires emergency surgery to repair.

Bowel Infarction - irreversible injury to the GI tract from insufficient blood flow that results in a medical emergency that requires surgical repair.

Gastric Perforation - spontaneous or congenital formation of holes all the wya through the wall of the GI tract that requires emergency surgery to repair.

Cleft Lip/Cleft Palate - most common defect of the 1st arch that may involve the hard and/or soft palate.

Torticollis - head tilt at birth from spasm of the SCM muscle that maybe due to trauma, fracture, dislocation or subluxation of the cervical spine.

Dysraphia (dysraphicus) - the failure of a raphe to fuse, incomplete closure of the neural tube.

Anecephaly - absence of the cerebral hemispheres and a major portion of the skull that occurs during embryonic development that results from a neural tube defect with the rotary portion fails to close (23-26 day of development).

Encephalocele - a neural tube defect that results in a sac like protrusion of the brain and meninges through an opening in the skull. Incomplete closure of the cranial vault (cranium bifidum).

Porencephaly - cysts or cavities within the cerebral hemisphere that communicates (connects) with a ventricle.

Hydranencephaly - extreme porencephaly in which the cerebral hemispheres are absent or nearly absent and the cranial cavity is filled with cerebrospinal fluid.

Spina Bifida - failure of the vertebral column to close. 3 main types.

1. Spina Bifida Occulta - mild to no symptoms. No protrusion of the spinal cord, spinal nerves or meninges.
2. Menigocele - least common form of spina bifida that allows the meninges to herniate (protrude) with no involvement of the nervous system.
3. Myelocele - the most sever type of spina bifida with formation of a myelomeningocele, protrusion of the spinal cord, spinal nerves and meninges.

Hydrocephalus - ventricular enlargement with excessive CSF producing an abnormally large head in neonates.

Genitourinary (GU) Defects are the most common organ system to be affected by congenital anomalies.

Horseshoe Kidney (ren arcuatus/super kidney) - often asymptomatic, the kidneys are joined at their corresponding poles forming a big (super) kidney.

Pancake Kidney (Fused Pelvic Kidney/discoid kidney/lumpy kidney) - rare deformity resulting in the fusion of the kidneys at the upper and lower poles giving it a pancake appearance. Gives rise to 2 separate ureters that enter the bladder. Often asymptomatic.

Renal Ectopia - abnormal position of the kidney(s) due to a failure of ascent and/or rotation.

Potter's Syndrome (Renal Agenesis) - failure of both kidneys to form.

Hypospadias - displaced urethral opening.

Epispadias - the dorsal fusion of the urethra that is either partial or complete.

Phimosis - constriction of the foreskin.

Crytorchidsm (undecended testes) - incomplete or improper prenatal descent of one or both testes.

Testicular Torsion - twisting of the testis on its spermatic cord reducing blood flow resulting in a medical emergency.

Cystinuria - congenital defect of the renal tubules that impairs resorption of cystine. Autosomal recessive trait that can result in cystine calculi in the urinary tract.

Diptheria - Cornybacterium diptheriae infection that produces a thick covering in the back of the throat (pseudomembrane) making it difficult to breath.

Pertussis (Whooping Cough) - highly communicable (contagious) bacterial infection of the respiratory tract that presents with sever hacking cough with high pitched (crowing) inhalation that sounds like whoop.

Acute Infectious Gastroenteritis - recessive diarrhea and committing that can result in dehydration and electrolyte imbalance that can be caused by a variety of pathogens. Dehydration in a baby can occur quickly and become sever.

Impetigo - superficial vesiculopustular (both vesicles and pustules) skin infection.

Ecthyma - ulcerative form of impetigo.

Measles (Rubeola) - highly contagious disease that presents with a dangerously high fever, cough, coryza (inflammation of the mucous membrane in the nose), conjunctivitis, Koplick's Spots and spreading maculopapular cutaneous rash.

Subacute Sclerosing Panencephalitis - a rare form of chronic progressive brain inflammation that is caused by the measles virus that usually presents 6-10 years after the measles infection that presents with mental deterioration, myoclonic jerks and seizures.

German Measles (Rubella) - contagious viral infection that presents with mild illness with symptoms that include low grade fever, sore throat, enlarged neck lymph nodes and rash that starts on the face and spreads to the rest of the body. Rubella is extremely dangerous to pregnant women and their developing baby. Maternal infection can result in abortion, stillbirth or congenital defects.

Chicken Pox (varicella) - acute viral disease that presents with eruptions that are characterized as macules, papule, vesicles and crusting caused by Vericella-Zoster virus. Can present as shingles later in life.

Hand Foot and Mouth Disease - enterovirus infection that presents with sores on the mouth and a rash on the hands and feet that is most commonly caused by a coxsackievirus.

Poliomyelitis (polio) - a viral infection that affects the central nervous system and can cause temporary or permanent paralysis.

Mumps (Epidemic Parotitis) - viral infection that presents with painful enlargement of the salivary glands most commonly the parotid glands.

Croup - upper respiratory viral infection that presents with swelling of the larynx, trachea and bronchi that causes the characteristic barking cough.

Kawasaki Syndrome - rare condition that causes inflammation of the walls of some blood vessels in the body. Most common affects kids under the age of 5 presents with exanthem, enanthem, fever, lymphadenopathy and polyarteritis with variable severity.

Pinworm - intestinal infection caused by Enterobius Vermicularis that presents with perianal itching. Pinworm is the most common parasite infesting children in temperate climates.

Wilm's Tumor (Nephroblastoma) - a rare kidney cancer that affect children most commonly from 3 to 4 years of age becoming less common after age 5. While rare it is the most common cancer of the kidney in children. Signs and symptoms vary widely.

Neuroblastoma - a common childhood tumor arising from the adrenal gland or the extra adrenal sympathetic chain including the retroperitoneum or chest that develops from immature nerve cells.

Retinoblastoma - a malignant tumor that arises from the immature retina is the most common primary malignant intraocular cancer of children that is almost exclusively found in young children.

Congenital Goiter - enlarged thyroid that is present at birth that may or may not present with hypothyroidism.

Leukemia - the most common cancer of children, also the most common cancer seen with Down's Syndrome.

Pituitary Dwarfism - abnormally slow growth resulting in short stature with normal proportions due to decreased function of the anterior pituitary gland.

Galactosemia - Galactokinase deficiency results in abnormal metabolism of galactose to glucose leading to elevated levels of galactose in the blood.

Fructose Intolerance - metabolic disorder caused by the absence of the enzyme phosphofructoaldolase resulting in the inability to utilize fructose is an inherited autosomal recessive trait.

Fructosuria - the harmless excretion of fructose in the urine caused by the autosomal recessive trait that results in the absence of the enzyme fructokinase.

Phenylkeytonuria (PKU) - inherited metabolic disorder that results in the absence of phenylalanine hydroxylase activity producing an elevated of plasm phenylalanine which often causes retardation.

Marasmus - general malnutrition

Kwashiorkor - protein malnutrition

Caput Succadeum - unusual shape of the baby's head at birth caused by swelling between the scalp and periosteum. considered benign, self resolving.

Cephalhematoma - swelling on the skull caused by the extravasation of blood between the periosteum and the underlying cranial bone due to birth trauma.

Myopia - nearsighted, image formed before retina due to longer eye.

Hyperopia - farsighted, image formed behind retina due to shorter eye.

Astigmatism - irregular curvature of the cornea or lens causing diffusion of light rays on the retina.

Emergency Care

Head Injuries - Call EMS (911) if the patient presents with; Sever head or facial bleeding, fluid leaking from the nose or ears, sever headache, changing levels of consciousness, Battle Sign, Raccoon Sign, confusion, irregular breathing, loss of balance, unequal pupil size, slurred speech, seizures or the inability to move the arms or legs or they move but in an uncoordinated fashion.

Battle Sign - head injury producing large black and blue areas around the mastoid indicating a possible skull fracture.

Raccoon Sign - back and blue areas around the eyes can indicate a skull fracture.

Head/Spine Injuries - do not move the patient. Movement can cause harm, the purpose of first aid it prevent further harm. Do not move the patient unless they are in imminent danger. If the patient is unconscious and head/spinal injury is possible assume it is present. Signs and Symptoms include pain the head, spine, abdomen, numbness and tingling in arm(s) or leg(s), weakness, inability to move, loss of bladder control, shock. If the patient is choking or vomiting roll them onto their side.

Bleeding - apply firm pressure to the wound with sterile gauze or clean cloth. DO NOT apply pressure to suspected skull fractures. Maintain pressure until the bleeding stops.

Thermal Injuries (burns) - can be caused by dry heat (fire), wet heat (steam, water), radiation, friction, electricity or chemical irritants. The severity of burns are determined by size and depth. May produce shock.

First Degree Burn - produces redness

Second Degree Burns - produce blisters.

Third Degree Burns - produce deep charing of the skin.

Unconscious patient - check breathing first.

Levels of Consciousness:
Grade 0 - Normal consciousness
Grade 1 - Confused, awake but does not know date, location etc.
Grade 2 - Not awake, DTR present, reacts to moderate stimuli.
Grade 3 - Not awake, only responds to strong painful stimuli.
Grade 4 - Not awake, comatose, no response to any stimuli.

Poisoning - ingestion, inhalation, skin contact or injection of a poison. Patient becomes suddenly ill with no apparent cause.

Ingestion Poisoning - Try to identify the poison ingested contact poison control, local EMS for advise. The goal is to remove the poison before it can be absorbed. Patient becomes suddenly ill for no apparent reason.

Inhalation Poisoning - remove patient from the smoke, gas, fumes or whatever poison is being inhaled. Contact poison control and/or local EMS.

Reaction of Venom - increased pain on the site, numbness, tingling, slurred speech, weakness, labored breathing, nausea, sweating. Try to identify what the patient was bitten by, contact EMS. Do not apply tourniquet, do not give the patient aspirin. Wash the bite, apply ice, remove rings or other constricting items. May produce shock.

Chocking - the airway is completely or partially blocked, the choking reflex is the body attempting to clear the airway. Two hands grabbing the throat is the international/universal sign for choking. Do not interfere if the patient is coughing forcibly with good air exchange. Assist immediately if the patient cannot breath by performing the Heimlich maneuver, remove the obstruction, thrust to the mid back with heel of the hand to children.

Mild Obstruction - good air exchange, patient can speak, DO NOT INTERFERE, stay with patient, encourage them to cough.

Sever Obstruction - patient cannot speak, no/poor air exchange, identify yourself, ask if they can speak, call 911, initiate subdiaphramatic abdominal thrusts (Heimlich maneuver).

5 and 5 Approach - The American Red Cross is suggesting this approach to helping a person that is chocking. Stand behind the PT and place one arm across the PT chest for support. Bend the PT at the waist so that the upper body is parallel withe the ground and deliver 5 sprat blows to the back between the scapula with the heel of your hand. Then deliver 5 abdominal thrusts (Heimlich maneuver) by standing behind the PT with one foot slightly inferno of the other for balance. Wrap your arms around the PT's waist and tip them forward slightly. Make a fist and place it slightly above the PT's navel and grasp the fist with your other hand. Press hard directly into the abdomen with a sharp upward thrust as though lifting the person up.

Cardiopulmonary Arrest - patient is not breathing with no pulse (heartbeat). First determine if the is breathing or not and if they have a pulse or not. Ask somebody to call 911 for emergency services while you assist the victim (patient). The faster they receive medical care the greater the chance of survival.

CPR

1. Check the scene for safety and check the person by touching and shouting. "Are you OK?"

2. If the person needs help, call 911 or ask somebody to call 911. If there is a bystander ask them to get an AED if one is available, if not bystander is present stay with the person in need of help.

3. Open the Airway. Position the person on their back and tilt the head back slightly to left the chin.

4. Check for Breathing. Listen, watch for no more than 10 second for the person to breath. If there is no breathing begin CPR.

5. CPR - place one hand on top of the other in the middle of the chest. Using your body weight administer compression that are at least 2 inches deep at a rate of at least 100 compression per minute. Push and and push fast.

6. Rescue Breaths - With the persons head titled back slightly and the chin lifted pinch the nose closed and place your mouth over the

person's mouth making a complete seal. Blow in the person's mouth making the chest rise. Deliver two resume breaths and then resume check compressions.

7. Continue - keep performing cycles of chest compression and rescue breaths until the person starts breathing, an AED become available or EMS/trained medication professional arrives on the scene.

Automated External Defibrillator (AED) - used to help those suffering from sudden cardiac arrest. Follow the automated instructions.

Breathing - occasional gasping or struggling to breath is not breathing.

Shock - when something happens that reduces the flow of blood though out the body, limiting the mount of oxygen the blood carries. This is a life threatening condition that requires immediate medical treatment. Signs and symptoms include weakness, dizziness, restlessness, anxiety, confusion, cold and clay skin, pale extremities, blue lips, chest pain, shallow breathing, nausea, numbness, intense thirst and unconsciousness.

5 Main Types of Shock

1. Anaphylactic - an extreme allergic reaction that can be triggered by medication, bee stings and foods such as nuts or shellfish. PT presents with decreased blood pressure, constricted airway, swollen tongue or lips, hives, flushed skin, tingling in the extremities and maybe confused. PT needs an Epi-Pen (shot of epinephrine).

2. Cardiogenic - most commonly caused by a myocardial infarction (MI) that presents with labored breathing, pale skin, sweating and increased heart rate.

3. Hypovolemic - results from an extreme loss of blood, more than 20% of all blood in the body. Presents with labored breathing, sweating, dizziness, confusion and commonly profuse bleeding but the hemorrhage can be internal which presents with abdominal pain and/or vomiting blood. Medical emergency that requires immediate attention.

4. <u>Neurogenic</u> - Typically caused by trauma to the brain/spinal cord (CNS) that presents with a dramatic drop in blood pressure, warm flushed skin from vasodilation and a decreased heart rate.

5. <u>Septic</u> - systemic bacterial, viral or fungal infection that leads to sepsis resulting in shock. The signs and symptoms mimic that of sepsis; cyanosis, confusion, dizziness, increased heart rate, increased respiration.

All Types of shock are medical emergencies that require immediate medical attention contact EMS (call 911).

<u>Muscle sprains and strains</u> - use the **RICE** approach.
Rest - do not use the injured muscle or joint.
Ice - Apply for 20 minutes and remove for 20 minutes. Do not apply ice directly to the skin.
Compression - Wrap the muscle, joint that has been sprained/strained.
Elevate - move the injured part above the heart to reduce swelling.

<u>Dislocation/Fracture</u> - contact EMS and attempt to immobilize the area.

Juris Prudence

<u>Lingo</u> - specialized vocabulary of a particular field or discipline.

<u>Fiduciary</u> - a person that holds a legal or ethical relationship of trust with one or more parties.

<u>Fiduciary Relationship</u> - a relationship when one person places special trust, confidence in and and reliance upon to act for their benefit. A patient places complete confidence and trust in the provider in regards to their care.

<u>Fiduciary Duty</u> - provide the highest standard of care by law, act for the benefit of the patient; subordinating personal interests to that of the other person.

<u>Law</u> - rule(s) established by authority and the body/system of those rules.

Keep all records for at least 7 years. Minors until they are adults, which could be more than 7 years.

<u>Statute</u> - a law enacted by the legislature.

The legislature makes laws, the courts interpret those laws and the jury applies the laws.

<u>Abandonment</u> - the transfer of a patient to another doctor without the patient's consent. After care has begun and the provider walks away while the patient is in need without securing the services of another doctor or affording the patient time and opportunity to find one.

<u>Slander</u> - verbal, to say something false about another person, the act of making a false statement(s) damaging to a person's reputation.

<u>Libel</u> - a false statement or claim made that is damaging to a person's reputation that is written or published. To recover damages one must prove damages.

<u>Evidence</u> - anything presented in court used by the judge or jury in making a decision.

Due Diligence - the research done before entering into an agreement to confirm the facts. If you google light bulbs and compare light bulbs and light bulb sellers and check reviews before buying any light bulbs you are preforming due diligence.

Hearsay - evidence which does not derive its value from the witness itself, but gained or acquired from another party. "I heard him say…"

Deposition - a sworn statement of fact given before a notary public, can be used as evidence. A question and answer session with attorneys performed under oath done during the discovery phase after a lawsuit has been filed before the trial begins.

Binding Arbitration - has no appeal process, alternative to trial, conducted by a mediator.

Principal - one who retains an agent to act for him.

Contract - a promise to perform for which consideration is given and for which the law recognizes a duty to perform.
Must have: 1) mutual consent, 2) consideration, 3) competent parties, 4) object of contract must be legal. 5) reality of consent to contract.
Offer + Acceptance = Contract.

Offer - A promise of good or services for exchange.

Consideration - the benefits bargained for between the two parties of a contract.

Acceptance - assent to the terms of an offer that is either express or implied by intentional action.

Bilateral Contract - both parties agree to perform or make a promise of performance.

Unilateral Contract - A service is provided for a promise. The classic example is a reward. The promise of a reward for finding a lost pet is not an expressed agreement between the parties. One person that lost their pet offers a reward to anyone that find their pet, that is an example of a unilateral contract. If they hire Ace Ventura the pet detective to find their pet for a fee that is an agreement between two parties, a bilateral contract.

Expressed Contract - is a specific agreement to terms. This type of contract is usually written but it can be oral if the exact terms are agreed to in detail.

Implied Contract - a legally binding obligation that is derived from the actions of one or more parties. The agreement is assumed to exist while there may not be a verbal or written agreement.

Quasi Contract - a legal obligation of one party to another imposed by law independent of any agreement between the parties. These are usually created but the courts to enforce things such as restitution.

Advertisement - an invitation to make an offer. The Federal Trade Commission requires that all claims made in advertising be evidence based. Every state has laws that pertain directly to the advertising of chiropractic services.

Counter Offer - when one party requests changes to one or more terms of a contact before giving consent implies rejection of the original offer.

Informed consent - the patient must be competent and informed of the dangers (risks) inherent with a procedure and feasible alternatives before consenting to it. If the patient is a minor, consent must be gained for the parent/guardian. The exceptions to this rule are; pregnancy, venereal disease, drug abuse and an emergency.

Assault - the threat or attempt to commit an act that would result in physical harm or unwanted touching. Example, throwing a brick at someone is assault. If the brick his them it is battery, hence assault and battery.

Battery - unlawful touching of another person. Adjustment without consent.

Sexual Transgression - inappropriate sexual act.

Sexual Impropriety - a behavior, gesture or expression that is seductive, sexually suggestive or sexually demeaning to a patient or other party regardless of whether it occurs inside or outside of a profession setting.

Sexual Violation - engaging in any conduct with a patient or key third party that is sexual in nature or maybe reasonably interpreted as being sexual in nature.

Sexual Misconduct - a healthcare provider's behavior toward a patient, former patient, or key third party that is sexually inappropriate or engaging in a romantic or sexual relationship that violates the professional code of ethics or professional code of conduct.

Consensual sex between two adults can be considered rape if there is an imbalance of power such as a doctor patient relationship. Do not have sex with patients.

Sexual Harassment - unwanted, unwelcome, inappropriate sexual behavior including remarks, suggestions or physical advances.

HIPPA - Health Insurance Privacy and Portability Act fo 1996 was created to modernize how healthcare information is shared and stipulate how healthcare professionals should protect personally identifiable information from theft and fraud.

Expert witness - a person qualified by special studies in special areas of knowledge, allowed to give their opinion.

Reasonable Man Standard - the action would be performed by any reasonable person.

Privileged communication - confidential communication that does not have to be revealed in court. (Husband/wife, doctor/patient, lawyer/client).

Contributory negligence doctrine - a person may not collect damages if their own negligence contributed to the cause.

Partnership responsibility - all partners are liable for the negligence of one another or of an employee. Release of one partner from liability releases liability for all.

Termination of partnership - In the event of death surviving partner can buy interest from the deceased estate.

Subpoena - a written legal order requiring one to appear in court to give testimony.

Summons - an official order to appear in court to respond as a defendant to a charge.

Plaintiff - The party bringing a complaint that bear the burden of proof.

Respondent superior - an employer is responsible for the torts (civil wrong) of their employee.

Good Samaritan Statute - Doctor assisting an individual in an emergency situation who is otherwise not their patient most states offer protection for the doctor from suit. Prevents doctors from being sued because they acted as a good samaritan.

Vicarious Liability - the responsibility of the superior for the actions of subordinates. If your assistant assaults a patient you are liable.

Civil Court - noncriminal court.

Tort - wrong doing that leads to civil legal liability, not criminal.

Tortfeasor - the person(s) that commits the civil wrong.

Intentional Tort - a civil wrong resulting from an intentional act by the tortfeasor.

Negligence - to act in a careless manner that violates the standard of care.

Malpractice case - tried in a tort (civil wrong) court.

Malpractice - the doctor must take the action a reasonable doctor would take.

Elements of Malpractice; (4 Ds of Malpractice)

Duty - the responsibility bore by accepting a patient. Once the doctor patient relationship is formed the doctor has the duty to treat the patient in a reasonable and prudent manner.

Dereliction - negligence of duty. Must be a specific act or omission (failure to act).

Directness - causation. Did the act directly cause harm?

Damages - Did the harm cause an out of pocket expense, pain and suffering or loss of earnings?

Breach of Duty - failure to meet/follow the standard of care resulting in harm, damage or loss.

Proximate Cause - an act or omission is the cause of loss or damage.

Restitution - the restoration of something lost, stolen, damaged to its proper owner; to compensate for injury or loss.

Mandatory Reporting - most states require the chiropractor to report; child abuse, communicable diseases and gunshot wounds (other suspicious wounds).

Risk Management - the anticipation and evaluation of risk with the identification of procedures to avoid or minimize their impact. You open a practice on the banks of a rive. What do you if/when the river floods? You purchase flood insurance in anticipation and evaluation of this risk.

Duress - any action taken against a person to make (force) them to do something against their will or against their better judgment.

Never take the risk, never drink and drive. You should be familiar with your state's laws and regulations. In some cases if there is any chance you could potentially fail a field sobriety test, it is possible that refusing the test could result in the loss of your driver's license and not your chiropractic license but every situation and every jurisdiction is different. Never drink and drive. Know your state's laws especially if you intend to consume alcohol.

Healthcare Laws are regulated by the states. Many of the laws and definitions as they relate to the practice of chiropractic are defined by the state.

<u>Voir Dire</u> - to speak the truth.

<u>Res ipsa loquitor</u> - the thing speaks for itself.

<u>Res adjudicata</u> - the matter has been decided.

<u>Most Common Mistakes Made during Deposition:</u>
Not answering the question asked.
Offering extra information beyond the questions asked.
Offering opinions outside the area of expertise.
Not keeping a written record, detailed history and/or accurate notes.
Not documenting exam results, anything and everything, write it down.
Improper use of terms or wording, not saying what you meant to say.
Not being directed confident by using statements such as, "I think so."
Becoming emotional, stay clam.

Healthcare Models

Cybernetic Model - analyzes systems interactions and considers patterns of interaction and groups of variable. AKA Schachter Model.

Linear - looking for direct cause and effect relationships (James Lange).

Reductionistic - the whole is equal to the sum or the parts. The medical model of healthcare.

Cartesian Dualism - separation of the mind and the body.

Vitalistic - the whole is great than the sum of the parts. No one part is acted upon without affecting all other parts. This is the chiropractic model of healthcare.

Chiropractic Practices

Goniometer - used to measure the range of motion of the arms and legs.

Inclinometer - used to measure range of motion of the spine.

Dynamometer - used to measure grip strength.

Static Palpation - digital palpation for assessment of static alignment and point tenderness by pressing on the hard and soft tissues using the pads of the fingers.

Soft Tissue Palpation - assess the para-spinal tissues for signs of inflammation (heat and swelling) and superficial edema. Asses muscle for hyper-tonicity indicating nerve irritation or dysfunction in areas of fixation. Boggy or doughy consistency near the spinous process indicates trophic changes.

Motion Palpation - assess the range of motion in a joint including end feel with and without patient assistance (active/passive). Intersegmental range of motion is the palpation of the intervertebral motion during passive and active range of motion (ROM).

Active Range of Motion - the patient (PT) moves the joint(s) through a full range of motion, making note of any painful motion.

Passive Range of Motion - the examiner move the joint(s) through a normal range of motion taking note of any painful motion.

Tenderness - the etiology of the PT pain is often associated with the most tender segment. Use digital palpation to find the most painful segment by pressing on the spinous process (SP) and surrounding tissues.

Muscular Palpation - normal muscle is soft and pliable. Spasm and/or hypertonicity of para-spinal muscles maybe related to segmental dysfunction, nerve irritations, point fixation. Assess the area for trigger points.

Postural Analysis - Observe the patient from all sides taking note of symmetry and the relationship of anatomical structures including; shoulders, hips, scapulae, gluteal folds, ears, spine and knees. Observe the patient standing with the eyes closed. Compare their posture to the ideal posture, lateral plum line, normal anatomic curves and ares of stress.

Leg Length Inequality - assisted by x-ray or with the patient in a prone or supine position the DR must determine if the inequality is structural or functional.

Functional Short Leg - is a leg length inequality due to a muscle imbalance, pelvic tilt, scoliosis or any other reason that is not an anatomical anomaly.

Structure Short Leg - is a leg length inequality that is do to an anatomical anomaly or osseous inequality.

Trophic Changes - boggy or doughy consistency detected with digital palpation near the spine indicate neurological dysfunction.

Planes of motion:
Sagittal plane (longitudinal) = flexion/extension
Transverse (axial) plane = rotation
Coronal (frontal) plane = lateral flexion

Axis of motion or Cartesian coordinate system;
X-axis = flexion/extension; +X is flexion and -X is extension
Y-axis = rotation; +Y is left rotation and -Y is right rotation
Z-axis = lateral flexion; +Z is right lateral flexion and -Z is left lateral flexion

Coupled motion - Cervical spine and upper thoracic spine spinous processes rotates toward (into) convexity and the body rotate toward (into) the concavity. While in the lower thoracic and lumbar spine spinous processes rotates toward (into) the concavity and the body rotates toward (into) the convexity.

Grade reflexes (0-5)
0 - absent
1+ - hypoactive
2+ - normal
3+ - hyperactive
4+ - hyperactive with transient clonus
5+ - hyperactive with sustained clonus

Deep Tendon Reflexes;
Biceps - C5-C6
Triceps C7
Brachioradialis - C6
Patellar - L4
Achilles - S1 nerve root

Babinski - pathological reflex indicating UMNL presents with ankle clonus in dorsiflex ankle.

Motor evaluation - Grade muscle strength (0-5)
5 = full ROM with resistance, normal
4 = full ROM with some resistance, good
3 = full ROM with gravity, fair
2 = ROM present without gravity
1 = no ROM, traceable, palpable contraction
0 = no ROM, no traceable, palpable contraction, no joint motion

Dermatome(s); an area of skin that is mainly supplied by an individual spinal nerve:

Cervical Spine dermatomes;
C1 - none
C2 - above occiput
C3 - below occiput
C4 - nape of neck
C5 - lateral brachium
C6 - lateral antebrachium, thumb, 1st finger
C7 - middle finger
C8 - medial antebrachium, 4th & 5th fingers

Thoracic spine dermatomes:
T1 - medial brachium
T4 - nipple
T7 - xiphoid process
T10 - umbilicus
T12 - above inguinal crease

Lumbar spine dermatomes:
L1 - below inguinal crease
L4 - medial leg to foot and big toe
L5 - dorsum of foot
S1 - lateral leg and foot (Achilles)

The web between the great and second toe is a key sensory areas used to test the L5 dermatome.

Cervical Facets - in the Transverse plane guide Rotation.
Thoracic Facets - in the Coronal plane guide Lateral Flexion.
Lumbar Facets - in the Sagital plane guide Flexion/Extension.
Lumbosacral Facets - in the Coronal plane guide Lateral Flexion.

Anterior Longitudinal Ligament (ALL) - Runs down the anterior aspect of all vertebral bodies and intervertebral discs (IVD) of the spine.

Posterior Longitudinal Ligament (PLL) - Situated within the central canal the PLL runs down the posterior surface of vertebral bodies from axis to sacrum. It is continuous with the tectorial membrane of the atlanto-axial joint. Thickest in the thoracic region, broader superior compared to inferior, wider at IVD compared to vertebral body. Prevents hyper-flexion of the spine.

Ligamentum Flavum - Yellow ligaments of the spine that connect adjacent laminae from axis to the first sacral segment. Elastic tissue with increased elastin, attach to the anterior inferior aspect of the lamina above to the superior posterior aspect of the lamina below. Hypertrophy can cause spinal stenosis in patient's with Diffuse Idiopathic Skeletal Hyperostosis (DISH).

Ligamentum Nuchae - Continuous with the supraspinous ligament, extends from the External Occipital Protuberance (EOP) and medial nuchal line to the spinous process of C7. Attaches to the posterior tubercle of atlas to the spinous processes of the cervical spine forming a septum between muscle of the neck. The traps and splenius capitis muscles attach to the nuchal ligament.

Posterior Atlanto-Occipital Membrane - a broad, thin membrane that attaches above the posterior margin of the foramen magnum and below the upper border of the posterior arch of atlas. The Vertebral artery transmits this membrane. Calcification at the posterior arch is called posterior ponticus that could possibly compress the vertebral artery.

Apical Ligament - Attaches the Apex of the Dens to the anterior margin of the foramen magnum. Commonly poorly developed thought to be rudimentary intervertebral fibrocartilage as traces of the notochord may persist with in it.

Alar Ligaments - Connect the lateral aspect of the dens to tubercles on the medial aspect of the occipital condyles. Short, tough, fibers ligaments that limit (check) side to side movement of the head with rotation. AKA Check Ligaments of the Odontoid.

Transverse Ligament of Atlas - is thick band that arches across the ring of the atlas and retains the dens in contact with C1. Clinically significant because this ligament may become compromised with rheumatoid arthritis, Down's Syndrome and Ankylosis Spondylitis.

Surface Anatomy, Palpable Landmarks:

External Occipital Protuberance (EOP) - base of the skull, knob at the most posterior aspect of the skull.

Axis (C2) - the first palpable spinous process (SP) below the EOP.

C3 - the smallest SP in the cervical spine, at same level as Hyoid Bone.

C4 - Superior aspect of the Thyroid Cartilage.

C5 - Inferior aspect of the Thyroid Cartilage.

C6 - Cricoid cartilage, carotid tubercle, last moveable spinous process (SP) in the flexion and extension.

C7 - Vertebral Prominence

T2 - Jugular Notch

T3 - Spine of the Scapula

T5 - Sternal Angle, Angle of Louis

T6 - Inferior angle of the scapula in recumbent position.

T7 - Inferior angle of the scapula in an upright position.

L4 - at same level with the iliac crests

S2 - at same level with the PSIS

The Scotty Dog;
Ear - Superior Facet (SupEARior Facet)
Tail - Transvers Process (TP) (T-tail)
Leg - Inferior Facet
Eye - Pedicle (spedicle like spectacles)
Nose- Transverse Process (TP) (blow your nose in TP)
Body - Lamina
Collar - Fracture of the Pars.

Scoliosis - abnormal sideways (lateral) curve (deviation) of the spine.

Scoliosis is based upon the convexity, always stand on the side of the convexity.

Structural Curve - fixed segment does not correct with lateral flection

Functional Curve - no structural change, curve corrects or over corrects with lateral flexion when the patient is probe.

Primary Curve - First abnormal curve to appear.

Major Curve - the abnormal curve with the greatest angulation.

Minor Curve - any abnormal curve less sever than the major curve.

Secondary Curve - compensatory abnormal curve to the primary curve.

Simple scoliosis the spinous process is on the side of convexity

Rotatory scoliosis the spinous process is on opposite side of convexity

Lovett Postive (rotatory) - vertebral body rotation and convexity toward and proportional to the low side of the sacrum.

Lovett Positive in Excess - vertebral body rotation and convexity toward the low side of the sacrum to a greater degree that would be expected most likely due to muscle spasm. (open wedge on convexity)

Lovett Negative (simple) - the convexity of the curve is toward the low side of the sacrum and vertebral body rotation is toward the high side of the sacrum.

Lovett Static - the convexity is toward the low side of the sacrum with no body rotation.

Lovett Failure - there is no compensatory scoliosis, there is no body rotation. Associated with disc problems.

Lovett Reverse - the convexity is away from the low side of the sacrum indicating disc hypoplasia.

Most important factor in the treatment of scoliosis is early detection.

Lateral Plum Line pass through:
External Auditory Meatus
Anterior Body of C7
Center of the Shoulder
Anterior 1/3rd of the Sacral Base
Center of the Hip Joint
Posterior to the Patella
1 inch anterior to the Lateral Malleolus

Lumbar Hyper-Lordosis - Tight erectors, tight quads, weak abs, weak hamstrings.

Lumbar Hypo-Lordosis - Tight abs, tight hamstrings, weak erectors, weak quads.

Contraindications to Chiropractic Care;

Vascular Conditions - vertebrobasilar artery insufficiency, severe atherosclerosis, aneurysm.

Tumors - primary or metastases to bone predispose patient to pathological fractures. Asses for integrity of bone before adjusting the patient.

Bone Infection (osteomyelitis) - can result in osteopenia and predispose the patient to pathological fracture.

<u>Trauma</u> - fractures, joint instability, hyper-mobility, sever sprain/strain injuries, any instability in general is a contraindication.

<u>Arthritis</u> - Rheumatoid Arthritis (RA), Ankylosing Spondylitis (AS), Prosriatic Arthritis, transverse ligament involvement, neurological compromise, joint instability.

<u>Metabolic Disorders</u> - clotting disorders, osteopenia can predispose the patient to pathological fractures.

<u>Neurological Complications</u> - Disc protrusion/herniation can involve the nerve root and result in permanent neurological deficits, same for any other space occupying lesion (SOL) involving the nerve root or spinal cord are contraindicated for chiropractic care.

Advanced Bone softening or demineralization (osteoporosis) can decrease the bones resilience to compressive focus. High Amplitude Low Amplitude (HVLA) corrective thrust are contraindicated in patient with "brittle bones."

Paradoxical Breathing, chest or abdominal motion is a contraindication to chiropractic care and warrant a medical referral. If due to trauma or illness could indicate an emergency.

The purpose of chiropractic care is to remove the subluxation complex, meaning chiropractic care is indicated when any of the components of subluxation exist.

Stable fractures may not be a contraindication to chiropractic care. <u>Clay Shoveler's fracture</u> of the C7 spinous process (SP) is a stable fracture and is <u>not a contraindication</u> for chiropractic care.

<u>Unstable Fractures of the Cervical Spine (contraindications);</u>

<u>Flexion Tear Drop Fracture</u> - anterior inferior aspect of the cervical vertebral body due to hyper flexion with axial compression, associated with spinal cord injury unstable fracture considered sever injury.

Extension Tear Drop Fracture - forced cervical extension causes the avulsion of the ALL at the anteroinferior corned for the cervical vertebral body. This fracture is stable in flexion and unstable in extension, not considered as sever as a flexion teardrop fracture.

Hangman's Fracture - fracture of both pedicles of axis (C2).

Jefferson's Fracrture - fracture of the anterior and posterior arches of atlas (C1). Caused by axial force and/or hyper-extension of the neck.

Type II Dens Fractrure - a fracture through the base of the dens at the junction of the base of the dens and the body of C2, is considered an unstable fracture.

Classification of Dens Fractures;

Type I - avulsion fracture of the apex, considered stable.

Type II - fracture at the base of the dens considered unstable.

Type III - fracture extend from the dens into the body of C2, considered unstable.

Flexion Malposition - wedging at the anterior aspect of the vertebral body increases the spacing between SP of the involved motion segment and enlarges the IVF.

Lateral Flexion Malposition - lateral wedging of the vertebral body is visible on A-P X-ray.

Extension Malposition - wedging at the posterior aspect of the vertebral body with the SP of the involved segment move closer together making the IFV smaller.

Rotational Malposition - vertebral rotation visible on X-ray.

Retrolisthesis - sever posterior displacement, break in George's Line, due to the degeneration of the IVD, decreasing the size of the IVF.

Paraphysiological Zone - described as the portion of range of motion that is beyond the active and passive ranges of motion prior to the anatomical restriction of the joint. Joint Mobilization occurs within the passive range of motion while manipulation occurs within the paraphysiological zone.

Gonstead emphasizes posteriority (P) of the spinous process as the primary basis for the subluxation listing. Right (R) or Left (L) indicate spinous process rotation. Superior (S) or Inferior (I) indicate lateral flexion or open wedge.

Posteriority - according to Gonstead all vertebra expect Atlas (C1) must first subluxate posterior in relationship to the bone below. All listing (except C1) start with P.

PRS: **P**osterior spinous **R**ight spinous, **S**uperior vertebral body (open wedge)

PRI: **P**osterior spinous **R**ight spinous rotation, **I**nferior vertebral body (closed wedge)

PLS: **P**osterior spinous **L**eft rotation spinous, **S**uperior vertebral body (open wedge)

PLI: **P**osterior spinous **L**eft spinous, **I**nferior vertebral body/ (closed wedge)

Anterior Superior (AS) Ilium - According to Gonstead; shorter innominate, smaller obteruator foramen, decreased lumbar lordosis, raised femur head level, spongy edema at the posterior inferior margin of the SI joint, Sacrum is posterior on the involved side.

AS Ilium - According to other techniques; low iliac crest, high femur head, PS sacrum, Lumbar SP rotation, Lumbar concavity, long leg, corrected with sole lift.

Posterior Inferior (PI) Ilium - Longer innominate, Larger obturator foramen, increased lumbar lordosis, lower femur heads level, spongey edema at the posterior superior margin of the SI joint, sacrum anterior on the involved side.

PI Ilium - According to other techniques, high iliac crest, low femur head, AI sacrum, Lumbar body rotation, Lumbar convexity, short leg, corrected with heel lift.

External (EX) Ilium - Decreased width producing a narrow ilium, Increased width at the base of the obturator foramen, Anterior lumbar curve increased, Lowers the femur head.

Internal (IN) ilium - Increased width of the ilium making it wider, appears to narrow the base of the obturator foramen, decreases normal anterior curve, may cause foot flare away from the midline.

PRS-SP or PLS-SP - indicate contact spinous process contact point in the thoracic or lumbar spine.

PRI-T or PLI-T - indicate transverse process contact point in the thoracic spine.

PRI-M or PLI-M - indicates to contact mammillary process in the lumbar spine.

Thoracic and Lumbar Listing can have either a Spinous (SP) contact or Transvers Process (T) contact.

The doctor stands on the side of open wedge for adjustment, torque closes open wedge. Do not cross the mid-line of the spine to make adjustment.

Atlas subluxations - According to Gonstead primary direction of subluxation is anterior. As the atlas rotates on the lateral mass the anterior side widens on an AP x-ray and the posterior side appears narrower.

Four letter Listings of Atlas subluxation:
First   - A for anteriority. (A is for Atlas)
Second   - S or I for superior or inferior anterior tubercle. (Torque)
Third   - R or L for Right or Left for laterality. (line of drive)
Fourth   - A or P for Anterior or Posterior TP on side of laterality.

Atlas Listings: ASRA, ASRP, ASLA, ASLP, AIRA, AIRP, AILA, AILP

4th letter is not required.

The segmental contact point for an ASR atlas listing is the right transverse process. The posterior arch is the contact only if rotation is present. (P or A at end of listing)

PRS - Right Rotation with open wedge on the right and spinous contact.
PRI-M - Right Rotation with open wedge on the left and left mammillary contact.
PR-M - Right Rotation with no open wedge scoliosis on the left and left mammillary contact.

<u>Intersegmental Range of Motion (IROM)</u> - a type of motion palpation used to identify segmental loss of full range of motion in any of the 6 degrees of freedom compared to standard motion palpation that assess a joint for end feel.

<u>Subluxation (Gonstead)</u> - a vertebral misalignment that results in nerve interference; the dis-relationship of the facets is the result of and secondary to the misalignment of the intervertebral disc.

<u>Compensation</u> - a misalignment in the spine that is created as a result of the body attempting to offset or overcome the imbalances created by the subluxation.

<u>Disc Plane Line</u> - the practice of Gonstead places great importance on adjusting vertebra from posterior to anterior with a thrust parallel to the disc plane line.

<u>Types of Fixation according to Gillet</u>

<u>Type I Muscular</u> - due to chronic involuntary hypertonicity of muscle. Deep digital palpation reveals taut and tender muscle fibers. Motion palpation demonstrates restricted mobility with rubbery end feel. Commonly secondary or minor subluxation.

<u>Type II Ligamentous</u> - A chronically fixated segment results in shortening of the associated ligaments. Motion palpation reveals hard end feel with no end play and normal range of motion.

<u>Type III Articular (Capsular)</u> - Intra-articular adhesion results in an immobile joint. Active range of motion is limited and painful in all directions. Commonly primary or major subluxation.

<u>Type IV Bony</u> - Due to exostosis motion palpation reveals free motion to the point of abrupt hard end feel.

Public Health Organizations;

<u>World Health Organization (WHO)</u> - AN agency of the United Nations that is dedicated to international public health was established on April 7, 1948 based in Geneva Switzerland.

<u>Center for Disease Control and Prevention (CDC)</u> - the leading national public health institute of the United States that is dedicated to the protecting the public health and safety through the control and prevention of disease, injury and disability.

<u>American Public Health Association (APHA)</u> - a professional organization of public health professionals in the US founded in 1872 by a group of physicians. Their goal is to influence federal healthcare policy for all people in all communities to "improve the health of the public and achieve equity in health status."

<u>National Institute of Health (NIH)</u> - the primary agency of the US government responsible for biomedical and public health research that was founded in the 1870s and is now a part of the US Department of Health and Human Services. NIH both conducts and funds research.

<u>Food and Drug Administration (FDA)</u> - protects public health by ensuring the safety, efficacy and security of the both human and veterinary drugs, biological products, medical devices and ensuring the safety of our nation's food supply, cosmetics and products that emit radiation.

<u>Center for Medicare and Medicate Services (CMS)</u> - a federal agency within the US Department of Health and Human Services that administers the Medicare and Medicaid programs in partnership with state governments.

<u>American Red Cross</u> - a humanitarian organization that provides emergent assistance, disaster relief and preparedness education in the United States.

America Medical Association (AMA) - Founded in 1847 the AMA is the largest association of MD, DO and medical students in the US who's stated mission is to promote the art and science of medicine and the betterment of public health.

Tobacco - a plant that is grown for its leaves that contain the addictive ingredient nicotine that once in the blood stream stimulates the adrenal glads to release epinephrine which stimulates the CNS, increases blood pressure, respiration rate and heart rate. Nicotine also increases dopamine levels stimulating the brains reward center.

Tobacco can be introduced in the the blood stream by smoking, chewing, or sniffing it in various forms.

Nicotine - is a stimulant and potent parasympathomimetic alkaloid that is naturally produced in the nightshade family of plants.

Parasympathomimetic - A substance that stimulate the parasympathetic nervous system. AKA; cholinomimetic drug, cholinergic receptor stimulating agent or cholinergic drugs because acetylcholine (ACh) is the parasympathetic neurotransmitter.

Smoking Tobacco - while nicotine is addictive most of the sever health effects of smoking tobacco come from other chemicals that can cause; lung cancer, chronic bronchitis, emphysema, COPD. Smoking also increases the risk of heart disease, stroke, leukemia, cataracts and pneumonia.

Chewing Tobacco - increases the risk of cancer in the body especially the mouth and throat. Chronic use can result in other dental issues.

Tobacco Withdrawal - long term use of tobacco changes brain chemistry that results in addiction and withdrawal symptoms that include; irritability, lack of attention, problems sleeping, increased appetite and powerful craving to use tobacco.

Healthy People 2020 Tobacco Use Initiative; Increase the price of tobacco products, implement hard hitting anti-tobacco media campaigns. Control (reduce) access to all tobacco products including e-cigarettes. Adopt policies and strategies to increase the access, affordability and use of smoking cessation services and treatments. Establish policies to reduce exposure to secondhand smoke, restrict tobacco advertising and reduce illegal sales to minors.

FDA has the authority to regulate the sales, marketing and manufacturing of all tobacco produces sold in the US.

CDC launched the first ever pain national education anti-tobacco marketing campaign that resulted in 1.6 million people attempting to quit smoking in 2012.

Effects of Alcohol - reduced inhibitions, slurred speech, impaired motor function, mental confusion, problem with memory and concentration.

Risks of consuming alcohol include; falling, car crashes, risk taking and violent behavior that can all result in death or injury.

Alcohol's effect on the Brain; the chronic abuse of alcohol can result in a deficiency of Thiamine (B1) leading to wernicke-koraskoff syndrome.

Alcohol's effect on the Heart; drinking too much over time or on a single occasion can result in cardiomyopathy, arrhythmias, stroke and/or high blood pressure.

Alcohol's effect on the Liver; heavy drinking the result in steatosis (fatty liver), hepatitis, fibrosis and cirrhosis of the liver.

Alcohol's effect on the Pancreas; drinking causes the pancreas that produce toxic substances that inflammation. Chronic inflammation of the pancreas is dangerous and leads to swelling fo the blood vessels in the pancreases that prevent proper digestion.

Cancer and Alcohol Consumption; the consumption of 3.5 drinks per day or more increased the risk of developing cancer of the pharynx, larynx, esophagus, liver, breast, colon and rectum.

Alcohol Use Disorder (AUD) - a medical diagnosis of chronic relapsing, loss of control over the use of alcohol, compulsive alcohol use and a negative emotional state when not using.

AUD questions; in the past year;

Have you had time when you drank more or longer than intended?

Have you want to cut dow or stop drinking more than once but couldn't?

Have spent a lot of time drinking or being sick from drinking?

Have you experienced cravings or a strong need (urge) to drink?

Have you continued to drink when drinking was causing problems with friends or family?

Have you given up anything that was important or interesting to you in order to keep drinking?

Have you found that drinking or being sick from drinking interfered with your ability to take care of your home, family, job or school commitments?

Have you more than once found that drinking or the after effects of drinking increased your chances of getting hurt because of risk taking behavior? Examples driving or swimming drunk, having unprotected sex.

Have you continued to drink while drinking made you feel depressed, anxious or caused some other health problem (illness)?

Have you noticed that you need to drink more to get the desired effect or found the number of drinks you consumed no longer had the same effect?

Have you found that when the effects of alcohol wear off that you have withdrawn symptoms like; trouble sleeping, shaking, irritability, anxiety, depression, restlessness, nausea, sweating, itching or even sensed any thing you know was not there?

If the answers is yes to anyone of these questions their drinking is cause for concern.

15-20% of Americans develop protracted back pain.

Americans Spend at least $50 billion per year on low back pain (LBP).

1% of the American work force is completely and permanently disable as a result of LBP.

LBP is second only to the common cold for time lost at work.

LBP is the third leading cause of surgical procedure in the US and 5th most common cause of hospitalization.

Exercises

Isometric - muscle contraction with no change in muscle length.

Isotonic - resistance to muscle contraction remains constant through a range of motion.

Concentric - contraction with muscle shortening

Eccentric - lack of contraction with muscle lengthen

Isokinetic - full range of motion agains the rate of limiting device such as a dynamometer.

McKenzie Exercises - repetitions of slow controlled hyper-extension of the lumbar spine to the point of stretching or mild discomfort. Series of simple exercises used to maintain lumbar lordosis and decrease the symptoms of lumbar disc pathology based on the premise that lumbar flexion stresses the posterior soft tissue. Contraindicated for PT with facet syndrome and spondylolisthesis.

Willaim's Exercises - Flexion exercises (opposite of McKenzie) designed to reduce lumbar lordosis indicated for facet syndrome and spondylolisthesis.

Buerger Allen - peripheral vascular disease

Codman's Pendular Exercise - shoulder bursitis or tendinitis, rotator cuff rehabilitation.

Wall Climbing - PT faces the wall at a distance that the finger tips just touch it with the out reached arm. Keeping the shoulder down (no shrugging) PT walks their fingers up the wall as high as pain will allow and holds that position for 30 seconds before slowly walking the fingers back down the wall.

Bobath's Therapy - Aim of this approach is to increase range of motion and mobility of patients with damage to the CNS. Described as Neurodevelopment Treatment (NDT) neuromuscular and function re-education is based upon neuroplasticity. By facilitation of normal posture (alignment) and motion patters demand is placed on the involved side as somatosensory reinforcement is essential the recovery process. Think PNF.

DeLorme Technique (method) - strengthens muscle using repeated sets of repetition with rest in between each set. Progressive resistance (weight) builds muscle. The method involves using isotonic exercise typically in repeated sets of 10.

Frenkel Exercises - used to treat cerebellar ataxia this system of slow exercises of increasing difficultly with the patient observing their own motions and makes corrections as necessary.

Jocobson's Relaxation Technique - focuses on contracting and relaxing specific muscle groups in a sequence described as progressive relaxation therapy. The goal is to gain body awareness and reduce stress.

Kegel - repetitive contraction of the pubococcygeous muscle often suggested for postpartum females.

Hilton's Law - the nerve supplying the muscles extending across and acting upon a joint not only supplies the muscle but also innervates the joint and the skin overlying the muscle.

Bell-Magendie Law - the anterior spinal nerve roots contain motor fibers and the posterior roots contain sensory fibers and nerve impulses are conducted in one one direction in each case.

Heuter Volkmann Law - bone growth is retarded by increased mechanical compression, and accelerated by the reduced loading of the growth plate in comparison with normal values. This law is often used to explain scoliosis and is related to the growth of maturing (growing) bone, not mature bone.

Wolff's Law - bone in a healthy mature person will adapt to the loads placed upon it. Specific load (stress) in specific direction will result in remodeling of bone along the lines of stress. Explain changes in normal healthy bone.

Davis's Law - soft tissues models along imposed demands. Mechanical stress dictates how soft tissue will heal. This the soft tissue version of Wolff's Law.

Six classifications for Degenerative Disc Disease

D1 disk – seen on lateral films, increased disk space due to increase in fluid uptake within disk (acutely swollen disk). In lumbar spine injury 90% of the damage is posterior to nucleus pulposis.

D2 disk – first stage of disk degeneration shows small decrease in posterior part of disk space with slight retrolisthesis.

D3 disk – very thin posterior with little change occurring anteriorly.
D4 disk – early disk thinning, reduced to 2/3 original height, also narrows Z-joint.

D5 disk – reduction to 1/3 original height (5-20 years after injury).

D6 disk – disk nearly gone; natural fusion.

The Occupational Safety and Health Administration (OSHA) - an agency of the US Department of Labor established by congress under the Occupation Safety and Health Act signed into law by President Nixon in 1970 to assume safe, healthy working conditions for men and woman by enforcing standards, providing training, education and assistance.
Under federal law (OSHA) workers have the right to; be trained in a language they understand, use machines that are safe to operate, be provided the required safety equipment to work safely, be protected from toxic chemicals, review copies of the workplace injury/illness log, review copies of test results done to find hazards in the work place.

All employees have the right to a safe and healthy workplace. The means the employer must take action to insure the workplace is clean, has sufficient lighting, sanitation (bathrooms) and proper ventilation.

<u>Proper Lifting</u> Technique - Do not attempt to lift anything by bending forward, always bend at the hips and knees squatting down to the load you are attempting to lift. Keep the load close to your body and lift with your legs. Never lift heave objects above the shoulder level and always avoid turning or twisting the trunk of your body while lifting or holding a heavy object (load).

<u>Eight Steps to Proper Lifting</u>;
1. Plan your lift. Check you path, check the weight and ask, "Can I do this alone?"
2. Ask for help. If there are obstacles in your path, the weight is too much or the awkward if there is any reason you might need help, ask for it.
3. Get good footing before lifting. Injuries from falls are more common that injuries from lifting.
4. Bend at the hips and knees, never bend at the waist.
5. Engage your core, tighten your stomach muscles.
6. Lift by straightening your knees, lift with your legs.
7. Keep the load, objects being lifted, as close to your body as possible.
8. Avoid twisting or turning your truck while lifting.

<u>Good Computer Ergonomics</u>;
Hands, wrists and forearms in a straight line roughly parallel to the floor.
Head is level, forward facing and balanced "in-line" with the torso.
Shoulders relaxed with the arms hanging normally at the side of the body.
Elbows stay close to the body with 90-120 degrees of flexion.
Feet are fully supported (not hanging) by either the floor or foot rest.
Lumbar curve is fully supported and the spine is vertical.
The hips and thighs are fully supported and roughly parallel to the floor.
Knees are at the same level as the hips with the feet slightly forward.

Small adjustments to the chair, desk, computer or other office equipment can help to dramatically improve posture while working.

Brief period of stretching the fingers, hands, forearms and torso can help prevent injury/symptoms from repetitive micro-trauma.

Standing - take the time to stand and walk periodically and try to do some tasks while standing.

Air Pollution - particulate and gases released into the air that may originate from car emissions, industrial use of chemicals, dust, pollen, mold, ozone (smog) can all cause an allergic reaction or have a harmful effect on human health.

Primary Pollutant - emitted directly into the atmosphere. Ex. SO_2, CO

Secondary Pollutant - form in the air by chemical reaction with other gasses in the atmosphere. Ex. Ozone, free radicals

Sources - cooking, combustion, burning, smoking, heating, suspension.

Suspension - dusted settled on the ground is not harmful. Disrupting the dust, distributing and suspending it in the air you breath is harmful.

Ozone - can lead to decreased lung function by inducing pulmonary inflammation.

Free Radicals - causes oxidative stress by reacting with metal and other compounds in the body.

Covalent Modification - a pollutant can bind to key intracellular proteins and/or enzymes rendering them useless.

Biologically Active - pollutant can be toxic and initiate an inflammatory reaction, interfere with autonomic nervous system activity, activate coagulants or suppress not immune response.

Essential Nutrient - a chemical required for normal physiological function that cannot be synthesized in the body.

Amino Acids - organic compounds that contain amine and carboxyl functional groups with a specific R group (side chain). Amino acids play an important role in a number of physiological functions including, protein synthesis, neurotransmitter transport and hormone production.

9 Essential Amino Acids - histidine, isoleucine, leucine, lysine, methionine, phenylalanine, threonine, tryptophan and valine.

Fatty Acid - a carboxylic acid with a long aliphatic chain that can be either saturated or unsaturated and divided into 3 main classes; esters, triglycerides, phospholipids and cholesterol esters. All are important as sources of fuel in the body and structural components of cells.

Saturated Fatty Acids - have no C=C double bonds.

Unsaturated Fatty Acids - have one or more C=C double bonds.

Vitamin - organic molecules that are essential micronutrients required for proper function and metabolism.

Antioxidant - molecules (compounds) that inhibit oxidation by free radicals in the body.

Fat soluble vitamins - A,D,E and K are stored for long period of time in the body (liver and fat) therefore pose a risk of toxicity. Fat soluble vitamins will not be lost in food containing them are cooked.

Vitamin A - Retinol, retinal, retinoid acid are all forms of Vitamin A which is import to helping the eyes adjust to changes in light, bone growth, tooth development, cell division, gene expression, maintaining a moist mucus membrane and regulation of the immune system. Vitamin A is also an antioxidant. Dairy Products (milk and butter), fish and liver are good sources of Vitamin A. Beta-carotene is converted to Vitamin A in the body is found in carrots, pumpkin, winter squash, apricots and dark green leafy vegetables

Vitamin A Deficiency (Xerophthalmia) - can present with dry rough skin, faulty tooth development, slow bone growth, decreased immunity (opportunistic infections), night blindness and if left untreated complete blindness.

Vitamin A Toxicity - presents with dry itchy skin, headaches, nausea, dizziness, slow growth, bone loss and pathologic fractures.

Vitamin D (Cholecalciferol) - a secosteroid plays an important role in the absorption of calcium, magnesium and phosphate. By regulating the absorption of these elements Vitamin D helps to maintain bone, control cellular growth and prevents osteoporosis, high blood reassure and cancer. The main source of Vitamin D is synthesis of cholecalciferol in the skin from cholesterol through a chemical reaction that depends upon exposure to UV light. Vitamin D is biologically inactive and must be converted by hydroxylate in the liver and kidneys into its active form where it is released. Vitamin D is stored in chylomicrons in the liver.

Vitamin D Deficiency - in young children is called Rickets which presents with soft bowed legs and flattening of the skull. In adults a lack of vitamin D can result in osteomalacia (bone softening) and/or osteoporosis (loss of bone density) and has been associated with an increased risk of developing cancer. It has been estimated that 50% of the global population suffers from Vitamin D deficiency as sunscreen is becoming more popular and outdoor activities are being less popular. Breast milk is very low in vitamin D and it is suggested that all breast fed infants be given vitamin D supplementation (400 IU/Day).

Vitamin D Toxicity - can present with sign of poisoning, nausea, vomiting and loss of appetite along with increased serum calcium levels.

Vitamin E (Tocopherol) - an antioxidant that protects Vitamin A and C, RBC and essential fatty acids from destruction. The main source of dietary vitamin E is vegetable oil but it is also found in fruits, vegetables, grains, nuts and seeds.

Vitamin E Deficiency - while rare is can occur in those unable to absorb fats or people that excessively reduce their fat intake. Vitamin E deficiency may present with disorientation, vision problems, muscle weakness and decreased immunity.

Vitamin E Toxicity - Again rare because relatively large does of vitamin E can be taken for years without any apparent harm or side effect but muscle weakness, fatigue, nausea, diarrhea and bleeds or bleeding problems are all possible. People taking statin drugs or blood thinning meds are the most prone to bleeding problem from mega does of vitamin E.

Vitamin K (Phytonadione) - is produced by gut flora and plays an important role in blood clotting and producing proteins for the blood, bones and kidneys. Vitamin K is found in turnip greens, spinach, cauliflower, cabbage, broccoli and some vegetable oils.

Vitamin K Deficiency - failure of the blood to clot or hemorrhaging can occur in those that are deficient in vitamin K. Infants lack gut flora that produce vitamin K and typically receive supplementation in the first week of life to protect them from uncontrollable bleeding. Adults my also suffer a similar effect from the long term use of antibiotics that kill off gut flora. However everyone should consult a doctor before supplementing vitamin K to avoid toxicity.

Vitamin K Toxicity - may present with liver damage and the destruction of RBC.

Water Soluble Vitamins - are not stored in the body (except for B12 that is stored in the liver) and any excess is excreted in the urine therefore must be replenished everyday.

B1 Thiamine - found in pork, liver, whole grains, peas, meats, legumes B1 helps release energy from food, promotes appetite and plays an important role in the nerve system.

B2 Riboflavin - found in liver, milk, dark green vegetables and eggs B2 helps to release energy from food and promotes good vision and healthy skin. Deficiency can result in dermatitis around the the nose and lips, cracks at the corners of the mouth and make the eyes sensitive to light.

B3 Niacin - found in liver, fish, chicken, meats and peanuts B3 helps release energy from food, aids in digestion, promote appetite and healthy skin. Deficiency can result in skin disorders, diarrhea, weakness, confusion and irritability.

B5 Pantothenic Acid - found in liver, kidney, meat, egg yolks, whole grains, legumes and more deficiency is rare because of the wide range of food it is found in but if it does occur it may present with fatigue, loss of appetite, nausea, abdominal cramps and difficulty sleeping.

B6 Pyridoxine - found in pork, meats, legumes, green leafy vegetables B6 aids in protein metabolism of fats, adsorption and RBC production. Deficiency can cause skin problems, kidney stones, irritability, anemia, nausea and smooth tongue.

B7 Biotin - found in liver, egg yolk, milk and it is also made by gut flora. B7 helps release energy from carbohydrates and aids in fay synthesis. Deficiency is rare but can present with fatigue, loss of appetite, nausea, vomiting, depression, muscle pain and anemia.

B9 Folate (folic acid, folacin) - found in liver, kidney, dark green leafy vegetables, meat, fish, whole grains, legumes and citrus fruits, B9 aids in protein metabolism, promotes RBS production, prevent birth defects of the spine and brain. Deficiency causes anemia, smooth tongue and diarrhea.

B12 Cobalamin - found only in animal products, meat, liver, kidney, fish, milk and eggs B12 aids in development normal RBC, DNA replication and maintenance of the nervous system. Deficiency causes pernicious anemia, anemia, neurological disorders, degeneration of peripheral nerves that results in numbness and tingling starting in the fingers and toes.

Vitamin C Ascorbic Acid - is found in citrus fruits, is an antioxidant that plays a role in tissue repair, the production of some neurotransmitters and it important to the functioning of several enzymes. Deficiency is called Scurvy that can present with weakness, fatigue, decreased RBC, gum disease, and changes to the hair and bleeding skin. Children may present with a flexed posture and scorbutic tongue.

Minerals - a chemical element required for the normal functions of life. Oxygen, Hydrogen, Carbon and Nitrogen are the most abundant of these elements and account for more than 90% of the weight of the human body.

Major Minerals (macrominerals) - Calcium, phosphorus, potassium, sodium and magnesium.

Trace Elements (minor minerals) - sulfur, iron, chlorine, cobalt, copper, zinc, manganese, molybdenum, iodine and selenium.

Potassium - an electrolyte that co-regulates ATP with sodium, found in potatoes, tomato, beans, lentils, dairy products, seafood, bananas, prunes, carrots and oranges.

Hypokalemia - decreased potassium in the blood resulting in lethargy, cramps, weakness, constipation and in extreme cases cardiac arrest.

Hyperkalemia - excessive kale in the diet, not really. It is actually elevated levels of blood potassium above 5.5 mmol/L. In sever cases resulting in palpitations, muscle pain, numbness and in extreme cases cardiac arrest.

Sodium - an electrolyte that co-regulates ATP with potassium, found in table salt, sea weed, milk and spinach.

Hyponatremia - low sodium levels in the blood can result in headaches, nausea, confusion and in sever cases seizures and coma.

Hypernatremia - high sodium levels in the blood that can result in strong thirst sensation, weakness, nausea, loss of appetite and in sever cases confusion, muscle twitching and bleeding on or around the brain.

Chromium - involved with the metabolism of glucose and lipids found in broccoli, grape juice, meat and whole grains.

Chromium Deficiency - lack of dietary chromium can result in impaired glucose tolerance, weight loss, peripheral nerve neuropathy and confusion.

Chromium Toxicity - in theory chromium could be toxic but cellular metabolism prevents it.

Chlorine - an electrolyte used to produce hydrochloric acid (gastric juices) and plays an important role in cellular pump functions. Main dietary source is table salt.

Hypochloremia - low levels of chlorine in the blood while rare it has been associated with chronic respiratory acidosis.

Hyperchloremia - elevated serum chlorine above 110 mEq/L indicates kidney dysfunction.

Calcium - important for muscular, cardiac and digestive functions, building bone found in dairy products, eggs, green leafy vegetables, nuts, seeds, tofu, dill and cinnamon.

Hypocalcaemia - low serum calcium levels below 2.1 mmol/l presents with numbness, muscle spasm, seizures, confusion and in extreme cases cardiac arrest.

Hypercalcaemia - high serum calcium levels above 2.6 mmol/l that presents with abdominal pain, bone pain, depression, confusion, kidney stones, abnormal heart beat and in extreme cases cardiac arrest.

Copper - important to redox enzyme function found in liver, seafood, oysters, nuts, seeds and legumes.

Copper Deficiency - a neurodegenerative syndrome that can parallel vitamin B12 deficiency presents with anemia, myelopathy, neuropathy and optic neuropathy.

Cooper Toxicity - exposure to a toxic dose of copper can present with vomiting, hematemesis, hypotension, coma, jaundice and if left untreated will result in live and kidney damage.

Phosphorus - a component of bones, cells used in processing DNA and ATP as well as many other physiological functions, found in red meat, dairy products, fish, chicken, bread, rice and oats.

Hypophosphatemia - electrolyte imbalance of low serum phosphorus that presents with weakness, loss of appetite, trouble breathing and in sever cases seizures, rhabdomyolysis and bone softening.

Hyperphsphatemia - elevated serum phosphate that indicates kidney failure, hypoprathyoridism, diabetic ketoacidosis, and rhabdomyolysis.

Iodine - is important in the production of thyroid hormones found in kelp, grains, eggs and iodized salt.

Iodine Deficiency - most common result is a goiter, decreased thyroxine, increased TSH leading to the goiter,

Iodism (iodine toxicity) - The lethal dose of iodine in an adult is 30 mg/kg because of the oxidizing properties of iodine that denature proteins.

Magnesium - required for processing ATP and bone production found in spinach, legumes, nuts, seeds, whole grains, peanuts and avocados.

Hypomagnesemia - low serum magnesium levels that presents with tremors, poor coordination, muscle spasm, loss of appetite, personality changes and nystagmus.

Hypermagnesemia - high serum magnesium levels that presents with weakness, confusion, depressed respiration, decreased reflexes and in extreme cases cardiac arrest.

Manganese - an important enzyme cofactor found in grains, legumes, seeds, nuts, leafy vegetables, tea and coffee.

Manganese Deficiency - rare condition that may present with poor boon growth, skeletal defects and slow or impaired growth.

Manganism - toxic exposure to excessive manganese presents with psychiatric and motor disturbances including irritability, mood changes, compulsive behaviors physical presentation can mimic ALS, MS and idiopathic Parkinson's disease.

Molybdenum - important to oxidase enzymes found in legumes, whole grains and nuts.

Molybdenum Deficiency - rare occurrence indicates a genetic disease.

Molybdenum Toxicity - again rare has been seen in Armenian populations and presents with gout like symptoms.

Iron - important to many proteins and enzymes especially hemoglobin, found in meat, seafood, nuts and beans and fortified foods.

Iron Deficiency (sideropaenia) - anemia, decreased RBC, irregular heartbeat, delayed or retarded growth of infants and children with impaired cognitive and behavioral development.

Iron Overload - excessive accumulation of corn in the body indicates hereditary haemachromatosis (HHC), also associated with liver cirrhosis, heart failure or hormonal issues.

Selenium - important to antioxidant enzymes found in brazil nuts, seafoods, meats, dairy products and eggs.

Selenium Deficiency - rare but when found in combination with coxsackievirus leads to Keshan disease that can be fatal. In conjunction with iodine deficiency can lead to Kashin-Beck disease. Selenium deficiency can produce the symptoms of hypothyroidism, fatigue, goiter, cretinism, recurrent miscarriage.

Selenosis - consumption of more than 400 micrograms per day and result in toxic effects including; garlic breath, GI disorders, hair loss, fatigue, irritability, and in extreme cases cirrhosis of the liver, pulmonary edema and death.

Zinc - required for normal function of several enzymes found in oysters, red meat, chicken, nuts, whole grains and dairy products.

Zinc Deficiency - inadequate zinc to meet demands of the body that presents with diarrhea, acne, eczema, xerosis, stomatitis, angular cheilitis, decreased immunity, loss of appetite, irritability, lethargy, depression, delayed growth in children. Symptoms typically only present in extreme deficiency.

Zinc Toxicity - overdose of zinc is define as ingestion of more than 225 mg of zinc that can result in nausea, vomiting, pain, cramps and diarrhea.

DASH Diet - Dietary Approach to Stop Hypertension is promoted by the National Heart, Lung and Blood Institute (part of NIH) to prevent and control hypertension.

Studies show that without any change in weight, alcohol or sodium consumption the DASH diet can reduce systolic pressure by 7.2 mm Hg and diastolic pressure by 2.8 mm Hg. In PT with hypertension the DASH diet can reduce systolic pressure by 12 mm Hg and diastolic pressure by 7 mm Hg.

Daily Servings of DASH Diet:
7-8 Grains
4-5 Vegetables
4-5 Fruits
2-3 nonfat or low fat dairy product(s)
2 or few servings of meat.
1-2 servicing of nuts, seeds, legumes

Cryotherapy - use of cold, ice packs, ice massage, can reduce edema, act as an analgesic and reduce muscle spasm. Icing is indicated for the first 72 hours after a sprain or strain, an acute inflammatory process or chronic bursitis and tendonitis.

Massage;

Effleurage - superficial stroking parallel to the muscle fibers promotes circulation.

Petrissage - kneading or rolling of the muscles.

Tapotment - tapping, slapping or cupping the skin to increase circulation.

Shiatsu - trigger point massage- deep relaxation.

Rolfing - deep tissue massage the breaks down fibrous bands.

Cross Friction Massage - used to break up adhesions with deep stroking across the muscle fibers.

Diagnostic Imaging

Y Epiphysis - Acetabulum.

Fabella - Sesamoid bone found in the lateral head of the gastrocnemius tendon proximally.

Capitulum - Distal humerus, articulates with the radial head.

Olecranon fossa - Posterior distal humerus, accepts olecranon process of the ulna.

Coronoid process - Located on the anterior ulna, articulates with the trochlea.

Coracoid process - Located on the scapula.

Supracondylar fossa - Located on the humerus.

Supraglenoid sulcus - Located on the humerus.

Paraglenoid sulcus - Female pelvis lateral to SI joints, usually postpartum, often seen with OCI.

Medial oblique - View taken to visualize the proximal talofibular joint.

Os trigonum - Accessory ossicle posterior to the tibia, superior to the calcaneus.

Os vesalianum - Sesamoid bone proximal to the fifth metatarsal.

Hahn's venous fissure - Horizontal radiolucent cleft on lateral thoracic film.

Source to Image Distance (SID) - is the distance from the tube to the film.

General Rule, for every 5 degrees of tube tilt reduce SID by one inch.

Radio Graphic positioning, like orthopedic tests, is composed of multiple elements that can all earn points on the remaining board exams. Where to measure PT thickness, SID, Film Size, tube tilt, where to point the Central Ray (CR) and PT position, breathing instructions, what the film demonstrates are all an opportunity for you to earn the points necessary to pass boards.

Cervical Spine X-rays;

AP Open Mouth (APOM) - Measure A to P at C4, Use 8 x 10 or 10 x 12 film, 40 inch SID, PT back against the bucky with their mouth open as wide as possible. PT Har Palate parallel to the floor. CR at uvula, or align the base of the occiput and inferior aspect of the PT upper teeth. Film taken with suspended respiration. Best film to observe burst/Jefferson fracture(s) of Atlas (C1).

AP Lower Cervical (APLC) - Measure A to P at C4, use 8 x 10 or 10 x 12 film, 40 inch SID, 15 degree cephalic tube tilt. PT back agains the bucky, CR at C4, film centered to CR. This film demonstrates the joints of Luschka.

Lateral Cervical - Measure laterally at base of the neck, use 10 x 12 film, 72 inch SID, there is no tube tilt, PT side against the bucky. CR at C4 posterior to the ear through atlas. Film is taken with full expiration.

Cervical Obliques - measure obliquely at C6, use 10 x 12 film, 40 inch SID, Tube tilt is *15 degrees cephalic for Posterior obliques* and *15 degrees caudal for anterior obliques.* PT positioned at 45 degree angle facing the film for anterior obliques and with their back to the film for posterior oblique. PT extends head slightly (10 degrees) and rotates toward the film to open the IVF.

Always take Right and Left posterior obliques or Right and Left anterior obliques, never mix anterior and posterior obliques in one series.

Supine Cervical Film (Pillar View) - Measure A to P at C4, use 8 x 10 film, 40 inch SID, 35 degree caudal tube tilt, CR at C4. PT is supine, Chin tucked, and head rotated 45 degrees away from the side of pillar being viewed. Must do bilateral films to compare.

Lateral Cervicothoracic (Swimmer's) view - Measure PT at T6, use a 10 x 12 film, 40 inch SID, CR through the sternal notch just anterior to the tube side shoulder. PT is standing in lateral position with arm closest to the bucky flexed and the hand on or behind the head. Use caution with recent trauma. Best view to visualize C7 which maybe obscured on lateral cervical.

Cervical Stress Films (Lateral Cervical Flexion/Extension) - Measure PT at C6, use 10 x 12 film, SID is 72 inches, there is no tube tilt. PT is upright is same position at Lateral Cervical film. Flexion stress film PT tucks chin and flexes neck maximally or to the point of pain. Film is taken with suspended full expiration. Extension stress film PT juts chin and maximally extends neck to point of pain. Film is taken with suspended full expiration.

Davis Series - in cases of whiplash, all cervical spine films are done, this is called a "Davis Series."

Thoracic Spine X-rays;

AP Thoracic - Measure PT across the shoulders from the sternum to spinous processes in the mid thoracic. Use a 14 x 17 film, SID is 40 inches, there is no tube tilt, CR is at the midline of the body at T6. PT is standing upright with back against the bucky, shielding is optional. Film is taken at full inspiration.

Lateral Thoracic - Measure PT below the arms, use 14 x 17 film, SID is 40 inches, there is no tube tilt, PT is standing upright with side against the bucky and arms above the head. If PT has significant scoliosis the convexity should be agains the bucky. Film taken at full inspiration.

Swimmer's View - Measure laterally at the inferior angle of the scapula. Use a 8 x 10 or 10 by 13 film, 40 inch SID, 2.5 cm superior to the jugular notch at T1 film during suspended inspiration. Best film to visualize C7.

Thoracic Spine Films - SID is 40, film is 14 x 17, no tube tilt, full inspiration.

If the gonads are in the general area being exposed assume shielding.

Lumbar Spine X-rays

AP Lumbopelvic - Measure A to P at thickest part of the abdomen or at ASIS, use 14 x 17 film, 40 inch SID, no tube tilt, CR 1 and 1/2 inches below the iliac crest, film taken during suspended expiration. This is a chiropractic film.

AP Pelvis - Measure through path of CR, use 14 x 17 film, 40 inch SID, CR midway though the pubic symphysis and the iliac crest. Center the film to the CR. Film taken with suspended expiration. PT is standing with back agains the bucky, internally rotate the feet approximately 15 degrees (heels apart toes together).

Lateral Lumbar - Measure PT at ASIS, use a 14 by 17 film, 40 inch SID, there is no tube tilt, CR is between the ASIS and PSIS at the top of the iliac crest, the film is centered to the CR. Film is taken with suspended expiration. Best film to visualize the Lumbar IVF.

Lateral Lumbrosacral - Measure just below the iliac crests, use 14 x 17 film, 40 inch SID, CR at iliac crest, take film durning suspended expiration.

Lumbar Obliques - measure at L3 obliquely, use a 10 x 12 film, 40 inch SID, No tube tilt, PT is upright at 45 degrees facing the film for anteriors and at 45 facing the tube for posterior obliques. Shield the gonads. CR for anterior films is one inch lateral from L3 SP not he side closest to the tube. CR for posterior films is 2 inches medal the ASIS on the side closest to the tube. Film is taken with suspended expiration. The Scotty Dog Films.

Lumbar Films - SID is 40 inches, films taken with suspended expiration.

Sacral Posterior Oblique - Measure PT through the path of the CR. Use a 10 x 12 film, 40 inch SID, *no tube tilt*, PT is standing at 25-30 degrees from the bucky, CR is one inch medial to the ASIS on the side closest to the tube. Shield Gonads, film is taken with suspended expiration. *No tube tilt*.

L5/S1 Spot (Sacral Base) - measure PT through the path of the CR. Use a 10 by 12 film, 40 inch SID, *tube tilt is 30 degrees cephalad for males and 35 degrees for females*. AP films the CR is midways between the ASIS and pubis. PA films the CR is at L5/S1 about 1.5 inches below the iliac crest. The film is taken with suspended expiration.

AP/PA Sacrum - measure PT through the path of the CR, use a 10 x 12 film, SID is 40 inches. *Tube tilt is 15 degrees cephalic* for AP film and 15 degrees caudal for PA film. CR is aimed midway between the ASIS and pubis for AP and PA films. Film is taken with suspended expiration.

Lateral Sacrum - measure PT at the ASIS, use a 10 bt 12 film, 40 inch SID, *no tube tilt*, PT is standing with side against the bucky, CR is 2 inches anterior to the posterior body surface at the level of the ASIS. Film is take with suspended expiration.

Sacrum Films - 40 inch SID, 10 x 12 film, suspended expiration.
AP Coccyx - measure PT 2 inches superior to the pubic bone, use 8 x 10 film, 40 inch SID, <u>10 degree caudal tube tilt</u>, PT is standing back against the bucky, CR is midway between the ASIS and pubis. Film is taken with suspended expiration. *AP Coccyx - Caudal tube tilt.*

Lateral Coccyx - measure PT at the sacrococcygeal junction, use 8 x 10 film, 40 inch SID, no tube tilt, PT is standing with side against the bucky, CR is 2 inches anterior to the posterior body and one inch above the greater trochanter. Film is taken with suspended expiration. *No tube tilt.*

Coccyx films - 40 inch SID, 8 x 10 film, suspended expiration.

Lower Extremity Films - SID is 40.

Hip Frog Leg - SID is 40 Hip is flexed and externally rotated CR aimed at the hip joint.

AP Hip - internally rotate the ankles 15 degrees to best observe the greater trochanter with CR aimed the hip joint.

AP Knee - SID is 40, PT is supine, 5 degree cephalic tube tilt, CR at the inferior aspect of the patella.

Lateral Knee - SID is 40, PT is lateral recumbent, CR at mid patella.

Inter-Condyal Knee (Tunnel View) - PT is prone, knee flexed at 45 degrees with 45 degree caudal tube tilt with CR aimed at the center of the knee.

Tangential Patella View (Sunrise View) - PT is prone with knee in full flexion, 10 degree cephalic tube tilt and CR aimed at the center of the knee.

AP Ankle - PT is Supine, ankle is centered on the film, foot is internally rotated 5-10 degrees and dorsiflexed to 90 degrees. SID is 40.

Medial Oblique Ankle - same as AP with foot internally rotated 35 degrees.

Lateral Ankle - PT is lateral recumbent with ankle dorsiflexed to 90 degrees wit hate CR just inferior to the medial malleolus. SID is 40.

AP Foot - PT is supine, knee flex with foot flat on center of film, tube tilt is 15 degrees cephalic.

Oblique Foot - Same as above with foot internally rotated 35 degrees, lateral aspect the foot will be elevated.

Lateral Foot - PT is lateral recumbent with foot dorsiflexed at 90 degrees CR is 2 inches above the base of the hell.

Spot Projection - Measure the PT through the path of the CR. Use an 8 x 12 film for one vertebra and 10 x 12 film for two vertebra. SID is 40 inches, no tube tilt, CR is directly through the area of interest (the spot).

PA Chest - measure PT in the mid sternal area, use a 14 x 17 film, 72 inch SID, no tube tilt, PT is upright facing the film with chin resting on top of the bcuky with hands over buttocks. CR is at T7 (inferior boarder of the scapula upright). Film is taken with full inspiration.

Lateral Chest - measure the PT under the arms (same as lateral thoracic) use a 14 x 17 film, 72 inch SID, no tube tilt, PT is standing upright with side agains the bucket and arms above their head. Bucky is raised to the bottom the PT ear, CR is centered on film. Film is taken with full inspiration.

Chest Films - 72 inch SID, no tube tilt, 14 x 17 film, taken with full inspiration.

Dorsiplantar foot - 5 degree cephalad tube tilt. Anterior fat pad normally seen on an AP elbow.

Apical Lordotic view - best view to observe the *Lung Apices*, the most common location of a *Pan Coast Tumor*.

Pleural effusion - Best seen with the lateral decubitus view.

Pneumoperitonium - Best seen with erect abdomen view.

Megenblase - Stomach gas.

Towne's View (occipital Skull View) - best film to visualize the *Foramen Magnum*. PT is supine, 35 degree caudal tube tilt, CR at the external auditory meatus. SID is 40.

Caldwell View (PA Skull) - PT is prone, 15 degree caudal tube tilt, 40 inch SID, best film to observe the *Frontal Sinus*.

Water's View - Best film to observe the Maxillary Sinus. PT is upright with mouth closed and chin resting on the bucky and the nose 2-3 cm away creating an 37 degree ands between the bucky and the cantomeatal line CR is through the midsagittal plane of the skull.

Increasing KVP - increases shades (low contrast) - best for *Chest Films*.

Decreasing KVP - decreases shades (high contrast) - best for *Bone Films*.

Contrast is the difference between the shades.

Order of radiographic densities (least to most)- **A**ir, **F**at, **W**ater, **B**one and **M**etal. (**A**ll **F**at **W**omen **B**uy **M**arshmallows)

Normal air density on plain film are the stomach and large intestine.

Radiolucent - the degree of blackness on the film.

Radiopaque - the degree of whiteness on the film.

Hyper-lucency - excessive blackness in area that should have some degree of whiteness. Example is the appearance of the lung field on chest film of a patient that has Emphysema.

mA x time x kVp = heat

Increased filament heat increases the amount of electrons being emitted.

mA - is the setting that regulates temperature of the filament.

Film Focal Distance (FFD) - is the distance from the x-ray to the film.
Source Film Distance (SFD) - is the distance from the x-ray to the film.
Source Image Distance (SID) - is the distance from the x-ray to the film.
Tube to Film Distance (TFD) - is the distance from the x-ray to the film.

Decreased FFD, SFD, SID, TFD will increase blur and magnification.
Increased FFD, SFD, SID, TFD will increase sharpness and decrease, magnification (decrease distortion).

Object Film Distance (OFD) - is the distance from the patient to the film.
Decreased ODF increases sharpness and decreases magnification.

Decrease Magnification - can be accomplished by either increasing the FFD, SFD, SID, TFD or decreasing the OFD.

Geometric Factors - focal spot, FFD, OFD, motion, screen size, patient position, tube position and the relationship of all.

Latitude - the range between the maximum and minimum exposure.

Linearity - is the ability to manipulate mA and Time to get the same result.

Bucky - holds the x-ray cassette (film).

Latent Image - the image that is on an exposed film that has not been made visible by developing.

Filtration - primary purpose is to reduce skin dosage by removing lower energy x-rays with long wave length before reaching the patient. Composed of aluminum the filter is inside the tube. Removing the longer wave, non penetrating x-rays the patient dose is decreased.

Aluminum filtration - Absorbs the less penetrating X-rays to decrease dose to the patient. No effect scatter radiation.

Thermionic emission - the process of electrons being boiled off the tungsten filament in the focusing cup (not an interaction between X-rays and matter).

Collimation - decreases patient dose by limiting the size of the x-ray beam and increased film quality by decreasing scatter radiation.

X-ray Machine - composed or 3 general parts. The tube, the voltage generator and control console.

X-ray Tube - an electronic vacuum tube with glass envelope ti withstand tremendous amount of heat being generated.

Rectifier - changes AC power into DC power.

Transformer - either increases or decreases voltage.

Autotransformer - measures the voltage coming into the machine and automatically makes adjustments to insure it is constant.

Quantum Mottle - "Noise" displayed on the film. Increased with faster film screen combinations. Refers to the random nature of x-rays interacting with the bucky/film. Faster the screen the more quantum mottle. High MSA low KVP decrease radiographic noise (quantum mottle).

Screens - Fluorescent crystals (salt) changes x-rays into visible light photons decreasing the patient dose. The screens are inside the cassette.

Small Crystals - Increase detail, increase patient dose because they produce less light.

Large Crystals - Decrease detail, decrease patient exposure because they produce more light.

The function of intensifying screens is to increase the penetration of the x-rays decreasing the patient dose.

High energy - Implies high frequency and low wavelength.

kVp - Refers to the quality of the X-ray beam, the penetrating power and contrast. kVp and contrast are inversely proportional. The more energy in the beam the more *penetrating power* determines *contrast*.

The optimal kVp for spine x-rays is between 70-90.
The optimal kVp for extremities under 10 cm is 50-60.

Milliampere (mA) - Determines the number of electrons produced in the cathode and regulates the temperature of the filament.

Milliampere per second (mAs) - Quantity of x-rays, determines the density (darkness) of the image. mAs and density are directly proportional.

A 15% increase in kVp is equivalent to doubling the mAs.

Density - Degree of film darkness, increased mAs equals an increase in density.

Contrast - the range of density variations among the dark and light areas. Scale of Contrast - Short scale of contrast results from decreased kVp.

Short scale of contrast - high contrast or abrupt transition of densities. Low KVP, used for Bone.

Long scale of contrast - low contrast or gradual transition of densities. High KVP, used for soft tissue.

Detail - the degree of sharpness/definition and radiographic contrast.

Penumbra - shaded outer region of a shadow, fuzziness. The size of the penumbra is indirectly related to image sharpness. Increased penumbra is increased fuzziness. The umbra is the darkest part of the shadow often used as a distractor.

Increased Penumbra - Large focus spot, decreased sharpness, decreased FFD, increased OFD, increased fuzziness.

Decreased Penumbra - Small focal spot, increased sharpness, increased FFD decreased OFD, decreased fuzziness.

Emulsion - Active component of the X-ray film, contains thin layer of silver halide crystals and binding agent.

Gelatin - hold the silver crystals on the film but it is NOT active.

Film tint - Blue or green tint added to film to improve contrast and reduce glare.

Attenuation - the reduction in intensity of an x-ray beam as it passes through matter.

Rectification - Conversion of AC to DC allows for unidirectional tube current.

Focal Spot - Tungsten target that is bombarded by electrons and generates the x-rays, does not affect patient exposure dose. Small focal spot leads to increased heat, 99% of energy is lost as heat - only 1% is transferred as x-radiation.

Cathode - negative (-), electrons boiled off tungsten element in focusing cup. Opposite charge of anode attracts electrons at about ½ the speed of light. Generates/produces electrons. Composed of the Filament and Focusing Cup.

Focusing Cup - negative (-) charge, surrounds the filament(s) to focus the the stream of electrons toward the anode.

Filament - tungsten produces electron cloud when extremely high heat is applied, AKA Thermionic emission. Most X-ray tubes have two filaments, one large and one small. Electrons are emitted from the filament.

Large Filament - large target, short exposure time, increased penumbra, less sharp (less detail).

Small Filament - small target, long exposure time, decreased penumbra, increased sharpness and detail.

mA - determines which filament is used.

Anode - positive (+), serves as a conductor, composed of a tungsten target buried in copper. Electrons strike anode and x-radiation produced with heat at the focal spot. X-rays travel from the anode to patient/film at approximately the speed of light. The anode spins or rotates to increase the target size and dissipate heat. The adobe side as the greatest geometric sharpness.

Anode Heel Effect - Angulation of the anode leads to decreased intensity of the beam from the outside of the anode. The intensity of the x-ray is higher on the cathode side demising the FFD and increasing KVP. Most likely used in the imaging of the thoracic and abdominal regions.

Anode side - less energy, few x-rays, smaller focal spot, increased detail, typically used for thinner body parts.

Cathode Side - more energy, more x-rays, larger focal spot used for thicker body parts.

Focal Film Distance (FFD) - long focal film distance increases definition, reduces magnification and distortion. Defined as the distance from the focal spot to the film.

Decreased Magnification - Decreased object to film distance(OFD) or increased tube to film distance(TFD).

Object Film Distance - Is the distance from the patient to the film. The greater the OFD the greater the magnification and distortion.

15% Rule - Increase kVp 15% will need to decrease mAs 50% to maintain density. Minimum change in mAs needed to note change density on plain film is 50%.

Roentgen (R) - unit for describing exposure dose of x-ray or gamma radiation.

RAD - Radiation absorbed dose, the energy transfer of 1 rad = 0.01 Gy = 0.01 J/kg.

Gray (Gy) - the SI unit for absorbed radiation.

Milliradian, Millirad, MRad - SI unit defined as 1/1000 of a RAD.

REM - Roentgen Equivalent to Man, used to determine occupational worker dose,. Maximum Permissible Dose MPD is 5(N-18) rads or 5 rads/year. 13 week period = 3 rads. The SI unit for REM is a Sievert.

Sievert - the SI unit of dose that is equivalent to an effective dose of a joule of energy per kilogram of recipient mass (the biological effect of ionizing radiation).

Coulombs - the SI unit of electrical charge equal to the quantity of electricity conveyed in one second by a current of one ampere.

Coulombs/Kg - the SI unit for R.

Maximum Permissible Dose (MPD) applies to everybody.
5 rads or 5 rads/year. 13 week period only 3 rads maximum

Radiation Equivalent in Men (REM) applies to workers.
Equivalent to absorption of 1 rad

Radiation Absorbed Dose (RAD) applies to the patient.
The energy transfer of 100 ergs/gram of the absorbing material.

The x-ray technician or person taking the x-ray receive the most radiation from the patient.

Grid - Found in the bucky, made of lead or aluminum strips that absorb scatter and decrease film fog. Increased the patient dose, increased film contrast, helps to absorb scatter from reaching the film.

Grid ratio - Height to Width, the height of the strip to the distance between the strips. Higher the ratio increases dose to the patient to produce a quality radiograph.

Air Gap Technique - Space between the body and the film cause scatter radiation. No grid is necessary, the patient dose is decreased but air gap does result in magnification and distortion of the image. (Lateral Skull)

Photoelectric Effect - Diagnostic x-rays that interact with inner shell elections and the x-rays is absorbed. Characteristic x-rays are produced following a photoelectric interaction.

Sequence of Development :
1. Wetting - emulsion permits chemical penetration of the film.
2. Development - creation of a latent image.
3. Rinse - (stop bath) end development, remove excess chemicals.
4. Fixing - removal of silver halides that were not exposed and hardening of the emulsion.
5. Washing - removal of any additional chemicals from previous steps.
6. Drying - removal of water to allow the film to be handled (viewed)

Fixing - Removes unexposed silver halides from the film, hardening the emulsion and preserves the image. This processes maybe referred to as fixation.

Fixer exhausted results in yellow spots with a faint image or discoloration.

Silver Reclamation - Recover silver from the fixer.

Washing - typically the longest stage of manual processing.

Developer - Purpose is to reduce the exposed silver halide crystals to metallic silver. Turns the latent image to a visual image.

Developing Agents are phenidone, hydroquinone sodium carbonate, sodium sulfate.

Long parallel streaks on the the film arm most likely related to the rollers on the processor affecting the film.

It is not suggested to use gonadal shielding when it will interfere with the purpose of the film you are taking because then there is no point in exposing the patient at all.

5 Developer Components:
1. Activator - swells the gelatin, that allows for chemical penetration, contains sodium carbonate.

2. <u>Restrainer</u> - prevents unexposed crystals from contamination, potassium bromide.
3. <u>Preservative</u> - controls (limits) oxidation, sodium sulfite.
4. <u>Hardner</u> - limits (controls) emulsion swelling, glutaraldehyde.
5. <u>Solvent</u> - dissolves chemicals, dihydraoxide, universal solvent, water.

<u>Increased temperature</u> of developer will <u>increase density</u> of the film.

<u>Decreased temperature</u> of developer will <u>increase development time</u> and also *decrease* the *density* of the film.

<u>Developing/Processing</u> - can effect the contrast of the film.

<u>Normal temperature</u> of the developing fluid to produce optimum density is <u>68° Fahrenheit</u>

<u>Excessive oxidation</u> of developer fluid turns the <u>film brown</u>.

<u>5 Components of the Fixer</u>:
1. <u>Activator</u> - Acetic Acid, Neutralizes the developer and stops that step.
2. <u>Clearing Agent</u> - Ammonium Thiosulfate, removes the underdeveloped silver bromide from the emulsion.
3. <u>Hardener</u> - Potassium Alum, hardens and shrinks the emulsion.
4. <u>Preservative</u> - Sodium Sulfite, prevents oxidation.
5. <u>Solvent</u> - Dihydraoxide (water) the universal solvent.

Sequence; Develop, rinse, fix, wash, dry.

<u>Wash</u> - Longest stage of manual development.

<u>Dark Room Light (safelight)</u> - Red 15 watt max light build for orthochromatic film.

Always avoid coming in contact with any of the chemicals used in processing the films.

4 Types of Radiation:

1. <u>Characteristic Radiation</u> - the useful beam, most of the radiation produced when an electron is "knocked out" of an inner shell, creating an unstable atom. When an outer shell electron fills the void left the electron that was knocked out an x-ray is emitted.

2. <u>Bremsstrahlung Radiation</u> - The projectile electron interacts with the nucleus that results in an x-rays being emitted. The electron slows and changes direction, so called "**b**raking" radiation. Most the X-rays in the diagnostic rang originate this way.

3. <u>Classical Scatter Radiation</u> - low energy x-rays which have undergone a change in direction after interaction with other x-rays and/or matter. No loss of energy, means no ionization. AKA - Secondary radiation, film fog.

4. <u>Compton Scatter/Effect</u> - Moderate energy x-rays "knock out" an outer shell election that results in loss of energy and ionization of the atom. Compton Scatter is the primary form of scatter caused by the interaction of x-rays with matter.

Principle of Radiation Protection
- Limit exposure as much as possible. (shortest possible time)
- Maximize distance between the source of the radiation and the person.
- Using shielding to protect the person being exposed on non-study areas.

<u>Magenbalse</u> - gas bubble in the funds of the stomach on film.

<u>Pneumoperitoneum</u> - abnormal finding on plain film that indicates air is trapped between the diaphragm and liver.

<u>Kissing Artifact</u> - Wet film touched together creating artifacts on the film.

<u>Black Branching Artifact</u> - Static electricity, increased with dry cold climates. Removing the film from the carton quickly can produce static electricity.

Tiny white specs on film are commonly the result of dust or dirt on the film.

Inverse square law - intensity of the beam is inversely proportional to the square of the distance. $I_1/I_2 = (D_2/D_1)^2$

Wolff's law - bone develops strength along the areas of greatest stress.

Women of child bearing years, X-ray within 10 days following onset of menses. 10 day rule.

Electromagnetic Radiation - the 2 primary types are X-rays and gamma rays. They are called photons because they have no mass, no charge and travel at the speed of light.

X-rays are produced outside of the atoms nucleus in the electron cloud. X-rays have a low specific ionization and high penetrability making them well suited for medical imaging.

Gamma Rays are produced in the nucleus of an atom. This is the major distinction between x-ray and gamma ray.

Photon - the smallest quantity of any type of electromagnetic radiation with constant velocity.

Electromagnetic spectrum - the possible changes in frequency and wavelength of photons, velocity (mass and speed) is constant.

X-ray photons have more energy than visible light as the frequency is much higher and the wavelength is much shorter.

The frequency and wavelength of a photon are inversely related.

Photo-disintegration (photo-transmutation) - occurs when high energy elections are absorbed directly by the nucleus causing the instantaneous emission of a nucleon or other nuclear fragment (subatomic particle).

The intensity of an x-ray decreases with distance from the source that created it. When the distance from the source doubles the intensity of radiation is reduced by one quarter, this is an example of the inverse square law.

Positioning the cathode side of the tube over the thicker part of the anatomy provides a more uniform radiographic density. This is an application of the anode heel effect.

The law of conservation of matter states that mater can be neither created nor destroyed only change forms.

The law of conservation of energy state that energy can neither be created nor destroyed, only change forms.

99% of the kinetic energy of the projectile electrons is converted to thermal energy (heat).

Plank's Quantum Theory - Photons created at the speed of light exist at the speed of light or they fail to exist.

Hemopoietic Cells - are rapidly dividing bone marrow stem cells that give rise to all all blood cells. Damage to these cells from radiation could result in leukemia.

Increased number of x-rays increases the photoelectric effect which increases the characteristic effect (characteristic radiation).

Cataracts can develop in the eye when exposed to radiation.

Law of Bergonie and Tribondeau - a fundamental law of radiation biology that states the radio-sensitivity of a tissue is increased the greater the number of undifferentiated cells in that tissue. The greater the mitotic activity and the greater the length of time the cells are actively proliferating increase the tissues radio-sensitivity.

ALARA (As Low As Reasonably Achievable) - Federal regulation that means a provider must make every reasonable effort to maintain exposure to ionizing radiation as far below the dose limits as practical while being consistent with the purpose for which the licensed activity is undertaken.

Gurney-Mott theory - a widely accepted theory that explains the formation of a latent images that metallic silver is formed at sensitivity centers (Sensitivity Spec) located at imperfections in the structure of silver halide crystals.

Stochastic Effect - the effects that occur by chance and may occur without a threshold level of dose and who probability is proportional to the dose and severity is independent of the dose. In the context of radiology the primary stochastic effect is cancer.

MRI - Used to evaluate the soft tissues and bone for pathology. Aides in the determination of radicular lesion and either verifies or negates the need for surgical consultation. Demonstrates disc dehydration, protrusion and degenerative joint disease without exposing the patient (PT) to ionizing radiation and has no known harmful effects. Offers the best low contrast resolution of imaging options. Produces multi-planar images.

T1 weighted MRI Hyper-intense (white):
Bone Marrow, Subcutaneous fat, menisci, tendons, ligaments, calcifications, sclerosis.

T1 Relaxation Time (longitudinal relaxation/spin-lattice relaxation) - is the return of net magnetization along the x-axis to its normal state.

T2 weighted MRI hyper-intense (white):
Water, neoplasm, deems, inflammation, cerebral spinal fluid (CSF)

T2 Relaxation Time (spin-spin relaxation/transverse relaxation) - the phase of coherence that occurs among Hydrogen nuclei after excitation by RF pulse.

Anything that is hyper-intense on T1 is hypo-intense on T2.

Bone is Black on both T1 and T2.

Using T-1 weighted MRI is best to visualize adipose (fat densities)

MRI - best imaging to evaluate the brain for a tumor and disc lesions. MRI is also the least invasive study to evaluate meniscal tears.

MRI - composed of imagine magnets, secondary coils, surface coils shim coils, gradient coils, and an RF probe.

MRI - should be done on PT with basilar invagination demonstrated on on plain film.

MRI - is better to detect early erosion of cortical bone compared to plain film x-ray. Significant changes of density (30%) are required before those changes are observable on plain film x-ray.

MRI - takes slice images in one plane.

Tomography - used when structures are superimposed on one another. A vertical fixing rod links the tube and bucky allowing the film and tube to move at the same time. High contrast films that are useful in the spine, TMJ, chest and wrist.

Linear Tomography - same as above but the tube moves in one direction and the bucky moves in the opposite direction. The Tomographic angle determines the thickness of the slice.

Multidirectional Tomography - produces sharper image than plain tomography.

Computerized Tomography (CT) - exposes the PT to ionizing radiation (x-rays). CT is preferred for viewing bony changes where MRI is preferred for visualizing soft tissue lesions. Takes slice images (like MRI) that are complied by the computer. There is no image receptor (bucky). Has a Gantry that includes the x-ray tube, detector array (instead of bucky), high voltage generator, patient support, computer and control console.

Single Photon Emission Computerized Tomography (SPECT) - a gamma imaging method that can be used to visualize structures in the body (organs) like the brain or heart.

Zonography - is when the topographic angle is less than 10 degrees.

Fluoroscopy - a continuous x-ray (like a movie) that visualizes the movement of internal structures and fluids in the body.

Contrast Exam - a contrast media is introduced into the specific structure being visualized and then radiographed. Examples, orthography, angiography, myelography and more.

KUB - Kidney, Ureter, Bladder, a plain film x-ray of the abdomen.

Electromyographic Tests (Needle EMG) - used to assess neural function can verify nerve damage but has a high rate of false negatives.

Surface EMG - used to assess the electrical activity of the para-spinal muscles. Less accurate than Needle EMG as the sensors on the surface of the skin.

Conduction Velocity Test - measure the speed at which a nerve delivers an electrical impulse to determine the presence and location of a nerve lesion.

Radionuclide Imaging - a radio-isotope is injected intravenously and areas of increased vascularity or bone growth will demonstrate greater uptake with imaged, so called Hot Spots.

Bone Scans - a physiological test that measure the amount of radioactive isotope uptake into bone. Used to identify abnormal bone physiology such as neoplasm or infection.

Thermography - a physiological test for sensory/neural abnormalities and myofascial irritations. A negative thermogram is consider a strong indicator for the absence of an organic cause for the PT's pain.

Diagnostic Ultrasound - a longitudinal sound wave with a higher frequency than audible sound. Echocardiogram imaging of the motion and position of the walls, valves and pericardial tissue using ultrasound.

Doppler - another type of diagnostic ultra sound used to evaluate blood flow in major veins and arteries.

Continuous Wave Ultrasound - used to examine fetal heart beat and blood flow.

Pulse Wave Ultrasound - used to produce imaging studies.

Ultrasound frequency - is inversely proportional to wavelength. High frequency, short wave length ultrasound yields better resolution and shallow penetration.

Spondylosis - ankylosis of a vertebral joint.

Spondylolysis - separation of the pars interarticularis.

Anterolisthesis - anterior displacement in relation to the bone below.

Retrolisthesis - posterior displacement in relation to the bone below.

Spondylolisthesis - spondylosis with anterior displacement.

Basilar Invagination - displacement of the cervical spine into the posterior cranial fossa due to pathological softening of the skull. Conditions includes, Paget's, osteomalacia, Ricket's and osteogenesis imperfecta. Demonstrated by Chamerlain's, McGregor's and MacRae's lines.

Sesamoid bone(s)- embedded in a tendon; example patella.

Inverted Napolean hat sign - AKA bowline of Brailsford, seen w/ advanced grade IV anterolisthesis or spondyloptosis.

Isthmic Spondylolisthesis - a fracture of the isthmus causes a greatest degree of forward slippage of a vertebra in relationship to the bone below that is also known as type 2 spondylolisthesis.

Cleft vertebra - failure of closure of the vertebral posterior arch.

Hemivertebra - lack of development of half a vertebra, can lead to development of scoliosis.

Spina bifida - developmental anomaly of the neural arch.

Spina Bifida Occulta - usually insignificant, no protrusion of the cord or meninges. Occulta means hidden.

Sp[ina Bifida Manifesta - cystic swelling of the meninges (menigocele), cord (myelocele), or both (menigomyelocele).

Knife clasp deformity - Elongated L5 spinous with spina bifuda occulta at S1 and pain with extension.

Bertolotti's Syndrome - unilateral lumbosacral transitional segment that results in disc herniation and may likely include sciatica and scoliosis.

Blocked vertebra - non segmentation or congenital fusion of two or more spinal segments.

Klippel Feil Syndrome - Multiple blocked vertebra with Springle's Deformity, an elevated scapula.

Tropism - asymmetrical or anomalous zygapophyseal joints.

Baastrup's - elongated spinous processes. AKA kissing SP.

Wisp of Smoke Sign - Medial knee, calcification of the medial collateral ligament (MCL) indicating Pelligerini Steidia Diseaes.

Slice of Pie Sign (Pie Sign) - suggestive of an anterior lunate dislocation. Lunate has a triangular shape on film because of dislocation.

Terry Thomas Sign - dislocation with ligamentous rupture widens the space between the scaphoid and lunate (gap).

Blade of Grass sign - lucent leading edge in a long bone seen during lytic phase of Padget's disease. AKA Candle Flame sign.

3 Types of Finger Nodes (boney knob)
Heberden's Nodes - Distal Inter Phalangeal (DIP) Joint
Bouchard's Nodes - Proximal Inter Phalangeal (PIP) Joint
Haygarth's Nodes - Meta Carpo Phalangeal (MCP) joint.

He-Bo-Ha from finger tip to hand.

Osteochondrosis - AKA Avascular Necrosis (AVN), AKA Aspectic Necrosis, AKA Osteonecrosis is degeneration affecting the epiphysis due to lack of blood supply.

Blount's - AVN of the Medial Tibial Condyle.

Kohler's - AVN of the tarsal, Navicular.

<u>Keiboch's</u> - AVN of the Lunate (carpal)

<u>Legg Calve Perthes</u> - AVN of Femoral Epiphysis (males)

<u>Osteochondritis Dessicans</u> - AVN of the articular surface of the medial femoral condyle.

<u>Osgood Schlatter's</u> - AVN of the Tibial Tuberosity

<u>Panner's</u> - AVN of the capitulum of the Humorous.

<u>Freiburg's Disease</u> - AVN of any metatarsal.

<u>Preiser's</u> - AVN of the carpal bone scaphoid.

<u>Scheuermann's</u> - AVN of the vertebral endplate.

<u>Sever's</u> - AVN of the calcareous (heel)

<u>Madlung's deformity</u> radial deviation of the hand medially, volar translation of the hand and wrist.

<u>Volar</u> - related to the palm of the hand or sole of the foot.

<u>Lenois deformity</u> - Fibular deviation of the toes.

<u>Gout</u> - Increased uric acid concentration leading to deposition of crystals and tophi formation. Overhanging edge sign, avascular necrosis, juxta-articular erosions. Grossly inflammatory condition works from outside into the joint space. AKA lumpy bumpy arthritis.

<u>Rheumatoid Arthritis</u> - RA factor (+), C-reactive protein, increased ESR. Early radiographic signs most commonly found in the hands and feet. Uniform loss of joint space. Hands and fingers affected starts in MCP joints (Haygarth's nodes). Can also affect PIP joints (Bouchard's nodes) but never DIP joints. Bilateral and symmetrical distribution, periarticular soft tissue swelling, periarticular osteoporosis, periarticular erosions and cysts, with uniform loss of joint space. Ligament laxity predominantly in hands with ulnar deviation of the fingers. Can affect the SI joints unilaterally.

Pencil in cup deformity. Whittled appearance of periarticular bone. (AKA) Still's disease in children.

Osteoarthritis - AKA Degenerative Joint Disease (DJD). Progressive, non-inflammatory process. Asymmetric distribution, non-uniform loss of joint space, osteophytes, subchondral sclerosis, subchondral cysts, facet arthrosis, IVF stenosis, disc height and vacuum sign.

Uncovertabral arthrosis/facet arthrosis - seen on cervical spine oblique films the intervertebral foramen (IVF) has an hourglass shape (instead of normal round shape) indicating IVF encroachment.

Erosive OA - Inflammatory variant of DJD involving DIP's and PIP's. Erosions lead to gull wing deformity, sclerosis, osteophytes, periostitis, ankylosis, and non-uniform loss of joint space.

Psoriatic arthritis - Most commonly involves the DIP joints, also interphalangeal and PIP joint present with widened joint spaces, ray pattern, sausage digit due to increased swelling, pencil in cup deformity and rat bite erosions.

Reiter's - Triad of conjunctivitis, urethritis and polyarthritis usually following sexual exposure. Lateral foot heel spurs, SI joint erosion and sclerosis often unilateral, spine will have non-marginal syndesmophytes.

Calcium pyrophosphate deposition disease AKA CPPD - Crystals deposited within the articular cartilage leading to thin linear cartilage calcification parallel to and separate from adjacent subchondral bone.

Osteochondritis dessicans - Most common site is the lateral aspect of the medial femoral condyle. Joint mouse (Synoviochondrometaplasia).

Hydroxyapatite deposition disease(HADD) AKA Calcific bursitis - Calcification within a tendon, bursa, or other periarticular soft tissue. Most common sites include shoulder, hip, and the cervical spine.

Synoviochondrometaplasia - Synonyms include joint mice, synovial chondromatosis, osteochondromatosis, and osteochondral loose bodies. Most common sites include knee, hip, ankle and hip. Can lead to formation of a Baker's cyst (popliteal fossa).

<u>Baker's cyst</u> - Enlargement of the gastrocnemius-semimembranosus bursa, commonly seen in RA and synoviochondrometaplasia.

<u>Charcot's joint</u> - AKA neurotrophic joint. Lack of subjective and objective pain. Commonly seen with diabetes and syphilitic tabes.

<u>Six D's of Charcot's Joint</u>
Distension -from effusion
Density -subchondral sclerosis
Debris-bony intraarticular fragments
Dislocation
Disorganizaton-bag of bones
Destruction of articular bone.

<u>Scheuermann's disease</u> - juvenile kyphosis, vertebral epiphysitis. Visualized on lateral thoracic film, characterized as three contiguous vertebra with irregular endplates, decreased disc height, increased kyphosis. Most common in middle to lower thoracic spine primarily in teenagers.

<u>Myositis ossificans</u> - Post traumatic calcification of muscular tissue.

<u>Sequestrum</u> - Fragment of a necrotic bone that has become separated from surrounding bone.

<u>Involucrum</u> - Covering of newly formed bone enveloping the sequestrum with infection of the bone.

<u>Geographic lesion</u> - Circumscribed and uniformly lytic lesion.

<u>Ewings Sarcoma</u> - Tumor most common seen in the diaphysis, onion skin layering. Most common primary malignant bone tumor to metastasize to bone. Only primary malignant bone tumor that simulates infection. Often occurs before 20 years of age, clinical findings include local swelling, pain, fever, anemia and elevated ESR.

<u>Chondroblastoma (Codman's Tumor)</u> - Most common seen in the epiphysis, calcific matrix.

Enchondroma - Benign neoplasm of hyaline cartilage. Most common benign tumor of the hand, most common tumor of tubular bones. Usually asymptomatic. Geographic lucent lesions with punctate calcifications.

Ollier's disease - Multiple enchondromas.

Maffucci's Syndrome - multiple enchondromas with multiple soft tissue hemangiomas, malignant.

Giant Cell Tumor - Expansile Soap Bubble lesion, occurs at the metaphysis and extends into the epiphysis of long bones, can affect the joints. Geographic, eccentric, expansile, soap bubble lesion that can become malignant.

Osteochondroma - The most common benign bone tumor, occurs near the articular surface. Can be sessile (broad base) or (narrow base) described as mushroom cap appearance, points away from the joint. May become malignant Osteosarcoma. The cap is lined in hyaline cartilage (articular surface).

Nonossifying Fibroma (ages 8-20) Fiberous Cortical Defect (ages 4-8) - identical findings, PT age is the difference. Painless, asymptomatic, self limiting, benign tumor described as ovoid lucent centered lesion of the metaphysis.

Simple Bone Cyst (Unicameral Bone Cyst) - fluid filled expansile lesion of the diaphysis that goes from cortex to cortex. Predisposes the site to fracture. Usually diagnosed after spontaneous fracture.

Aneurysmal Bone Cyst - Blood (fluid) filled expansile eccentrically located tumor. Most common expansile lesion of the posterior elements of the spine (posterior arch of the atlas).

Chordoma - develops from the notochord, may occur anywhere in the spine, most commonly in the skull and sacrum. 40% of cases metastasize.

Pedunculated Osteoma - Paranasal sinuses.

Osteopoikilosis - Widespread multiple circumscribed round or ovoid lesions of increased density. AKA bone measles.

Hemangioma - Most common benign tumor of the spine, corduroy cloth vertebra. (also the most common tumor of blood vessels)

Osteopetrosis - Vertebra within a vertebra. Bone within a bone.

Sarcoidosis - enlargement of the hilar lymph nodes aka potato nodes.

Syndesmophyte - Bony outgrowth or ossification of a ligament that attaches to bone.

DISH - Diffuse Idiopathic Skeletal Hyperostosis (Forestier's Disease) Ossification of ALL with non-marginal syndesmophytes. Disc spaces and facets are spared. Diagnosed on lateral film, exam findings include difficulty swallowing, can be associated with diabetes.

Ankylosing Spondylitis (AS) - Initial marginal pencil thin syndesmophytes, can cause sclerosing of posterior motor units. Syndesmophytes thicken with time, bilateral SI joint obliteration, decreased chest expansion. HLA-B27(+). Orthopedic test is Schober's test. (Marie Strumpel's Disease)

Paget's - typically 50+ male, excessive and abnormal remodeling of bone results in coarse trabecular appearance with cortical thickening. Ivory vertebra, blade of grass sign, cotton wool skull, shepherd's crook deformity, picture frame vertebra, saber shin deformity, protrusio acetabuli, both blastic and lytic, bone expansion, increased hat size. AKA osteitis deformans. Lab Dx: Urinary hydroxyproline, alkaline phosphatase. Malignant degeneration to osteosarcoma.

Osteitis Condensans Ilii - triangular sclerosing (hyperostosis) of the ilium side of the SI joint. Most common in young multiparous females.

Brim Sign - Thickening of the cortex at the pectineal line and the pelvic rim. Seen with Paget's.

Multiple Myeloma - Most Common primary malignant bone tumor. Bone scans are cold. Most common sites; spine, pelvis, skull, ribs and scapula. Punched out lesions, raindrop skull (multiple small round holes). Lab findings include Bence Jones proteinuria and reversed AG ratio.

Fibrous dysplasia - Shepherd's crook deformity, ground glass appearance, septations of bone giving cobweb appearance. Expansile lesions with cortical thinning. Most common benign tumor of rib creating extrapleural sign. Rind of sclerosis around geographic lesion. AKA polyostotic fibrous dysplasia. Can be found in vertebral bodies.

Monostotic Fibrous dysplasia - Short zone of transition, sclerotic ring often found in the neck of the femur.

Tuberculosis - Likes the apices of the lungs, can have calcified density in the lung field or miliary type lesions. Can also produce lesions in the spleen. Pott's Disease is Tuberculosis (TB) of the spine resulting in Gibbus formation with angular kyphosis.

Pancreatic calcification - midline calcification frequently seen with alcoholics.

Sarcoidosis - Pulmonary signs include lymphadenopathy(1-2-3 sign, potato nodes), infiltrates and fibrosis.

Scleroderma - Acro-osteolysis, soft tissue retraction, calcification and tapered fingers. **CREST** - **C**alcinosis, **R**aynauds phenomenon, **E**sophageal abnormalities, **S**cleroderma and **T**elangiectasia.

Prostate metastasis - Primarily blastic, likes the spine and pelvis. Midline calcification AP pelvis above pubic symphysis.

Parasites - Multiple calcific densities in muscle.

Hyperparathyroidism - Rugger jersey sign, salt and pepper skull, increased serum calcium with soft tissue calcification.

90% of shoulder dislocations are anterior most hip dislocations are posterior.

Fracture - Need to have pieces (fragmentation) to diagnose.

Avulsion - a piece of bone is torn away by forceful muscular or ligamental strain (clay shoveler's or teardrop).

<u>Tear Drop</u> - A type of avulsion fracture of the anterior inferior aspect of the vertebral body. Most commonly seen at C2 with hyperextension injuries

<u>Comminuted</u> - a fractures with two or more boney segments (pieces).

<u>Impaction</u> - a portion of the bone is driving into another bone by compressive force.

<u>Stress Fracture</u> - repetitive stress leads to fatigue and fracture.

<u>Simple Compression Fracture</u> - Anterior step defect from thoracolumbar trauma.

<u>Occult</u> - a fracture with clinical signs and no radiographic evidence.

<u>Pathological</u> - Any fracture of any bone that is weakened by a disease process.

<u>Duverny</u> - A large fracture through the lateral surface of the iliac wing (crest).

<u>Jefferson's fracture</u> - C1 compression fracture, burst fracture ring of the atlas, unstable needs to be braced. Forceful axial compression on the skull. Rust sign, diving into a shallow pool.

<u>Hangman's fracture</u> - C2 decompression fracture, bilateral fractures through both pedicles caused by hyper-extension. This is a stable fracture but does need bracing.

<u>Odontoid fracture</u> - Three types: apical, transverse at the base, and transverse extending into the body of C2.

<u>Clay shovelers fracture</u> - Avulsion fracture of the spinous process of C6 or C7, T1 due to a flection injury or repeated stress on the spinous.

<u>Chance (Seatbelt Fracture or Fulcrum Fracture)</u> - A horizontal fracture through a single vertebral body and posterior arch that is most common in the lumbar spine (L2).

Horizontal Fissure Fracture - extends from the SP through the vertebral body.

Galeazzi fracture - radius is fractured at the junction of the middle and vital thirds with distal radioulnar dislocation.

Monteggia fracture - Proximal ulna with dislocation of the radius.

Hill-Sacks Lesion - Impaction fracture of the humor head creating hatchet deformity caused by anterior shoulder dislocation.

Bankhart - a type of avulsion fracture of the inferior glenoid rim caused by an anterior dislocation of the shoulder.

Flap Fracture - avulsion of the greater tuberosity from an anterior dislocation of the shoulder.

Colle's fracture - break of the distal radius with posterior inflation of the distal fragment most commonly caused by a FOOSH injury. Most common wrist injury in the elderly.

FOOSH - **F**all **O**n **O**ut **S**tretched **H**and.

Smith's fracture - Distal radius fracture with anterior angulation of the distal fragment. Most commonly caused by direct blow or fall with the wrist forced into hyper-flexion. Sometimes called a reversed Colle's fracture.

Green Stick - one side of the bone is broken while the other side is bent, seen in preteen children.

Torus Fracture - preschool child with an incomplete fracture of the distal radius with buckling (expansion) of the cortex and very little to no distal displacement.

Thurston-Holland Fracrture - Salter Harris Type II fracture of the distal radius.

Pott's fracture - fracture of the distal fibula above the lateral malleolus with disruption of the distal tibiofibular ligament.

Game Keeper's Fracture - avulsion of the ulnar collateral ligament of the thumb.

Mallet Finger (baseball fracture) - intra-articular fracture at the base of the proximal phalanx.

Bennett's - a fracture through the base of the 1st metacarpal.

Boxer's Fracture - 2nd or 3rd metacarpal fracture.

Rolando Fracture - comminuted intra-articular fracture of the back of the first metacarpal.

Bar Room Fracture - fracture of the 4th or 5th metacarpal.

Jones Fracture (dancer's fracture) - Fifth metatarsal avulsion fracture caused by the traction of the peroneus brevis muscle with the foot inverted and plantar flexed.

March fracture - Stress fracture of 2nd or 3rd metatarsal.

Bedroom fracture - break of any phalanx of the foot caused by a direct blow to the toe.

Diastatic fracture - Separation of a partially moveable joint.

Kummel's fracture - compression fracture of a vertebra associated with osteoporosis.

Anderson lesion - Fracture of pathologic calcification. Ex: Ankylosing spondylitis.

Freiburg's sign - Fracture of the 2nd and 3rd metatarsals avascular necrosis.

Freiburg's Disease - AVN of any metatarsal.

Keinbock's sign - Fracture of the lunate.

Monteggia Fracture - Shaft of the Ulna is fractured with displacement of the radius in any direction.

Malgaigne fracture - Ipsilateral vertical fractures of the superior pubic rams and ischiopubic ramus with a fracture or dislocation of the SI joint.

Bucket Handle Fracture - Fracture of the obturator ring and contralateral SI joint.

Straddle Fracture - Bilateral double vertical fractures at 4 sites in the obturator rings with displacement.

Diastasis Pubis - not a fracture but separation of the pubic symphysis.

Sprung Pelvis - Diastasis Pubis with dislocation of both SI joints.

Stable Hip Fractures - single breaks though the ischial or pubic rami, single iliac wing fracture or an avulsion fracture of the hip.

Subcapital Fracture - fracture at the must superior or proximal aspect of the femoral neck.

Mid Cervical Fracture - a fracture near the mid point of the femoral neck.

Subtrocanteric Fracture - a fracture of the femur below the trochanters.

Intertrochanteric Fracture - a fracture located between the trochanters of the femur.

Trochanteric Fracture - a piece breaks off a trochanter.

Basocervical Fracture - a fracture at the most distal or inferior aspect of the femoral neck.

Capsular Hip Fractures - are fractures that are within the joint capsule; Midcervical, Basocervical and subcapital.

Extra Capsular Hip Fractures - fractures outside of the joint capsule; Trochanteric, Intertrochanteric and subtrachnteric

Salter Harris fractures:
Type 1 - through growth plate only; ex: slipped capital femoral epiphysis.
Type 2 - through growth plate and metaphysis.
Type 3 - through growth plate and epiphysis.
Type 4 - through growth plate and both metaphysis and epiphysis.
Type 5 - compression deformity.

3 Complications of Fractures

Nonunion - arrest of the healing process before the fragments of bone form a union (join together).

Infection - the fracture does not appear to heal with progressive bone loss.

Osteonecrosis - non healing fracture with radiolucency (necrotic bone) due to a lack of blood supply (avascular necrosis)

Stress Fracture - abnormal stress to normal bone.

Insufficiency Fracture - normal stress applied to abnormal bone.

Risser's Sign - Diffusion of iliac crest apophysis, used to determine skeletal maturity as the epiphyseal closure of the iliac crest moves from lateral to medial.

Myerding Spondylolisthesis classification:
The sacral base is divided into quarters and the position of the posterior inferior aspect of L5 is measured for a percentage equivalent of anterior displacement.

Grade 1 = 0-25%
Grade 2 = 25-50%
Grade 3 = 50-75%
Grade 4 = 75-99%

Spondyloptosis = 100% anterior displacement.

Grade 1 is most common, not contraindicated for chiropractic care.

Grades 2-4, stress films are required to determine stability.

5 Classifications of Spondylolisthesis
1. <u>Dysplastic</u> - congenital anomaly of sacrum or L5 neural arch.
2. <u>Isthmic</u> - lyric or fracture of the pars or elongation of the pars.
3. <u>Degenerative</u> - caused DJD and disc thinning; most common at L4.
4. <u>Traumatic</u> - fracture of the neural arch other than pars.
5. <u>Pathological</u> - bone softening diseases. (Paget's)

Skull Films

<u>Multiple Myeloma</u> - Swiss cheese skull, rain drop skull, multiple round small lesions.

<u>Paget's</u> - Black frontal lobe (lytic) with increased white areas with fuzzy edges (blastic)

<u>METS</u> - few large holes irregular shape, edge.

<u>Acromegaly</u> - excessive growth hormone after skeletal maturity. Widened joint spaces, increased mandible size and enlarged sella turcica.

<u>Osteomalacia</u> - bones softening disease caused my impaired metabolism calcium due to a lack of vitamin D resulting in coarsened trabecular pattern maybe the only findings on x-ray or in severe cases generalized bone softening (AKA Adult Rickets).

<u>Rickets</u> - Osteomalacia in children from a deficiency of vitamin D.

<u>Hyperpara-thyroidism</u> - salt and pepper skull.

Cervical Spine Films

<u>Lateral Cervical</u> - Atlantodental interspace (ADI), Retropharingeal interspace (RPI) under 7 mm, retrotracheal interspace (RTI) under 22 mm. If visible observe C7 for Clay Shoveler's fracture. Check for white, absent or eroded vertebrae. Observe the ALL and PLL for calcification.

<u>AP Cervical</u> - observe lung apices for blackness, rib and/or clavicle pathology. Observe tracheal deviation, carotid placing, uncinate process arthritis and cervical ribs.

APOM - Observe for Odontoid (Dens) fractures, Jefferson's fracture, Hangman's fracture and lateral overhang.

Cervical Obliques - Evaluate IVF, uncinate hypertrophy and cervical ribs.
Right Anertior Oblique (RAO) = Left Posterior Oblique (LPO) - RT IVF
Right Posterior Oblique (RPO) = Left Anterior Oblique (LAO) - LT IVF

Cervical Stress Films - evaluate for instability (anterior slide), Fracture near the lamina or lateral masses. Assess for Hyper-flexion or Hyper-extension injuries.

Unstable Cervical Spine Fractures - Flexion Tear Drop, Extension Tear Drop, Hangman's, Jefferson's and Type II fracture of the dens.

Chest Films

Pneumothorax - evaluate for bilaterally symmetry of blackness and blood vessels. No blood vessels can be seen with pneumothorax.

Miliary TB - multiple small densities, looks like bird seed.

Histoplasmosis multiple densities with rough borders, look like bone, all of similar size and equally separated (equal distribution).

Pneumonia - big white mass maybe an entire lobe or lobes.

Tumor - large white mass, usually round in shape.

Viral Infection - Bilateral increased hilar density.

Sarcoidosis - 1,2,3 potato sign aka pawn brokers sign or Garland's triad is defined as enlargement of the right paratracheal lymph nodes and the right and left hilar lymph nodes.

Emphysema - flat diaphragm.

Thoracic Films

AP Thoracic - scoliosis, count ribs, observe margins, calcified hilar nodes.

Lateral Thoracic - compression fractures, Apical tumor, wedge of pie opacity indicting pneumonia.

Lumbar Films:

AP Lumbar - count the pedicles (mets) observe TP for fracture.

Lateral Lumbar - observe for spondylolisthesis, gall bladder calcification, aneurysm.

Lumbar Obliques - best (only) film to visualize the pars (scotty dog).
Right Anertior Oblique (RAO) = Left Posterior Oblique (LPO) - LT PARS
Right Posterior Oblique (RPO) = Left Anterior Oblique (LAO) - RT PARS

AP Pelvis - Young PT evaluate for AVN of femoral head (Legg Calves Perth) and SCFE (Slipped Capital Femoral Epiphysis). Elderly PT evaluate for fractures, osteonecrosis, protrusion acetabula, and METS, soft tissue calcification.

Extremity Films

Long Bones - observe for fracture, expansive lesion, periosteal reaction.

Knee - Osteosarcoma in kids, fracture in adults (depressed plateau), Osteoarthritis (OA), osteochondritis dessicans (tunnel view).

Ankle - evaluate for fracture, heel spurs, accessory ossicles.

Shoulder - evaluate the lung field for white masses, proper alignment of bones and joints.

Elbow - Observe Fat Pad Sign for possible fracture or infection. Fat Pad should not be observable in normal healthy PT.

Lunate - Most common dislocation of the hand.

Scaphoid - most common fracture of the hand.

Abdominal Films;

Spleen - should be less than 14 cm from hemidiaphragm to tip of spleen. Hodgkin's disease presents with splenomegaly (enlargement of the spleen).

Kidney - 90% of kidney stones are radiopaque visualized obliquely to the spine. Best observed on AP film as stones overlap spine on lateral film.

Gallstones - 20-25% are radiopaque, best seen on lateral film anterior to the spine as opaque ring with lucent core. 4 F's of most common presentation, Fat, Female, Fertile, Flatulant. Very common in Native populations.

Phleboliths - are small calcifications in the veins that are very common.

Abdominal Aortic Aneurysm - asymptomatic, normal measurement is 2 cm, risk of rupture is high at 7 cm, diagnosis is made with ultrasound.

Splenic Artery Calcification - wiggly worm in the left upper quadrant.

Congenital Diagnosis

Achondroplasia - defect of enchondral bone formation results in bones that are short with normal diameter (normal trunk with short limbs).

Osteogenesis Imperfecta - abnormal collagen formation, clinical findings include; blue sclera, translucent skin, hyper-mobile joints. Osteoporotic fragile bones that fracture easily resulting in deformity. Sever osteopenia and stippled epiphysis.

Osteopetrosis - failure of the osteoclasts resulting in incomplete or lack of resorption of the primary spongiosa. Bone within a bone appearance without enlargement, sandwich vertebrae sign, Erlyenmeyer flask deformity or metaphysical flaring is described as constriction of the diaphysis with flaring of the metaphysis. Uniformly dense bones with no distinction between the cortex and spongiosa (medullary).

Osteopoikilosis - multiple bone islands, areas of increased density. Not clinically significant with no clinical signs or symptoms.

Osteopenia - decreased bone mass due to a diminished rate of osteoid synthesis.

Osteoporosis - loss of bone density that occurs as bone resorption exceeds bone deposition.

Primary Osteoporosis - idiopathic and not associated with any other disease process that can occur in juveniles and the elderly.

Juvenile Osteoporosis - is a subtype of primary osteoporosis with no known cause. Most often an underlying disease process can be identified in children with loss of bone density, making it secondary osteoporosis however while rare there are children with primary idiopathic juvenile osteoporosis.

Secondary Osteoporosis - the result of disuse, trauma, inflammatory process, neoplasm, disease process, corticosteroid or heparin therapy that results in the loss of bone density.

Type I Involutional Osteoporosis - postmenopausal females 55-75 YOA, increased osteoclastic activity leads to osteoporosis. Back pain is a common complaint without spinal deformity however compression fractures of the spine are a common sequela to Type I.

Type II Involutional (Senile) Osteoporosis - occurs in both men and women over 70 YOA due to a decrease in bone formation that presents with back pain and spinal deformity. Fractures of the femoral neck are common sequela of Type II.

Klippel-Feil Syndrome - congenital disease characterized by multiple non-segmentation of the cervicals with spina bifida, omoverterbral bone, sprengel's deformity and scoliosis. PT presents with short webbed neck, limited ranges of motion and low hairline.

Legg Calve Perthes - idiopathic osteonecrosis of the capital femoral epiphysis in a skeletally immature patient. More common in males than females with an average age of 7.

Slipped Capital Femoral Epiphysis (SCFE) - Displacement of the femoral head though the growth plate relative to the femoral neck. Occurs shortly before closure of the growth plate, evaluated with Klein's line.

Scheeuermann's Disease (juvenile kyphosis) - 3 or more consecutive vertebrae with undulating endplates, multiple level Schmorl's nodes. Most common in young males.

Arthritis

Osteoarthritis (OA) - uneven loss of joint space with subchondral sclerosis, osteophyte formation, subchondral cysts without osteoporosis or erosions. Also known as Degenerative Joint Disease (DJD), most commonly affects the joints of the hands, hips, knees, neck and lumbar spine.

Erosive Arthritis (Erosive Osteoarthritis) - DJD with acute synovitis, inflammatory erosions and ankylosis. Gull Wing deformity of the DIP joint(s).

Neuropathic Arthropathy - Joints that have lost proprioception and pain sensation resulting in progressive damage and derangement of the joint. Diabetic neuropath is the most common cause. Finding include; resorption of the bone ends, gross swelling, debris, extensive sclerosis, osteophytosis and subchondral cysts.

Gout - Hyperuricemia, most common in males, most common affects the 1st MTP (big toe) also found in interracial joints, ankle and knee. Radio graphic findings include, tophi, punched out lesions, overhanging edges, asymmetrical polyarticular distribution (juxta-articular erosions) large soft tissue masses and spotty appearance of the carpals.

Crystal Pyrophosphate Dihydrate Deposition Disease (CPPD) - clinically presents as pseudo-gout, crystal deposition in articular cartilage produces chonedrocalcinosis. Findings include, loss of joint space, proliferative bony changes and joint fragmentation. Classic presentation is isolated involvement of the patellofemoral joint or radoiocarpal joint.

Calcium Hydroxyapatite Deposition Disease (HADD) - recurrent painful, periarticular calcific deposits in tendon and soft tissue. Dense sharply defined linear or circular calcification in tendon (AKA Calcific Tendonitis). Presents as tendinitis or bursitis. Most common in middle aged patients, most common site is the supraspinatus tendon.

Diffuse Idiopathic Skeletal Hyperostosis (DISH) - Calcification of the Anterior Longitudinal Ligament (ALL) that does not affect the apophysis so there is no loss of joint space. Bone density is normal with large flowing ossifications over 3 (or more) contiguous level of the spine. More common in men than women.

Rheumatoid Arthritis (RA) - Inflammatory arthritis of the small synovial joints. Bilateral symmetrical involvement. Radiographic findings include, periarticular soft tissue swelling, osteopenia early and osteoporosis later, uniform loss of joint space, sever erosions, total joint destruction, ulnar deviation, swan neck deformity and boutionnieres deformity.

Scleroderma - Multi-system fibrotic connective tissue disease that is life threatening because it affects organs. Tuftal resorption, DIP joint erosions and soft tissue atrophy are characteristic.

Ankylosing Spondylitis (AS) - Inflammatory arthritis with subchondral sclerosis, squared vertebral bodies, sydesmophytes and ossification (calcification) of the posterior longitudinal ligament (PLL). Starts in the SI joints, affects the apophyseal joints, Shiny Corner sign.

Reiter's Disease - Triad of conjunctivitis (can't see) Urethritis (can't pee) and arthritis (can't dance)...Can't see, Can't Pee, Can't dance with me. Radiographic changes occur in synovial joints, symphyses and enthuses. Bony erosion with bony proliferation, symmetrical loss of joint space, periarticular osteopenia.

Psoriatic Arthritis - Predominately found in the upper extremity, involves the DIP joints, pencil in cup deformity.

Blood Disorders

<u>Hemophilia</u> - genetic deficiency of coagulation factor VII, radiographic findings are most common in the knee and include, overgrowth of the epiphysis, subchondral cysts and a widened intercondylar tunnel.

<u>Sickle Cell Disease</u> - genetic defect in hemoglobin that leads to abnormal shape of red blood cells (RBC). Classic radiographic finding in the spine is H shaped vertebrae. Infarcts and osteonecrosis is also common.

<u>Osteonecrosis (Avascular necrosis AVN)</u> - loss of bone due to lack of blood supply is more common in men than women.

<u>Keinbock's Disease</u> - AVN of the lunate

<u>Frieberg's Disease</u> - AVN of the head of the 2nd metatarsal.
<u>Kohler's Disease</u> - AVE of the immature tarsal navicular.

<u>Chandler's Disease</u> - idiopathic AVN of the femoral head.

Infections

<u>Osteomyelitis</u> - A pyogenic infection of bone and bone marrow most commonly caused by staph aureus. Permeative destruction of bone starting in the metaphysis and extending across joints and growth plates. Solid periosteal reaction.

<u>Brodies Abscess</u> - Local, subacute bone abscess. Well defined radio lucent area with smooth, rounded geographic margins with thick sclerotic rind. Pain relieved by aspirin.

Tumors

<u>Osteosarcoma</u> - most common primary bone tumor at 10-25 years of age, most commonly in the knee. Speculated or sunburst periosteal reaction, can be lytic, sclerotic or both. Expansile lesion that readily spreads to the viscera.

Chondrosarcoma - Patient typically 35-70 years of age with deep boring pain lasting for months to years. Radiographic findings include, endosteal scalloping, cortical thickening. Looks like enchondroma or bone infarct in a long bone making it easily misdiagnosed.

Osteoid Osteoma - benign bone forming lesion called a nidus that maybe found cortical, central or subperiosteal. Pain at night relieved by aspirin.

Osteoma - most commonly found in the skull, localized masses of dense mature bone that can be on the endosteal or periosteal surface of the cortex.

Osteoblastoma - most common in the posterior aspect of the spine. Considered a variant of osteoid osteoma giving it the AKA Giant Osteoid Osteoma. Clinically and histologically similar to osteoid osteoma.

Bone Island - normal cortical bone in and abnormal location. Margins have a speculated appearance.

Soft Tissue

Hamartoma - most common in the chest, mostly benign, mostly asymptomatic result from the abnormal formation of normal tissue.

Rhabdomyoma - tumor of striated or cardiac muscle.

Teratoma - tumor of all three germ layers. Tooth in the abdomen.

Adenoma - tumor of glandular tissue, often with excessive production of glandular products.

Papilloma - benign exophytically (outward growing) tumor of the epithelial tissue (nipple like).

Lipoma - benign tumor of fatty tissue.

Virchow's nodes - left-sided supraclavicular lymph node known location for mets go GI cancer.

<u>Krukenberg's</u> - cancer of the gut, GI tract, stomach (the primary site) that metastasizes to the ovaries.

<u>Seminoma</u> - malignant germ cell tumor of the testicles.

<u>Wilm's Tumor (Nephroblastoma)</u> - mixed tumor of the kidney found in children.

<u>Xanthoma</u> - tumor of connective tissue that is yellow in color can appear anywhere in the body.

<u>Leiomyoma</u> - benign tumor of smooth muscle known as fibroids that can occur in any tissue but are most common in the uterus (uterine fibroids).

<u>Hemangioma</u> - Benign tumor of infants described as an abnormal cluster of small blood vessels on or under the skin. Most common tumor of blood vessels.

<u>Spinal Hemangioma</u> - Most common benign tumor of the spine, corduroy cloth vertebra, found in the thoracic and lumbar spine in approximately 10% of the population.

<u>Myositis Ossificans</u> - Post traumatic calcification of muscular tissue.

Most shoulder dislocations are anterior, most hip dislocations are posterior.

<u>Lines of Mensuration</u>

<u>Eisenstein Sign</u> - Canal stenosis viewed from lateral film, posterior body line (George's) to the spinolaminar line. Connect the tips of the superior and inferior articular processes. The distance for the this line to the center of the posterior body is measured. If less than 15 mm indicates spinal canal stenosis. Normal should be approximately half or more than the width of the vertebral body.

<u>Chamberlain's Line</u> - Hard palate to the opisthion, > 7mm indicates basilar invagination.

Canal Body Ratio - The higher the ratio the smaller the canal. The ratio is determined using 4 lines; interpeducular distance, Eisenstein's line, transverse body dimension and the sagittal body dimension.

George's Line - Smooth continuous line at the posterior aspect of vertebral bodies. Disruption of the line indicates antero/retro-listhesis.

Shenton's Line - A curved line is drawn along the inferior femoral neck to the superior aspect of the obturator foramen. Any disruption or break in this line indicates a fracture or dislocation of the femoral neck or possible slipped capital epiphysis.

Macrae's Line (foramen magnum line) - from the anterior to the poster foramen magnum. If the dens is above this line, indicates basal invagination.

Ilio-femoral Line - a smooth curved line draw along the outer ilium across the joint onto the femoral neck. Disruption or bilateral asymmetry indicates fracture, dislocation or slipped capital epiphysis.

Atlantodental interspace (ADI) - Line from the anterior tubercle to the odontoid. Under 3mm in adults or 5mm in children indicates rupture of the transverse ligament as with trauma, Down's Syndrome, Rheumatoid Arthritis, (inflammatory arthritis)

McGregor's Line - Hard palate to the base of the occiput, > 7mm = to basilar invagination.

Martin's Basilar Angle - Root of the nasion/sella turcica to ant.foramen magnum, 128-152. Check for platybasia.

MacNab's Line - Facet imbrication, a parallel line along the inferior end plate extends posterior. This line should not cross the superior articulating facet of the inferior vertebra. Doing so indicates an extension malposition of facet imbrication, so called Rostrocaudal migration of the vertebra.

Jackson's cervical stress line - Lines at the posterior bodies of the C2-C7 in stress films (flexion and extension). The lines should intersect in extension (and neutral film) at C4/5 and in Flexion at C5/6. Muscle spasm, joint fixation, disc degeneration will alter this line. (AKA Ruth Jackson's Lines)

Spinolaminar Line (Posterior Cervical Line) - smooth arch like line connecting the spinolaminar junctions of the cervical spine. Disruption of the line indicates antero/retro=listhesis.

Ullmann's Line - (Garland Thomas Line) Draw line perpendicular at anterior portion of S1 endplate line, should not intersect L5 body. If it does indicates spondylolisthesis.

Skinner's Line - A line is drawn in the center of the fervor shaft and parallel its margin. A perpendicular line is drawn tangential to the superior tip of the greater trochanter. The fovea captious should be above at the trochanter line, if it falls below this line indicates coxa vara.

Shenton's Line - curved line drawn along the inferior border of the superior pubic rams along the inferior medial boded of the neck of the femur. This line should be smooth and continuous. Indicates, hip dysplasia or fracture.

Patellar Position Line - A line is drawn connecting the superior and inferior patellar poles. Another line is drawn contacting the inferior patellar pole to the tibial tubercle. These lines should be quasi-equivalent. If the length of the tendon is 20% or more greater than the length of the patella itself indicates patella alta (abnormally small patella).

Hadley's "S" curve - is a curved line drawn along the inferior aspect of the transverse process, inferior articular process and through the joint space to the superior articular process of the vertebra below. This line should be a smooth "S" shape, an interruption or break in this line indicates subluxation or facet imbrication.

Klein's Line - A line is drawn along the superior aspect of the femur neck. The femoral head should interest this line. If it does not indicates a slipped femoral capital epiphysis.

Kohler's line - is used to determine protrusio acetabulum. Lines are drawn along the pelvic inlet to the outer aspect of the obturator foramen. The acetabulum should not cross this line, if it does indicates protrusion acetabulum.

Heel Pad Measurement - Measure the shortest distance from the plant surface of the calcareous to the external skin. Greater than 25 mm in men and 23 in women indicate acromegaly.

Cervical Spine Gravity Line - Tip of odontoid to anterior C/7 vertebral body.

Lumbar Spine Gravity Line - (Ferguson's Line) A line drawn from center of the L3 body center vertically should intersect with the anterior 1/3 of sacral base. Anterior to the sacral base indicates hyper-lordosis, posterior to the sacrum indicates hypo-lordosis.

Lumbosacral Disc Angle - A line drawn along the inferior endplate is compared to another line drawn along the superior endplate of S1 to find an angle. Normal measurement is 10-15 degrees, indicates lumbosacral stability.

Boehloer's Angle - The 3 most superior aspects of the calcaneus are connected with two lines. If this angle of the ankle less than 28 degrees indicates fracture or dysplasia of the calcaneus.

Ferguson's angle - Weight bearing lateral lumbar film 2 lines are drawn. One along the sacral base and the other horizontal to the edge of the film. The inferior intersecting angle should be 41 degrees (+/- 2 degrees) in the average adult.

Femoral Angle (Mickulicz's angle) - two lines are drawn through and parallel to the mid-axis of the femoral shaft and the femoral neck. The angle is measured where they intersect. Normal angle is 120-130 degrees; femoral neck angle, angle of declination between epiphysis and diaphysis of femur. An angle greater than 130 is considered coxa valga, an angle less than 120 is considered coxa vara.

X-ray Evaluation **CAT BITES**

Congenital
Arthritis
Trauma
Blood
Infection
Tumor
Endocrine
Soft tissue

Radiographic Search (**The ABCs**)

Technical Factors
Alignment of (anatomy)
Bone
Cartilage (joint space)
Soft Tissue

Radiology Reports

<u>Identify Information</u> - Name of the doctor, name of the clinic with address and phone number along with the patient's full name date of birth (DOB) and any file indentation numbers should all be included in the radiology report.

<u>Findings</u> - This is a narrative description of what you can been seen on the film. If you cannot see it, you cannot diagnose it.

<u>Impression</u> - This is a numbered summary of the clinically significant findings.

<u>Recommendations</u> - the possible indications and contraindications to treatment and follow up procedures.

<u>Signature</u> - the doctor must sign the report and provide their qualifications. A chiropractor can read films and write a report but a radiologist is better at reading films. Signature with qualification indicate who is writing the report.

General Diagnosis

Chief Complaint - should be stated in the patient's own words as the problem they are most concerned with.

The purpose of the health history is to determine the parameters of the physical exam.

The patient's age, sex and race are all important information gathered during the case history that is helpful to form a differential diagnosis (DDX).

Health History
Inspection
Palpation
Percussion
Instrumentation
Range of Motion
Orthopedic test
Neurological tests
Imaging/Labs

HIPPIRONI

Present Illness - History of the patient's chief complaint in their own words.

Onset - When did the complaint begin? How? What is the **mechanism of injury**? Has it occurred before? What occurred the first time you had this complaint?

Provocative - What if anything makes the complaint worse?

Palliative - What if anything makes the complaint better? Previous care for this complaint, or recent care? What was the effect?

Quality - What does the complaint feel like? Sharp, throbbing, dull, deep.. best if in the patient's own words. What does it feel like to them?

Radiate - does the complaint travel, move or emanate from the site?

Severity - Pain is subjective, on a scale of 0-10 how much does the complaint bother you? Right now, at best, at worst?

Site - Where does it hurt? Where is in the complaint. Ask the patient to point to the actual spot. What they call the neck might be a shoulder or what they call the low back might be a hip.

Timing - When does the patient experience the complaint? Frequency, duration. Is there a cycle or pattern, it is related to anything in particular?

O,P,Q,R,S,T - Onset, provoke/palliative, quality, Radiate, site/severity and timing. How to investigate the present illness, or chief complaint.

Health History - Previous, serious injury, hospitalization, injury, trauma, accident (MVA ect), current medications, diagnosis.

Social History - Use of Alcohol, Tobacco, Daily Stress, Exercise, diet are also part of the patient health history and can assist in forming a DDX.

Family History - any condition within blood relatives that may be related to the patient's wellbeing or chief complaint. Are your parents alive, are they healthy, if not how did they die? Siblings?

Occupational History - Sports, working conditions, activities of daily life that maybe related to the patient's chief complaint or overall wellbeing.

Review of Systems - a general exploration of the various systems and parts of the body that may remind the patient of additional symptoms they do not believe are related and they may have failed to mention but could be important to forming a DDX.

When forming a differential diagnosis always consider the most likely possibilities first, the simplest solution is the most likely (Occam's Razor).

Open ended question requires more than a yes or no answer. What seems to the the problem? Is open ended. Do you have a problem? Is a closed ended question that only requires a yes/no answer.

A proper case history will reveal risk factors such as; hypertension, cardiovascular disease, diabetes, previous injury and medications.

Differential Diagnosis (VINDICATE)

V - vascular
I - inflammatory and infection
N - neoplastic
D - degenerative
I - intoxication and idiopathic
C - congenital
A - allergic and autoimmune
T - traumatic
E - endocrine/metabolic

Cage questions; Alcoholism

Have you ever felt like you needed to cut down on your drinking?

Have people annoyed you by criticizing your drinking?

Have you ever felt guilt about your drinking?

Have you ever felt the need to have a drink first thing in the morning (eye opener) to settle your nerves of recover from a hang over?

1 point for every yes, 2 points is a positive screening.

Vital signs:

The 4 primary vital signs are body temperature, blood pressure, pulse (heart rate) and respiration rate (breaths per minute).

Temperature - Normal Oral Temp is 98.6 F (37 C), Over 100 is a fever indicating an infection. Axillary temp is half a degree warmer, rectal is a full degree warmer.

Pulse - Normal resting heart rate is 60-100 beats per minute. Men 72 blm, Women 82 bpm, Child 90-140 bpm, Newborn 120-160 bpm, Elderly 70-80 bpm. The pulse is observed for rate, rhythm, amplitude and contour.

Respiration - 14-18 breaths per minutes is normal range for an adult, another source cited 12-20 breather per minute. Newborn baby, 44 breather per minute.

Blood pressure - 120/80 - 139/90 is considered a normal range for adult blood pressure (Systole/diastole) Children 90-100/60-70 is the normal range.

Pulse Pressure - the difference between systole and diastole, normally 30-40 mm Hg.

Auscultatory Gap - maybe heard with hypertensive patients.

The radial pulses are typically symmetrical with a myocardial infarction.

Heart failure presents with absence of femoral pulse.

Pulsus parvis - small systolic peaks

Pulsus magnus - big systolic peaks

Pulsus alternans - weak-strong-weak-strong

Pulsus bisferious - Pulse with two peaks for each systole.

Pulsus paradoxus - abnormally large decrease in stroke volume and systolic blood pressure that most commonly occurs with constrictive pericarditis.

Pulse pressure - Difference between systolic and diastolic blood pressure.

Coarctation of the aorta - Congenital deformity Dx by pulse/BP variations from upper extremity to lower.

Biot's Respiration - abnormal pattern of breathing with groups of quick shallow inspirations followed by regular or irregular periods of apnea caused by damage to the pons, stroke, trauma or increased intra-cranial pressure affecting the pons.

Cheyne Stokes - abnormal breathing pattern characterized by a period of apnea lasting 10-60 seconds, followed by gradually increasing then decreasing respirations that can be caused by heart failure or stroke. Is thought to be a component of sleep apnea syndrome.

Kussmaul Breathing - deep labored (gasping) respiration a form of hyperventilation associated sever metabolic acidosis especially diabetic ketoacidosis.

Paradoxical - chest contracts during inspiration and expands during exhalation, seen with rib fractures, infection, trauma, neurological disorder.

Stertorous Breathing - harsh noisy respiration characterized by rattling or rubs, most commonly seen in comatose patient.

Whisper pectoriloguy - increased loudness of whispering during auscultation of breath sounds. Whispers are not normally heard, this finding indicates lobar pneumonia (consolidation).

Diabetic coma - Increased respiration

Basal body temperature is increased during the menstrual cycle and after ovulation.

Increased body temperature increases the respiratory rate.

Bruit - Abnormal sound heard during auscultation of an artery produced by turbulent blood flow indicating partial obstruction of the artery or a localized abnormally high rate of blood flow in an unobstructed vessel. Typically bruits only occur during systole and frequently depend upon the heart rate. AKA vascular murmur.

Abdominal Exam Starts with the patient supine, exposed from the xiphoid process to the pubis with an empty bladder and arms at their side.

Order of Operations; Inspection, auscultation, percussion and palpation.

Inspection; color, masses, vascularization, contour, pulsations.

Auscultation - done before palpation. Use the diaphragm of the stethoscope to listen to all 4 quadrants for bowel sounds and use the bell in all 4 quadrants to list for bruits. The absence of bowel sounds can indicate peritonitis, paralytic ileus, bowel obstruction, intestinal ischemia or other condition of the GI tract.

Absence of bowel sounds indicates advanced intestinal obstruction and should be considered a medical emergency although the accuracy and importance of abdominal auscultation is open to debate.

Percussion - scan all regions/quadrants of the abdomen for a sense of tympani and dullness. Tympani should be heard over the stomach and intestines while dullness should be heard over organs and solid masses. Percuss from ASIS to ASIS.

Palpation, light (superficial) and deep.

Light Palpation - Lightly press, skin should be smooth and have a consistent density. Note any tenderness, muscle guarding or inspiration arrest, gasp for air, or apprehension with light palpation.

Deep Palpation - Have the patient raise their knee and place feet down on the table then press firmly 1 to 2 inches down or deeper into the abdomen.

Liver - at the midclavicular line at the 2nd or 3rd intercostal space percuss downward to the 5th to 7th intercostal space to locate the upper margin of the liver. Percuss upward at the midclavicular line to determine the location of the inferior margin of the scapula.

Spleen - posterior to the midaxillary line on the left side percuss the 6th to 10th intercostal spaces to find the spleen.

Stomach - percuss down the midclavicular line on the left side at the costal margin. The predominate sound is Tympani due to air in the stomach.

McBurney's Point - rebound tenderness half way between the ASIS and the umbilicus indicating acute appendicitis.

Robson's Point - great tenderness at the inferior margin of the liver indicating a gall bladder pathology.

Blumberg's Sign - rebound tenderness that suggest peritoneal inflammation indicting peritonitis. Pain upon removal of pressure instead of the application of pressure.

Rovsing's Sign - digital palpation of the left lower quadrant increase pain in the lower right quadrant, indicating appendicitis.

Rogoff's Sign - Pain with deep palpation near the 12th rib in the area of the adrenals indicating adrenal disease.

Kehr's Sign - acute pain in the tip of the left shoulder with the PT recumbent and their legs elevated indicating a ruptured spleen.

L'hermite's Sign - electric shock type pain shooting down the due to cord irritation, usually by bring the chin toward the chest associated with MS.

Murphy's Sign - inspiratory arrest that occurs with palpation of the upper right quadrant that indicates gall bladder involvement. DR palpates below the costal margin at the mid-clavicular line while the PT breathes in. Sudden arrest of inhalation only on the right side is a positive Murphy's Sign.

Right Upper Quadrant (RUQ): liver, gallbladder, duodenum, pancreas, right kidney.

Left Upper Quadrant (LUQ): stomach, spleen left kidney and pancreas.

Right Lower Quadrant (RLQ): cecum, appendix, right ovary, right fallopian tube.

Left Lower Quadrant (LLQ): sigmoid colon, left ovary, left fallopian tube.

Midline: Aorta, bladder, uterus.

Emmetropia - normal sighted eyes, no defects.

Myopia - near sighted

Hyperopia - farsighted

Ptosis - drooping of the upper eyelid (Horner's syndrome, CN III paralysis).

Horner's syndrome - a rare condition characterized by miosis, ptosis and anhidrosis caused by damage to the sympathetic nerves of the face.

Anhidrosis - a lack of sweating.

Miosis - excessive constriction of the pupil.

Exophthalmosis - budging of the eye anterior out of the orbit. Bilateral involvement indicates hyperthyroidism (Graves'), unilateral involvement indicates a tumor.

Ectotropion - outward turned eyelid, leaves the inner eyelid exposed and prone to irritation. Most common in elderly patients.

Entrpion - inward turned eyelid, most common in elderly patients.

Blepharitis - infection of the eyelid, commonly at site of eye lash, most commonly caused by obstruction of tiny oil glands.

Iridocyclitis - inflammation of the iris and ciliary body usually due to systemic disease.

Amblyopia (lazy eye) - unilateral development disorder which an eye fails to achieve normal visual acuity. Usually begins in infancy, early childhood.

Presbyopia - loss of sight due to aging (decreased lens elasticity, hardening of the lens)

Photophobia - pain or discomfort caused by exposer to light.

Migraine headache - is commonly described as moderate to sever throbbing head pain with an aura, nausea, weakness and sensitivity to light and sound.

Optic Disc - Normally yellow orange to creamy pink in color with well defined margins.

Papilledema (Choked Disc) - optic disc margins appear blurred indicating increased intracranial pressure causing "bulging" of the optic disc that is typically bilateral with minimal visual impairment.

Papillitis - sudden unilateral loss of vision and pain with movement of the eye presents with hyperemic edematous disc with blurred margins. Associated with optic neuritis, MS or maybe idiopathic.

Cupping of the Optic Disc - result of increased intra-ocular pressure, a hallmark of glaucoma.

White optic disc with lack of disc vessels indicates optic atrophy.

Blood Vessels of the Eye are normally light and thin.

Conjunctiva of the Eye - Pink is normal, pale indicates anemia, bright red indicates infection.

Sclera of the Eye - White is normal, yellow is jaundice and blue is osteogenesis imperfecta (brittle bone disease).

Copper wire appearance of blood vessels in the eye indicates early stage arteriosclerosis.

Silver wire appearance of blood vessels in the eye indicates late stage arteriosclerosis.

Dermatomyositis - violent flower lesion over eye with skin rash

Flame hemorrhages in the eye indicate hypertension are feather/flame shaped.

Hordeolum (Sty) - pimple on the eyelid, infection of the sebaceous gland(s).

Chalazion - sty like, but bigger. Granulomatous nodule on the eyelid that points inward caused by an infection of the meibomian gland.

Coloboma - congenital absence of ocular tissue.

<u>Pinguecula</u> - yellow plaques on the bulbar conjunctiva common with aging.

<u>Ciliary infection</u> of the eye is considered to be medical emergency

<u>Pancoast tumor</u> can present with unilateral meiotic (meiosis) eye.

<u>Meiotic (Meiosis) Eye</u> - excessively constricted pupil.

<u>Adie's Pupil (Tonic Pupil)</u> - A large regular pupil with sluggish accommodation and convergence and diminished or absent light reflex.

<u>Mydriasis</u> - dilation of the pupil.

<u>Anisocoria</u> - one pupil is more dilated than the other.

<u>Sinus infection</u> - headache with facial pain indicates a sinus infection.

<u>Cluster Headaches</u> - are made worse with alcohol ingestion.

<u>Bitot's spots</u> are keratin on the superficial conjunctiva of the eye associated with deficiency of Vitamin A.

<u>Temporal Arteritis</u> - headache over the eye with distended temporal artery. also known as Giant cell arteritis - temporal headache, tenderness of temporal artery, visual loss, facial pain and decreased blood to the optic nerve ultimately leading to blindness.

<u>Hordeolum</u> - AKA sty, inflammation of a sebaceous gland of the eyelid.

<u>Entropion</u> - Inversion of the eyelid.

<u>Ectropion</u> - Eversion of the eyelid.

<u>Dacryocystitis</u> - Localized pain and swelling to side of nose inferior to the inner canthus.

<u>Pterygium</u> - Triangular shaped structure extending from the inner canthus to the border of the cornea with the apex toward the pupil, an extension of a triangular vascular membrane.

Xanthelasma - patty plaques on the nasal surface of the eyelids indicates hypercholesterolemia or is a normal finding.

Pinguelcula - yellowish triangular nodule in the conjunctiva that is harmless and is common with advanced aging. Look like a pimp on the eye.

Direct Light Reflex - shine a pen light in the eye tests CNII (sees the light) and CNIII (constricts pupil). Shine directly into the eye.

Consensual Light Reflex - tests CN III, the opposite (contralateral) pupil constricts from shining a light in the other eye. Consensual with other eye.

Accommodation - Tests CN II and CN III, maintain focus on object as it moves away.

Visual Acuity - tested with a Snellen Eye Chart.

Cardinal Field of Gaze - Tests CN II, CN III, CN IV, CN VI, see the object, and follow it through all planes of motion (big H).

Internal Ophthalmoplegia - Dilated pupil with ptosis and lateral deviation that does not react to light and has no accommodation, indicates Multiple Sclerosis.

Argyll Robertson pupils - small, irregular, mitotic, accommodating, no consensual reflexes, does not react to light, associated w/ tabes dorsalis (syphilis). AKA Prostitute's Pupil.

Fixed Dilated Pupils - indicated anticholinergic drug use, magic mushrooms.

Fixed Small Pupils - indicates miotic (cholinergic) drug use.

Aphthous stomatitis (Canker sore, Aphthous ulcer) - Painful oral ulcers with yellow borders surrounded by yellow/crimson hyperemic zone.

Angular stomatitis (Angular Cheilitis) - a common inflammatory condition affecting the corners of the mouth (oral commissures) linked to a lack of riboflavin (B2). AKA; cheilosis, perleche.

Physical exam reveals erosion of tooth enamel and scars on the extensor surface of the index finger indicates <u>bulimia nervosa</u>.

Breath Sounds;

<u>Vesicular</u> - heard in most of the lung, especially at the base, inspiratory sound is longer than expiratory sound.

<u>Bronchovesicular</u> - heard on the anterior in the 1st and 2nd interspace and on the posterior between the scapula at the apex of the lung. Inspiratory and expiratory sounds are equal.

<u>Bronchial</u> - heard over the manubrium. Expiratory sound is louder than inspiratory.

<u>Tracheal</u> - heard over the trachea in the neck, inspiratory and expiratory sounds are equal.

<u>Wheezing</u> - abnormal breath sound that indicates chronic respiratory disease such as asthma, emphysema, sever allergies, COPD.

<u>Atelectasis</u> - collapse of lung with loss of volume presents with a lack of breath sounds in the area and flat or dull percussion.

<u>Rhonchi</u> - thick fluid in the alveoli produce a harsh sound indicating bronchitis.

<u>Emphysema</u> - hyper-resonant percussion of the lungs, air filled spaces. Wheezing and barrel chest.

<u>Pleurisy</u> - normal resonant percussion with abnormal breath sound crackles and friction rub caused by thin fluid in the alveoli.

<u>Pleural Effusion</u> - accumulation of fluid in the pleura seen with congestive heart failure.

<u>Pulmonary Edema</u> - left sided heart failure with pink frothy sputum.

<u>Stridor</u> - high pitched wheezing breath sound caused by disrupted airflow caused by an extra-thoracic airway obstruction in the lawny or trachea.

Biot's breathing - abnormal pattern of breathing characterized as groups of quick shallow inspirations followed by irregular periods of apnea.

mucoid - involving or resembling the nature of mucus.

Mucopurulent - emission or secretion of fluid that contains mucus and puss.

Sentinel Node - the first few lymph nodes that a tumor drains into.

Clubbing of the Fingernails - indicates chronic lung pathology (COPD)

Chest - Symmetry is normal, asymmetry indicates scoliosis.

Dyspnea - difficult or labored breathing

Tracheal Tug - the abnormal downward movement of the trachea during systole indicates aortic arch aneurysm or dilation. AKA Oliver's sign.

Pneumcoccal (lobar) Pneumonia - most common presents with productive cough, rusty sputum, caused by strep. pneumonia.

Friedlander's Pneumonia - presents with productive cough, currant jelly (red) sputum, caused by kledsiella pneumonia seen in elderly patient or immunocompromised patient. Often associated with esophageal varies (dilated veins in the esophagus).

Hemophilus Bronchopnumonia - presents with a productive cough caused by gram negative coccobacilli hemophilus influenza mot common in children.

Primary Atypical Pneumonia - presents with dry cough caused by Mycoplasma pneumonia most common 5-35 years of age.

Viral Pneumonia - presents with dry cough, headache, fever and myalgia. Caused by a virus.

Pneumocystis Carnii - caused by a protozoan most commonly found in HIV/Aids patients.

Cytomegalovirus - caused by virus of the same name, also found in HIV/Aids patients.

Blood Flow Through the Heart - Deoxygenated blood from the body enters the Right Atrium to the right ventricle to the lungs. Oxygenated blood from the lungs enters the left atrium to the left ventricle out to the body.

Systole - is the time when the ventricle contract.

Diastole - is the time when the ventricles rest and fill while the atria contract.

S1 heart sound - Mital and Tricsupid valves are closing

S2 heart sound - pulmonary and aortic valves closing (semilunar valves)

Korotkoff Sounds - the sounds observed while taking blood pressure.

Left Sided Heart Failure;

Left Ventricle enlargement. Fluid backs up into the lungs causing a shortness of breath because the left ventricle is not pumping efficiently preventing the delivery of oxygen rich blood to the body.

Pulmonary Edema - fluid accumulation in the tissue and air space of the lungs.

Nocturnal dyspnea - sever shortness of breath and coughing that occurs at night.

Exertional dyspnea - shortness of breath with exercise related to insufficient tissue oxygenation.

Tachycardia - heart rate above 100 beats per minute.

Systemic hypertension - high blood pressure in the body.

Orthopnea - shortness of breath with laying flat.

Rales - breath sound heard when the small airways become fluid filled. Same a crackles.

Right Sided Heart Failure (RSHF);

Pitting Edema - visible swelling caused by a buildup of fluid in tissue. Indention remains after skin is pressed. Bilateral pitting edema of the ankles is often an early sign of RSHF.

Ascites - abnormal build up of fluid in the abdomen.

Cor Pulmonale - enlargement of the right side of the heart as a result of a lung disease or the pulmonary blood vessels.

Hepatomegaly - enlargement of the liver.

Portal Hypertension - increase in the blood pressure within the portal venous system.

Jugular Venous distention - the jugular vein becomes visible, indicating increased central venous pressure a measurement of the pressure inside the vena cava.

Esophageal varices - enlarged veins in the esophagus that develop when the normal blood flow to the liver is blocked.

Hemorrhoids - distended veins of the anus.

Right Ventricular Hypertrophy - enlargement of the right ventricle.

Testicular varicosities - distended or enlarged veins of the testicles.

Takayatsu's Disease (Vasculitis) - Chronic inflammation of the aorta and its main branches that is most common in Asian women.

Male reproductive organs;

Scrotum - holds the testes, help regulate temperature.

Testes - produce sperm and secrete testosterone

Epididymis - collection tube for sperm, Tube of smooth muscle lined by pseudostratified epithelium.

Vas Deferens - straight end of the epididymis.

Seminal Vesicle - produces yellow recreation that contributes to the volume of semen and aids in nourishing the sperm.

Spermatic Cord - formed by vas deferens and surrounding tissue that transmits the inguinal ring to each testicle.

Prostate - is a gland that contributes fluid to semen and has an ejaculatory function. Stroma of prostate contains dense collagen, fibroblasts and haphazard smooth muscle fibers and innervated by sympathetics. Luminal layer tall columnar secretory cells with basal nuclei. Basal cell layer produces keratin.

Semen - seminal fluid that contains sperm.

Cowper's gland (bulbourethral glands) - exocrine glands produce mucous known as pre-ejaculate.

Sertoli cells - support and nourish spermatozoa, rests on basement membrane of seminiferous tubule. Secretes inhibin to regulate hormone production

Leydig cells of the testis - Found in interstitial supporting tissue between seminiferous tubules.

Male Genitalia Disorders:

Varicocele - Enlarged scrotal veins, feels like a bag of worms.

Hydrocele - Fluid accumulation in the testicle, will trans-illuminate.

Spermatocele - Cystic, painless will trans-illuminate, located superior and posterior to the testis.

Epididymitis - inflammation of the coiled tube on the back of the testicle that stores and carries sperm. Usually caused by infection secondary to chlamydia.

Orchitis - inflammation of the testicles caused by a bacterial or virus that affects both testicles but one is more common. Usually secondary to mumps infection but maybe caused by a STD (STI)

Seminoma - Cancer, a germ cell tumor of the testicle that is malignant but is one of the most treatable and curable forms of cancer if discovered early. It does not trans-illuminate and is often painless.

Cryptorchidism - One or both of the testes fail to descended.

Hypospadius - congenital birth defect in which the urethra is on the underside of the of the penis rather than the tip.

Epispadius - rare congenital birth defect in which the urethra is on top of the penis rather than the tip.

Phimosis - Inability to retract the foreskin that may appear as a tight ring or rubber band preventing the foreskin from being retracted.

Paraphimosis - Inability of retracted foreskin to return to its normal anatomic position over the glans penis. Early recognition of this condition is important to prevent complications resulting in amputation of the glans penis.

Peyronie's Disease - Similar to a Dupuytren's contracture, but of the fascia of the corpora. Scar tissue formation that results in an erect penis that is bent (curved) rather than straight. This can result in painful sex or erectile dysfunction.

Doppler Ultrasound - non-invasive test that bounces high frequency sound waves off red blood cells to estimate blood flow. The test monitors the pulse and amplifies the sounds of blood flow. Used to diagnose Buerger's disease, blood clots, venous insufficiency, blood vessel and valve defects, arterial occlusion, aneurysms, arterial stenosis and peripheral arty disease.

Ultrasound - high frequency sound waves are used to visualize organs, vessels and other water densities. The sound creates echos that the computer uses to create an image.

Angiography - Radiopaque dye is injected into arteries to be visualized on x-ray. Used to study the circulatory system and diagnose tumors.

Biopsy - a small amount of tissue is removed from a lesion and microscopically evaluated for pathology.

Joint Aspiration - a needle is used to remove fluid from a joint or lesion to be evaluated for pathology.

Myelography - Radiopaque dye is injected into the subarachnoid space and visualized on x-ray. Used to evaluate space occupying lesions of the subarachnoid space.

Spirometer - instrument that measures breathing, how much air is inhaled and exhaled and how quickly. Used to diagnose COPD, asthma, bronchitis or other conditions that affect breathing.

Tonometer - instrument measures pressure changes in the eye that would indicate glaucoma.

Nerve Conduction - Electrode over a nerve, another one the muscle the speed the stimulation reaches the muscle is measured testing for peripheral nerve entrapment.

Electromyogram (EMG) - electrical stimulus measures the extent of neuromuscular damage from muscle wasting diseases.

Magnetic Resonance Imaging (MRI) - diagnostic image used to visualize the soft tissue, can be used to "see" spinal discs, spinal tumors, muscle tears, ligament damage and more.

Bone Scan - is a type of x-ray that uses a dye to visualize changes in the bone and find hidden fractures or other bone pathology.

Dual Energy X-ray Absorptiometry (DEXA) - 2 x-rays beams pointed at bone used to measure its density. Changs in density as small as 1% can be detected with DEXA scan, more sensitive and accurate that normal x-ray which requires a 40% change in density to be observed on plain film.

Venogram - confirms signs of thrombophlebitis.

PET scan - positron emission test, used to measure blood volume, oxygen uptake, metabolism and glucose uptake.

CAT Scan (CT) - Multiple x-rays are enhanced using a computer to create a more detailed view of bone or soft tissue.

Plethysmograph - an instrument that measure the volume of organ and the amount of blood flow that information can be used to find disturbances in blood flow.

Increased Eosinophils (eosinophilia) - indicates allergic reaction.

Curshmann's Spirals - microscopic finding in sputum of asthmatic patient.

Charcot Leyden Crystals - microscopic finding of crystals composed of an eosinophil protein found in septum of patients with asthma or other allergic disease or parasitic infection.

Elevated Amylase and Lipase - indicates pancreatitis or pancreatic cancer. These enzymes are produced by cells of the pancreas and an increase of them in the blood stream indicates disease of pancreas cells.

Elevated BUN, Uric acid, creatinine - indicate kidney disease, renal disease.

Acid Phosphatase - if found in the blood stream it indicates the capsule of the prostate is broken like the result of prostate cancer.

Elevated CPK with decreased creatinine - indicates muscular dystrophy because of a loss of muscle. (there are many kinds of muscular dystrophy)

Fasting Blood Sugar - under 100 is normal, 100-125 is considered prediabetic, and if it above 126 or higher on two separate tests, indicate diabetes.

Prostate Specific Antigen (PSA) - blood test that measures the amount of PSA in the blood of a man. One of the screening methods for prostate cancer.

Glucose Tolerance Test (GTT) - Oral test, measures the body's reaction to sugar. Used to diagnose gestational diabetes and Type 2 diabetes. Patient consumes 2.6 ounces of solution containing 75 grams of sugar. Two hours later blood glucose is tested. Normal blood sugar level would be under 140, 140-199 is considered prediabetes and blood glucose of 200 or more indicates diabetes.

Lab Values with Myocardial Infarction;

CPK - first to appear, 3 to 6 hours after MI peaks in 24 to 36 hours and returns to normals by the 3rd day.

SGOT - 2nd to appear, 6 to 8 hours after MI peaks in 24 hours and returns to normal with in 4 to 6 days.

LDH - 3rd to appear, 10 to 12 hours after MI peaks in 48 to 72 hours and returns to normal after 14 days.

Urine Analysis; Straw color is normal.

Red urine - blood or food pigments, indicates infection, cancer, bleeding, or it was something you ate, beets.

Green urine - caused by biliverdin and indicates biliary duct obstruction.

Blue urine - caused by diuretic therapy.

Orange urine - caused by urobilinogen indicating hemolytic jaundice.

Brown urine - caused by bile pigments or blood in the urine indicating biliary duct obstruction or occult blood.

Black (dark brown) urine - caused by homogentisic acid from melanin indicating a melanotic tumor or urobilin indicating ochronosis, hemolysis or bacterial infection.

Cloudy urine - indicates pus from an infection

Specific Gravity - normally 1.01-1.03 will elevate with dehydration, bacterial infection, diabetes mellitus and all kidney diseases.

Protein - is not normally in urine, proteinuria indicates kidney disease (dysfunction) toxemia of pregnancy or diabetes mellitus.

Glucose - is not normally found in urine under 180 mg/dL (renal threshold), glycosuria indicates diabetes mellitus, shock, head injury or increased dietary sugar intake.

Ketones - are not normally found in urine, indicates diabetes mellitus or starvation (Ketosis).

Blood - should not be in the urine, hematuria indicates cancer, trauma, kidney infection or kidney stones.

Conjugated Bilirubin - indicates liver disease (hepatic disease) and/or biliary obstruction.

Bacteria and/or pus - indicate and infection of the kidney, ureters and/or bladder.

Shilling Test - a 24 hour urine test for pernicious anemia as it measures how well the patient is able to absorb B12 from their intestinal tract. Not to be confused with the Shilling Shift an increase in immature blood cells that indicates acute appendicitis.

Bence Jones Protein - a monoclonal globulin protein (immunoglobulin) found in the urine maybe suggestive of multiple myeloma.

Urine Casts;
Hyaline casts are normal.
RBC casts indicate glomerulonephritis.
WBC casts indicate pyelonephritis.
Waxy Casts indicate nephrotic syndrome.

Hematology

Red Blood Cells (RBC) - normal level is 4-6 million/ cubic cm. Decreased RBC is anemia of which there are several types.

Polycythemia Vera - increased number of RBC due to a slow growing blood cancer that results in the bone marrow producing too many RBC, thickening the blood slowing its flow, decreased ESR.

White Blood Cells (WBC) - normal level is 5k-10K/ cubic mm. Over 50K indicates leukemia. 20k to 30k indicates infection or inflammation. Any decrease indicates some form of anemia.

Hemoglobin (Hgb) - normal is approximately 15 g/dL an increase indicates dehydration or polycythemia vera a decrease indicates some sort of anemia.

Hematocrit (Hct) - This the is the ratio of the volume of RBC to the volume of whole blood, normal range is 42% +/- 5%, same as Hgb and an increase indicates dehydration or polycythemia vera while a decrease indicates some sort of anemia.

Erythrocyte Sedimentation Rate (ESR) - a measure of how fast RBC settle at the bottom of a test tube. Normally slow, a faster rate can indicate inflammation in the body. Increased ESR can indicate and infection while decreased ESR indicates sickle cell anemia or polycythemia vera.

Platelets - tiny blood cells in the body that form clots. Normal range is 200k to 350k per cubic mm. An increase indicates trauma, blood loss or polycythemia vera while a decrease indicates anemia, sever burns or thrombocytopenia.

Plasma - the liquid component of blood with the cellular components removed.

Serum - the liquid component of blood with the cells and fibrinogen removed.

C-Reactive Protein (CRP) - an abnormal protein found in blood with tissue inflammation or destruction.

Types of WBC

Neutrophils - 60% of WBC increased with bacterial infection.
Lymphocytes - 30% of WBC increased with Viral infection (Mononucleosis)
Monocytes - 8% of WBC increased with chronic infections (Hodgkin's)
Eosinophils - 2% of WBC increased with allergies (asthma) and parasites.
Basophils - 0% normally are not found in the blood, increased levels indicate an inflammatory reaction from an allergy. Basophils contain the anticoagulant heparin to prevent blood from clotting to fast and the vasodilator histamine that promotes blood flow to tissues.

60,30,8,2,0 **N**ever **L**et **M**y **E**ngine **B**low

Normocytic - the red blood cells are normal size and shape. Microcytic is small cells, macrocytic are large cells.

Normochromic - the concentration of hemoglobin in the red blood cells is within a normal range. Hypochromic is a decrease in the concentration of hemoglobin.

Anemias

Normocytic Normochomic Anemias - indicates acute hemolysis, hemorrhagic, aplastic or hypoplastic anemias.

Microcytic Normochromic Anemias - indicate infection, liver disease, malignancy, more.

Microcytic Hypochromic - iron deficiency is the most common cause.

Macrocytic, Normochromic Anemia - indicates Vitamin B-12 (folic acid deficiency) pernicious anemia.

Reticulocytes - immature RBC, indication of bone marrow function.

Decreased Reticulocytes - indicates aplastic/hypoplastic anemia, defective erythropoiesis or untreated iron deficiency.

Increased Reticulocytes - indicates hyperactive bone activity, post-hemorrhage, hemolysis or chronic bleeding.

Antistreptolysin O (ASO) titer - blood test that measures antibodies against streptomycin O, increases with any strep infection, rheumatic fever, acute glomerulonephritis.

AntiNuclear Antibody (ANA) Test - blood test that indicates autoimmune diseases Systemic Lupus Erythematosus (SLE), Rheumatoid Arthritis (RA), Scleroberma.

Blood Urea Nitrogen (BUN) - blood test that measures the amount of area and nitrogen in the blood. Increased BUN indicates Kidney Disease with decreased BUN indicates Liver Disease.

Immunoelectrophoresis - generalized name for biochemical separation of proteins. Spike of IgM indicates Multiple Myeloma (MM)

C Reactive Protein (CPR) - increased with inflammation, used to help diagnose inflammatory arthritis, RA, AS.

Blood Glucose - normal 70-99, an increase indicates Diabetes Mellitus, Cushing's Syndrome, a decrease indicates an overdose, Addison's disease.

CSF Glucose - decreased indicates bacteria meningitis.

CSF Protein - increased proteins in CSF indicate viral meningitis.

Dick Test - used to diagnose scarlet fever

Frei Test - lymphogranuloma venereum

Darkfield Microscopy - primary syphilis

VDLR - tertiary syphilis

Mantoux - intra-dermal test of tuberculosis (TB)

Coombs test - detects the presence of the Rh factor (antigens)

Schilling - used to indicate pernicious anemia, determines HCL production and Vitamin B-12 absorption.

Sputum - saliva and mucus coughed up form the respiratory tract.

Hemoptysis - coughing up blood indicates bleeding in the mouth or pharynx.

Pink Sputum - blood mixing with secretions often associated with pneumonia or pulmonary edema.

Rusty Sputum - dark reddish brown indicates pneumococcal pneumonia.

Frothy Sputum - Thin bubbly sputum indicates pulmonary edema and/or congestive heart failure.

Mucoid Sputum - Slimy grey-white translucent sputum indicates post asthmatic attack.

Purulent Sputum - yellow, green or dirty grey sputum associated with bacterial infection, tuberculous cavity, resolution of pneumonia, fistula and bronchiectasis.

Broncholiths - calcified particles in sputum seen with calcified lymph nodes, granulomas, or histoplasmosis.

Hematochezia - the passing of fresh blood in stool indicates lower GI bleeding.

Melena - bark tarry stool, indicates upper GI bleeding.

Steatorrhea - pale clay colored stool that results from malabsorption from a lack of bile pigments or an excess of fat intake that indicates obstructive jaundice or pancreatic insufficiency.

Electrocardiogram - records the electrical signals produced by the heart visualized by a p,q,r,s,t wave.

P Wave - atrial depolarization

QRS complex - ventricular depolarization

T wave - ventricular re-polarization.

T wave Inversion - non-specific finding that indicates possible diffuse myocardial ischemia, sub-endocardial infarctions or CNS lesion.

Q wave - "hallmark" of Myocardial Infarction (MI). Wider Deeper Q wave indicates chronic condition.

P wave - anomalies are of limited diagnostic value

U wave - increased amplitude indicates hypokalemia or inverted indicates myocardial ischemia.

Q-T interval - indicates prolonged ischemia.

New (recent) MI can be indicated by ST elevation and T inversion.
Old MI indicated by a large Q wave.

Paroxysmal Tachycardia - P:QRS ratio is normal 1:1 but very close together indicating a rapid heart rate (140-250 bpm)

Atrial Fibrillation - multiple ectopic foil are produced by rapid irregular atrial contraction (quivering). Extra waves in the wrong place.

Atrial Flutter - Rapid atrial contractions generate "saw-tooth" waves where the QRS is normal but the ratio to P is greater than 2:1 instead of the normal 1:1.

Ventricular Fibrillation - rapid uncoordinated ventricular contraction. The Electrocardiogram doesn't look like there is anything normal waves all over the place.

Ears;

When examining the ear of an adult with a otoscope the ear is pulled up and back.

When examining the ear of a child the ear is pulled down and back.

<u>Auricle</u> - Outer ear, tenderness indicates acute otitis externa.

<u>Otitis media</u> - inflammatory disease of the middle ear, presents with tenderness behind the ear.

<u>Ear Drum</u> - divides the middle ear from the external ear. Pink is the normal color, perforation of the ear drum indicates a purulent infection, amber fluid with bubbles indicates serous otitis media, red with dilated blood vessels and bulging of the tympanic membrane indicates purulent otitis media or bacterial infection, hemorrhagic vesicles indicate a viral infection and retraction of the ear drum indicates obstruction of the Eustachian tube(s).

<u>Ear drum;</u>
Blue - hemorrhage
Amber - acute serous otitis media
Red - acute otitis media
White - suppurative otitis media
Pink - myringitis
Retracted - blocked eustachian tube.

Tympanic Sclerosis white chalky tympanic membrane caused by chronic infection.

<u>Acute Otitis Externa</u> - inflammation of the ear canal most commonly caused by a bacterial infection, presents with tenderness of the auricle.

<u>Bullous Myringitis</u> - type of ear infection with small fluid filled blisters form on the ear drum.

<u>Purulent otitis media</u> - infection/inflammation of the middle ear that produces puss bulging the ear drum that appears red with dilated blood vessels.

Chemodectoma - a tumor of the gloms bodies in the middle ear that are visible as red mass behind the tympanic membrane.

Weber test - 512 Hz tuning fork is placed at the vertex of the head. Right lateralization indicates sensorineural loss of the left ear or conduction loss on the right. Sound should not lateralize.

Rinne's Test - 512 Hz tuning fork is placed on the mastoid process and time the patient when the stop hearing the vibration. Then repeat with the tuning fork infant of the ear and time when the patient stops hearing the tuning fork. Air Conduction of sound should be twice as long as bone conduction (on the mastoid). If air conduction is not twice as long indicates sensory hearing loss

Meniere's disease - patient complains of hearing loss, tinnitus and episodes of dizziness with progressive deafness, tinnitus, vertigo, feeling of fullness/pressure in the ears. This is an inner ear disease that typically affects one ear. This disease can cause pressure or pain in the ear, severe cases of dizziness or vertigo, hearing loss and a ringing or roaring noise, also known as tinnitus.

Acoustic Neuroma (vestibular schwannoma) - a benign tumor that develops on nerves leading from your inner ear to the brain. Early symptoms including hearing loss with tinnitus problems with balance may develop.

Vertigo - Room seems to be spinning, spinning dizziness, result of a disturbance to the equilibratory apparatus with many known causes.

DeMusset's Sign - oscillation of the head due to aortic aneurysm or insufficiency.

Viral Rhinitis (common cold) - red swollen nasal mucosa.

Allergic Rhinitis - clear mucus with pale, blue or red nasal mucosa.

Atrophic Rhinitis - foul odor, crust formation with sclerosis and atrophy of the nasal mucosa due to necrosis of tissue.

Angioma - benign growth of small blood vessels that can be located anywhere in the body.

Cherry Angioma - a red spot with white ring around it that appears with normal aging. AKA; red moles, senile angiomas, Campbell de Morgan Spots are most common after age 30, common skin growths the can occur on most areas of the body.

Spider Angioma - a vascular lesion with a central red spot with reddish extensions that radiate outward just below the surface of the skin. These are common and may be benign however having 3 or more is an indication of liver disease and suggests alcoholism. AKA; spider naevus, nevus araneus, vascular spider, spider telangiectasia.

Cauda Equina Syndrome - the most consistent symptom is urinary retention (weak or absent bladder control.) Unilateral or bilateral sciatica, sensory and motor deficits considered a medical emergency.

Multiple Sclerosis - Chronic neurological disease characterized by areas of demyelination scattered throughout the white matter in the spinal cord and brain. Presents with; nystagmus, scanning speech and intention tremors (Charcot's triad). Visual disturbances, hyper-reflexive and inability to recognize objects by touch alone. Tests; Lhermitte's, Hoffmann's, Babinski's and MRI may show periventricular and spinal cord plaques (multiple areas of sclerosis).

Parkinson's disease - a chronic, progressive neurodegenerative disease that affects the motor system with unknown cause that presents with Pill-rolling, resting tremor, cog-wheel spasticity, stiffness, slowness of movement, mask-like facies and depression.

Bell's Palsy - is paresis of a lower motor neuron involving the facial nerve that presents with sudden unilateral weakness of the facial muscles.

Nystagmus - a rhythmic uncontrolled oscillation of the eyeball resulting in reduced vision and depth perception affecting balance and coordination. Generally pronounced in one direction and then slowly returning to the center. It can be due to cerebellar and vestibular apparatus disease, congenital disease, eyestrain, or systemic disease but it can present without any underlying disease process.

Paget's Disease - Metabolic bone disorder characterized by repeated episodes of osteolysis and excessive but ineffective attempts at repair resulting a weakened bone of increased mass. Presents with pathological fractures, increased skull size, thoracic kyphosis, bowing of the legs, radicular pain and in sever cases compression of the optic nerve can result in blindness.

Ischemia (ischaemia) - local deficiency of blood supply or a restriction of the blood supply causing a lack of oxygen that is required for cellular metabolism resulting in tissue damage or dysfunction.

Infarction - necrosis of tissue following cessation of blood supply by the blockage, rupture, compression or the constriction of a blood vessel.

Hypoxia - deficiency of adequate oxygen to sustain normal function.

Embolus - a mass of undissolved matter or air present in the blood stream or lymphatic vessel that causes the sudden blocking of an artery.

Thrombus - a blood clot that formed within the vascular system and obstructs a blood vessel or cavity of the heart that is composed of aggregated platelets and red blood cells and a mesh of criss linked fibrin protein. The substance that a thrombus is composed of is sometime called a cruor (the clotted portion of coagulated blood).

6 types of Pneumonias:

1. Pneumococcol - caused by streptococcus pneumoniae a gram negative, facultative anaerobic bacteria. This is the most common bacterial pneumonia found in adults. Presents with sudden with all the classic signs and symptoms of pneumonia with characteristic lobar distribution and rusty (blood streaked) sputum.

2. Klebsiella - caused by klebsiella pneumoniae, a bacteria that normally lives in our gut and are normally harmless in the gut but can cause sever infections in other parts of the body. This gram negative, non-motile, encapsulated, lactose fermenting facultative anaerobic rod-shaped bacteria presents with current jelly (bloody) sputum, commonly seen with alcoholics and immunocompromised individuals. AKA Friedlander's Pneumonia.

3. <u>Hemophilus Influenza</u> - this gram negative, coccobacillary facultative, anaerobic bacteria commonly seen with children that presents with alveolar consolidation. A vaccine has been available since the early 1990s and is recommended for all children under the age of 5.

4. <u>Mycoplasma Pneumoniae</u> - an atypical bacteria that causes a "mild infection" give this type of pneumonia the common name, "walking pneumonia." Myco normally would mean fungal but this is a bacteria infection related to Cold Agglutinin disease.

5. <u>Pneumocystis Carinii</u> - Protozoan, yeast like fungus of the genus pneumocystis this infection is most commonly seen with HIV/AIDS patients or other immunocompromised hots.

6. <u>Viral Pneumonia</u> - Any viral infection of the lungs can be classified as viral pneumonia. Viruses are the most common cause of pneumonia in children. A dry cough in an early characteristic but a Mucopurulent productive cough is a key to differentiating viral from other forms of pneumonia.

<u>Ulcerative colitis</u> - chronic inflammation of the lining of the large intestine that results in open sores or ulcers that lead to bloody diarrhea, rectal bleeding, abdominal cramps and pain. Ulcerative colitis increases the patients risk of developing colon cancer.

<u>Crohn's Disease (Regional Enteritis)</u> - an inflammatory bowel disease that may affect any part of the GI tract that presents with chronic intermittent sometime bloody diarrhea, weight loss, abdominal pain, anemia, enteropathic arthritis and inflammation of the eye. The cause of Crohn's disease remains unknown. Additional terms for Crohn's disease include terminal or regional ileitis.

<u>Celiac Disease</u> - an immune reaction to eating gluten, a protein found wheat , barley and rye, that damages the lining of the small intestine. Presents with chronic diarrhea described as loose, pale and greasy. Weight loss from malabsorption, fatigue and anemia.

<u>Lactose Intolerance</u> - a lack of the enzyme lactase in the small intestine results in a decreased ability to digest lactose (sugar found in dairy products) producing abdominal pain, bloating, diarrhea, gas and nausea.

Inguinal Hernia - the most common type of hernia this is a protrusion of the abdominal cavity contents through the inguinal canal that presents with pain that increases with coughing and bending.

Femoral Hernia - the abdominal contents protrude through a natural weakness in the abdominal wall called the femoral canal (below the inguinal ring). This type of hernia is more common in men that women but is generally consider uncommon. Surgical repair is suggested even in the asymptomatic patient to prevent complications.

Umbilical Hernia - the abdominal contents (viscera) protrude through the abdominal wall behind the navel causing to bulge outward. In newborns these hernias can be large but typically self resolve by age 2 or 3. In adults this condition is not likely to self resolve and surgery is suggested to prevent complications (strangulation…)

Direct Hernia - develops over time to straining is caused by a leaking is the abdominal wall. More common in adult males that does not transmit the inguinal ring and forms to one side of the groin.

Indirect Hernia - caused by persistent opening that does not close during fetal development. More common in children and typically present at birth does pass through the inguinal ring into the scrotum.

Sports Hernia (athletic pubalgia) - most common in sports that require sudden changes in direction (cutting) results in damage to a tendon, fascia or ligament that results in an inguinal hernia.

Examination is performed with the patient standing the DR palpates the scrotum and asks the patient to cough. A bulge of tissue entering the scrotum at the inguinal canal indicates a hernia.

Incisional Hernia - any hernia that results for an incision.

Hiatal Hernia - protrusion of the upper stomach to the wrong side of the diagram.

Pectus Excavatum - congenital deformity of the anterior thoracic wall in which the sternum and rib cage are "caved-in" or sunken that can be present at birth or develop after puberty. AKA Dented Chest or Funnel Chest.

Pectus Carinatum - congenital deformity of the anterior thoracic wall in which the sternum and rib cage protrude, bulge or point out giving the chest a bird like appearance giving this condition the AKA Pigeon Chest or Keel of Ship appearance.

Barrel Chest - describes the increased anterior to posterior dimension giving the chest a barrel like appearance that is most commonly associated with emphysema.

Hematochezia - passing for fresh blood through the anus with or without stool indicating lower GI bleeding from hemorrhoids, diverticulosis or in rare cases cancer.

Rectorrhagia - is the passing of fresh blood though the anus that is not associated with defecation (no stool).

Palmar erythema - the palms turning red at the thenar and hypothenar eminences associated with chronic liver disease/failure.

Gastric/Peptic Ulcer - stomach acid damages the lining of the GI tract. Most common cause is H. Pylori followed by NSAID (Aspirin). Sores that form in the stomach and/or upper portions of the small intestine present with upper abdominal pain.

Duodenal ulcer - a type of peptic ulcer that occurs in the duodenum. Most common presentation is waking at night with postprandial pain relieved by eating.

Postprandial - changes that occur after eating, postprandial pain is pain after eating.

Portal hypertension - in high blood pressure in the hepatic portal system most commonly due to the cirrhosis of the liver.

Tympani - most common percussive note in the abdomen.

Liver enzymes - AST(SGOT), ALT(SGPT).

Pancreatitis - Inflammation of the pancreas that presents with pain, nausea and vomiting. The pain usually refers to the back and can be severe.

Acute Pancreatitis - typically presents with a fever and will resolve in a few days.

Chronic Pancreatitis - also presents with weight loss, fatty stool, diarrhea and does resolve in a few days.

The most common cause of pancreatitis are gall stones blocking the common bile duct and heavy alcohol consumption.

Pancreatic cancer - 85% of cases are pancreatic adenocarcinoma is a proliferation of the glandular tissues that produce digestive enzymes. Typically presents with abdominal and/or back pain, unexplained weight loss, dark urine, loss of appetite. Symptoms usually are not severe or specific enough to be diagnosed until the cancer has spread to other parts of the body.

Serum ferritin - Iron/phosphate/protein complex. Iron combines with apoferritin on interstitial mucosa and is stored in the reticuloendothelial cells of the liver, spleen and bone marrow. "Ferritin" iron away to store it.

Monckeburg's Medial Calcific Sclerosis (MCS) - Ring like calcification of small to medium sized arteries without thickening of the tunica intima. MCS is almost exclusively the underlying condition of Breast Arterial Calcification (BAC) that is found with routine mammography.

Leriche's Syndrome (Sign) AKA Aortoiliac Occlusive Disease - a form of Central Artery Disease that is characterized as blockage (obstruction) of the abdominal aorta at the bifurcation into the common iliac(s) that presents with claudication of the buttocks and thighs, bilateral leg pain, absent or decreased femoral pulses and impotence (erectile dysfunction).

Polyarteritis Nodosa (PAN) - systemic necrotising inflammation of the blood vessels (vasculitis) of medium sized arteries usually involving the arteries of the kidneys and other internal organs but typically sparing the lungs. Small aneurysms that are strung together like beads (rosary sign) are an important diagnostic feature of PAN.

Bacterial endocarditis (Infective Endocarditis) - is a bacterial infection that enters the blood stream and steels in/on he endocardium (heart lining), a heart valve or cardiac blood vessel that presents with; Splinter hemorrhages in nail beds, fever, malaise, heart murmur and more.

Essential hypertension (Primary Hypertension) - is defined as high blood pressure with no known cause that is diagnosed by recording/observing the patient with unexplained high blood pressure n three desperate occasions.

Secondary Hypertension - A known causes such as adrenal tumor, hormone abnormalities, thyroid disease, excess dietary salt, medications, and more. The key factor is that there is a known cause.

Thoracic aortic aneurysm - characterized by sub-sternal pain, dyspnea and tracheal tug.

Coronary artery disease - the narrowing or blockage of the coronary arteries most commonly caused by atherosclerosis, a build up of plaque on the inner wall of arteries.

Cardiac tamponade - accumulation of fluid in the pericardial space that decreases ventricular filling that presents with distention of the neck veins, low blood pressure, paradoxical pulse, decreased heart sounds.

Acrocyanosis - idiopathic vasospasm of the arterioles of the skin of the hands resulting in asymmetrical persistent painless cyanosis (blue hands).

Erythromelalgia - a paroxysmal, bilateral vasodilation of the lower extremities' blood vessels resulting in burning pain, redness and increased temperature of the feet (Red hot burins legs).

Thromoboangitis Obliterans (Buerger's) - an inflammatory occlusion of the arteries and veins of the legs that is more common in men that smoke ages 20-40 characterized as intermittent claudication (Pain with exertion in the legs received by rest).

Angina Perctoris - temporary myocardial ischemia with exertion that presents with retrosternal crushing pain that lasts for 1-5 minuets with normal EKG and ESR.

<u>Prinzmetal's Angina</u> - Pain at rest caused by spasm of a coronary artery EKG shows arrhythmia and ST elevation.

<u>Immunoglobulin (Ig)</u> - protein present in the blood serum and cells of the immune system that function as antibodies (AB).

<u>IgA</u> - The principle immunoglobulin in exocrine secretions such as milk, saliva, tears, respiratory and intestinal mucin.

<u>IgD</u> - Increased in persons with a high concentration of Rh AB, AKA erythroblastosis fatalis.

<u>IgE</u> - Atopic diseases increase concentrations, eg: allergies. Parasites. Binds to mast cells.

<u>IgG</u> - The principal immunoglobulin in human serum. Crosses the placenta. Major AB for antitoxins, viral and bacteria. Activates the complement cascade.

<u>IgM</u> - Controls the A,B, and O blood group AB responses, most efficient in stimulating the complement cascade.

Neuromusculoskeletal Diagnosois

Gait Cycle - Composed fo the Stance phase and Swing phase with two periods with double support (two legs) and one period of a single leg support.

Stance Phase - defined as when a foot is on the ground bearing weight. Composed of 5 sub phases; heel strike, flat foot, mid stance, heel off, toe off.

Swing Phase - defined as when the foot is non weight bearing and moving. Composed of 3 sub phases; initial swing, mid swing and terminal swing.

Double Leg Stance - the period of time in the gait cycle that both feet on the ground. Accounts for approximately 25% of the entire cycle. This period of time shortens as speed increased and completely disappears with running.

Single-Leg Stance - the period of time in the gait cycle that only one leg is on the ground. Accounts for approximately 30% of the entire cycle, occurs twice during normal gait.

Gait Length (Step) - normal range is 35 to 41 cm is defined as the distance between successive contact points on opposite feet.

Stride Length - defined as the distance in the plane of progression between the successive points by the same foot. Normal range is 70-82 cm (double gait length). Two steps equal one stride.

Types of Pathological Gait

Spastic Gait - indicates Upper Motor Neuron Lesion (UMNL) such as Multiple Sclerosis (MS).

Scissor Gait - indicates spastic paraplegia, cerebral palsy.

Motor Ataxic Gait - indicates cerebellar lesion, clumsy, staggering steps with a wide base. PT cannot walking heel to toe or in a straight line. Resembles acute alcohol intoxication (drunk).

<u>Fenestrating Gait/Propulsive Gait/Shuffling Gait</u> - indicates Parkinson's Disease

<u>Waddling Gait</u> - indicates muscular dystrophy (weak abductors and gluts), congenital hip dysplasia.

<u>Steppage Gait (Neuropathic Gait/Equine Gait)</u> - indicates Lower Motor Neuron Lesion (LMNL) commonly seen with foot drop caused by paresis of the Anterior Tibial Muscle from a lesion of the L4/L5 nerve root or peroneal nerve.

<u>Antalgic Gait</u> - patient alters gait to avoid pain, common with disc lesions.

<u>Sensory Gait (Slap Gait)</u> - sensory ataxia.

<u>Toe In Gait (pigeon toe)</u> - predisposes patient to medial knee injuries. Extensive toe in may result in femoral ante-version.

<u>Hemiplegic Gait (Circumduction Gait)</u> - unilateral weakness onto affected side the arm is flex, adducted and internally rotated while ipsilateral leg is in extension with planter flexion. PT tends to "drag" the affected leg in a semicircle (circumduction). Most commonly observed in stroke patients.

<u>Diplegia Gait (Scissor Gait)</u> - bilateral spasticity of the legs PT walks with narrow base, dragging both legs, scraping the toes. This gait indicates bilateral periventricular lesions (Ex. cerebral palsy). Extreme Tightness of hip adductors result in the legs cross the midline giving this gait the "scissoring" appearance.

<u>Myopathic Gait</u> - muscle weakness results in the contralateral side of the pelvis dropping with each step. It is possible to have bilateral hip/pelvis drop with bilateral muscle weakness making the PT appear to waddle (aka waddling gait)

<u>Choriform Gait (Hyperkinetic Gait)</u> - Irregular jerk involuntary movements of all extremities indicates basal ganglia pathology including; Sydenham's Chores, Huntington's Disease or any form of chorea, athetosis or dystonia.

Titubation - a nodding motion of the head or body caused by a nervous system disorder. A type of essential tremor descried as uncontrolled rhythmic motion of the head, neck ad trunk.

Trendelenburg Sign - the pelvis drops when lifting the opposite leg.

Scoliosis;

Cob Method - using the most "tilted" vertebrae above and below the apex of an abnormal lateral curve the angle of intersecting lines drawn perpendicular to the top of the vertebrae above and the bottom of the vertebrae below is the Cob Angle. This is a means of measuring bending disorders of the spine such as scoliosis or traumatic deformities.

70% of structural Scoliosis is idiopathic.

4% of the US population will develop idiopathic scoliosis, which means there is no known cause. Idiopathic scoliosis (most common form) typically does not present with pain.

Infantile Idiopathic Scoliosis - patient is 0-3 years of age (YOA); 80% of infantile idiopathic scoliosis will self resolve, the remaining 20% can be difficult to manage. These cases should be closely monitored. If any progression is noted aggressive non surgical intervention (chiropractic, therapeutic exercise) must be started, if progression continues there are number of invasive surgical methods to address infantile scoliosis.

Juvenile Idiopathic Scoliosis - patient is 3-10 YOA, less common and less severe than adolescent scoliosis.

Adolescent Idiopathic Scoliosis - patient is 10-16 YOA, accounts for 80% of all cases of idiopathic scoliosis. This is a period of rapid development, any abnormal curve fo the spine should be closely monitored for progression.

Adult Idiopathic Scoliosis - once the PT reaches skeletal maturity adolescent idiopathic scoliosis becomes adult idiopathic scoliosis. Pain is the most common reason PT will seek treatment as normal degenerative changes are accelerated by the abnormal curvature.

Adult Onset Scoliosis - is abnormal curvature of the spine caused by degeneration of the facet joints. Most common in adults over 65 years of age. Osteoporosis, arthritis of the spine (spondylosis), compression fracture(s) and degenerative disc disease are all possible contributing factors resulting in the most common form of scoliosis that develops is adults.

Scoliosis under 20 degrees - conservative treatment, no bracing an re-examine regularly.

Scoliosis greater than 20 degrees - refer for bracing.

Scoliosis of 50 degrees or more may require surgery because it can lead to cardio-pulmonary issues.

Structural Scoliosis (congenital scoliosis) - a fixed abnormal lateral curve of the spine, may have no known cause (idiopathic) or be a part of a syndrome or disease process. Typically present at birth, hemi-vertebra, tumors, metabolic disease, connective tissue disorder, neuromuscular disease or unknown cause (idiopathic) can result in structural scoliosis.

Neuromuscular Scoliosis - the result of a neuromuscular disease such as; birth defects, muscular dystrophy, cerebral palsy, Marfan's Syndrome typically present with a long "C" shaped curve of the spine because their muscles are unable to help their spine straight.

Functional Scoliosis (Non-structural Scoliosis) - an abnormal lateral curve without rotation that is reversible with resolution of the cause such as pain, muscle spasm or a difference in leg length. This type of scoliosis is a normal response to a problem somewhere else in the body.

Compensatory Scoliosis - an abnormal spinal curve in the coronal plane that disappears with the patient sits. This type of scoliosis maybe due to a short leg, pelvic tilt or contracture of hip muscles.

Dextroscoliosis - the most common presentation of scoliosis the when the PT is viewed from behind the abnormal lateral curve is to the right.

Levoscoliosis - less common presentation when viewed from behind the abnormal lateral curve is the to the left. In the thoracic spine may indicate pathology or spinal injury.

Kyphoscoliosis - the abnormal lateral curve presents with excessive forward bending.

Postural Scoliosis - is nonstructural, the abnormal curves are a slight and disappear with lying down, related to the PT posture.

Transient Scoliosis - not a true scoliosis that most commonly results from pain such as a disc herniation putting pressure on a nerve root, or inflammation (infection) of tissue or organ leading to side bending to relieve pain. This is a nonstructural type of scoliosis.

Hysterical Scoliosis - extremely rare, nonstructural, transient scoliosis that is manifested by the mind and can be corrected with psychiatric treatment.

Progression - defined as an increase of 3 degrees or more in one year using the Cob Method.

Skeletal Maturity - using the Greulich and Pyle Atlas, or approach, skeletal maturity is reached with the distal radial epiphyseal plate is fully fused.

Milwaukee Brace - is a Cervic-thoraco-lumbo-sacral orthosis (CTLSO), a full torso brace that extends from the pelvic to the skull. Typically used to stabilize adolescent scoliosis of 25 to 40 degrees. This is not a corrective brace, it is worn 23 hours pre day until skeletal maturity is reached to prevent progression. Scoliosis beyond 40 degrees requires a surgical consult.

Harrington Rod(s) - starless steel rods surgically implanted along the spine to reduce and stabilize severe scoliosis that immobilize the spine.

<u>Lateral Electrical Surface Stimulation (LESS) Therapy</u> - a non-invasive treatment for idiopathic scoliosis that uses electrical neuromuscular simulation for 8 hours per night on the involved side. The goal is not resolution or correcting but prevention of progression.

Pregnancy, osteoporosis, bone softening, facet joint arthritis and degenerative disc disease will exacerbate scoliosis.

<u>Orthopedics Examination principles</u>

Test normal side first.

Active ROM first, passive second, and resisted third.

Painful movements last.

Apply pressure/resistance with care.

Repeat or sustain movements if history indicates.

Do resisted isometric movements in resting positions.

With passive and ligamentous testing both degree and quality of opening are important.

With ligamentous, repeat with increasing stress.

With myotome testing, hold contractions for five seconds.

Warn the patient (PT) of possible exacerbations.

<u>End Feel</u> - the sensation perceived by the DR performing passive range of motion.

<u>Bone to Bone</u> - abrupt end feel as two hard surfaces meet.

<u>Springy Block</u> - a slight rebound at the end range of motion.

<u>Empty End Feel</u> - pain before the full range of motion is achieved.

Coxa - Hip
Genu - Knee
Cubital - Elbow

Cervical Spine DTR
C5 Nerve Root - C4/5 Disc - Deep Tendon Reflex: Biceps
C6 Nerve Root - C5/6 Disc - Deep Tendon Reflex: Brachioradialis
C7 Nerve Root - C6/7 Disc - Deep Tendon Reflex: Triceps

Lumbar Spine DTR
L4 Nerve Root - L3/4 Disc - Deep Tendon Reflex: Patellar
S1 Nerve Root - L5/S1 Disc - Deep Tendon Reflex: Achilles

Orthopedic Tests have multiple components that can all earn the points required to pass the remaining board exams. A muscle has 1. Origin, 2. Insertion, 3. Action, 4. Innervation. Knowing any one of the 4 facts about a muscle can earn points. Orthopedic tests are similar in that they are composed of 1. Patient Position, 2. Procedure, 3. Positive Findings and 4. Indications. The procedure can vary slightly, it can be difficult to memorize and recall from written descriptions in parts 2 and 3. In some cases multiple procedures have been described below but keep in mind that patient position, positive finding and indications are just as important as the procedure and much easier to memorize and recall later.

Cervical Spine Orthopedic Tests:

Barre Lieou Test - Patient (PT) seated, rotates head to end point from side to side, vertigo is the positive finding indicating Vertebral Artery Syndrome.

Barre Lieou Syndrom (posterior cervical sympathetic syndrome) - migraines, ringing in the ears, dizziness, ear and neck pain.

DeKleyn's Test - PT is Supine, hang head off the end of the table (hyper-extension) and examiner (DR) rotates the head. Positive finding include Nystagmus, Dizziness, Nausea... indicating stenosis or compression of the vertebral basilar insufficiency (VBI) or carotid artery.

George's Test - PT is Seated, Examiner extends and rotes the patient's cervical spine to end point. Positive findings include nystagmus, dizziness, nausea...indicating VBI.

Hautant's Test - PT seated, PT hold arms out in front while extending and rotating the head. Positive findings include nausea, vertigo... indicating VBI.

Compression Test - PT seated, DR places downward pressure to the top of the head. Positive finding is radicular pain indicating nerve root compression.

Maximum Compression Test - PT seated, PT laterally flexes head and brings their chin toward shoulder. Positive finding is radicular pain indicating nerve root compression.

Jackson's Compression Test - PT seated, DR places downward pressure on the superior aspect of the PT head with neck in lateral flexion. Pain is the positive finding indicating nerve root compression.

Cervical Distraction - PT seated, PT rotates head to point of pain and returns to neutral position. DR applied upward pressure on the head and passively returns the head to the same point of pain. Persistence of pain indicates muscle or ligament involvement, relief of pain indicates nerve root compression.

Maigne's Test - PT seated, DR instructs PT to extend and rotate the head fully for 30 second. Positive findings are vertigo, nystagmus... inducing VBI or carotid artery stenosis.

O'Donoghue's Test - PT is seated. DR performs resisted and passive ROM of the involved muscle(s) in the region of the PT complaint. Positive finding is pain. Pain with resisted ROM indicates muscular involvement while pain with passive ROM indicates ligament involvement. This test can be performed on any region, muscle or joint to test severity of sprain/strain injuries.

Soto Hall - PT is supine, DR stabilizes the sternum while passively flex PT neck to their chest. Positive finding is pain indicating boney lesion, ligament damage, and/or disc involvement. Anterior pain suggests fracture while posterior pain indicates ligamentous injury.

Shoulder Depression Test - PT is supine, DR applies downward pressure to the shoulder while the head is lateral flexed toward the opposite shoulder. Positive findings is radicular pain indicating dural sleeve adhesion or spinal nerve root involvement.

Spurling's - PT is seated, PT maximally rotates and flexes the head to the affected side. DR strikes the top of the head with firm blow. Positive findings are pain in the neck or shoulder indicating nerve root irritation.

Underburgh's - PT is standing, PT outstretches arms, supinates hands while extending and rotating the head the PT walks in place. Positive findings include, vertigo, dizziness, nausea…indicating VBI.

Bakody's Test - PT is seated, PT places palm of hand on the involved side flat on top of their head. Positive findings is relief of pain indicating IVF encroachment.

Reverse Bakody's Test - PT is seated, PT places palm of hand on top of the head, positive finding is increased pain indicating Thoracic Outlet Syndrome (TOS).

Naffzinger Test - PT is seated, DR applies pressure to the jugular veins bilaterally for 30 to 45 seconds increasing the PT's intrathecal pressure. Flushing of the face indicates proper PT position, positive finding is pain in the lumbar region indicating nerve root compression or SOL. Contraindicated for PT with cardiovascular conditions.

Cervical Spine Orthopedic Review;
Compression Tests - nerve root compression
Distraction - nerve root compression or sprain/strain
Spurling's - nerve root compression
Shoulder depressor - dural sleeve adhesion
Soto-Hall - fracture, sprain/strain
Bakody's - neuropathy
Lhermiette's - MS, spinal cord lesion
Rust Sign - instability.

Thoracic Spine Orthopedic Tests:

Adam's Test - PT is standing, DR instructs PT to bend forward while palpating and observing the spine. Positive finding is rib humping, asymmetry of the spine indicating scoliosis. This is a screening test.

Beevor's Test - PT is supine, DR instructs PT to perform a partial sit-up (crunch) with hands behind the head. Positive finding is lateral movement of the umbilicus (belly button) indicating a nerve root lesion.

Eden's (Costoclavicular) Test - PT is standing, DR establishes radial pulse and instructs PT to drawn their shoulder's down and back assuming a "military" posture giving the test another name the Military Brace Test. Positive finding is a diminishment of the radial pulse indicating subclavian artery or brachial plexus compression (TOS).

Schelepmann's Sign - PT is seated, PT abducts shoulders t o180 degrees and laterally flexes spine from side to side. Positive finding is pain that increases with lateral flexion on the unaffected side indicates intercostal neuritis while pain on the affected side indicates intercostal neuralgia.

Adson's Test - PT is seated, DR established placatory pulse PT then elevates chin and rotates the head toward involved side. Positive findings include absence or diminishing radial pulse indicating the compression of the neurovascular bundle (NVB). Paresthesia or radiculopathy are positive findings indicating compression of a nerve, both potentially could indicate Thoracic Outlet Syndrome (TOS).

Modified Adson's Test - PT is seated, same test as above but the PT rotates the head away from the side of involvement. Positive finding is a change in the pulse indicating involvement of the middle scalene muscle.

Allen's Test - PT is seated, DR occlude the radial and ulnar arteries, raises the PT arm and instructs them to open and close a clinched fist for about a minute then DR lowers the PT arm, relieves pressure and observes coloration of the palm. Positive finding is a delay in the return of normal color for more than 10 second indicating arterial insufficiency.

Roos' Test - PT Is upright (sitting or standing), DR instructs PT to "pump" their first above their head for 3 minutes, giving this test another name; Elevated Arm Stress Test (EAST). Positive findings include pain, paraesthesia and the inability to complete the test indicating TOS.

Halstead - PT is seated, DR establishes pulse, tractions the arm and PT hyper-extends their neck. Positive finding diminishment of the pulse indicating cervical rib or scalenus anterior syndrome.

Wright's - PT is seated, DR evaluates the pulse then hyper-abducts the arm. Positive finding is a change (diminishment) of the pulse indicating compression of the axillary artery.

Bikele's Test (sign) - PT is upright, DR instructs PT to abduct arm to degrees and then bring the arm back maximally. Positive finding is pain indicating meningeal irritation, nerve root lesion or brachial plexus irritation.

Thoracic Outlet Syndrome Review;
Allen's - latency of ulnar and radial arteries
Eden's - costoclavicular syndrome
Adson's - scalenus anticus syndrome
Wright's - pec. minor syndrome

Sacroiliac (SI) Joint Orthopedic Tests

Allis's Test - PT is supine, DR observes the height of PT knees with knees in flexion. Positive finding is a discrepancy in leg heights indicating a possible dislocation or tibial inequality (structural short leg).

Anvil Test - PT is supine, DR elevates the affected leg and strikes the calcareous sharping from inferior to superior. Positive finding is pain the hip, heel or leg indicating possible fracture at the site of pain or joint pathology.

Fabere Patrick Test - PT is supine, Flexion, abduction, external rotation of the thigh (figure 4) DR applies anterior to posterior pressure on thigh. Positive findings is pain. If the pain occurs before the DR applies pressure to the thigh indicates inflammation of the SI or hip joint, pain with pressure indicates SI joint or hip lesion.

Lageurre's Test - PT is supine, SAME AS ABOVE (Fabere Patrick) but the DR raises the leg and applies inferior to superior pressure to the femur (knee) to compress the femoral capsule. Positive finding is pain in the hip joint indicating lesion of the hip joint.

Gaenslen's - PT is Supine, test leg is extended over the edge of the table while bringing the opposite knee to the PT chest. Positive finding is pain on the side of the extended leg indicating an SI joint lesion.

Lewin Gaenslen's Test - PT is on their side, PT flexes inferior leg while DR extends superior leg positive finding is pain with extension indicating a SI joint lesion.

Hibb's Test - PT is prone, DR flexes leg to butt with abduction, positive finding is pain, indicating lesion at the site of pain. PT flexes knee to 90 degrees, DR stands on the opposite side and applies lateral pressure to the leg internally rotating the femur and stabilizing the pelvis with the other hand. Positive finding is pain in the SI joint indicating SI lesion while pain in the hip indicates hip joint pathology.

Nachlas - PT is prone, DR brings heel to ipsilateral buttock. Positive finding is pain. If pain is located in the SI joint indicates SI lesion, pain in the lumbar region indicates lumbar lesion, pain in the anterior thigh indicates femoral nerve lesion.

Trendelenburg's Test - PT is standing, DR places thumbs on the PT's PSIS while PT flexes thigh one at a time. Positive finding is the dropping of the pelvis on the side of the raised leg indicating weakness of gluteus medium on the stationary side.

Yeoman's - PT is prone, DR flexes the leg and extends the thigh. Positive finding is pain in the SI joint indicating sprain/strain of SI joint ligament.

Iliac Compression Test (SI Compression Test) - PT is side lying with the involved side up, DR places downward pressure on the superior ilium. Positive finding is pain in the SI joint indicating SI joint lesion.

Pelvic Rocking Test - PT is supine with leg flexed at the hip and knee. DR places palms iliac crests and rotates the pelvic with compression. Positive finding is pain the SI joint (region) indicating SI point pathology.

Lumbar Spine Orthopedic Tests

Belt Test (Supported Adam's Test) - PT is standing, PT is asked to bend forward to the point of pain. Then DR supports PT sacrum with DR's hip and hold the PT ASIS and the PT is asked to bend forward again. Positive findings are pain with support indicating a lumbar problem and relief of pain with support indicating a pelvic problem.

Bechterew's - PT is seated, DR instructs PT to extend one leg, then the other and then both. Positive finding is pain indicating IVD involvement.

Bowstring - PT is supine, DR performs SLR to the point of pain, then slightly flexes the knee and DR applies firm pressure to the hamstring and/ popliteal fossa. Positive finding is pain indicating nerve root compression one the sciatic nerve.

Forestier Bowstring Test - PT is standing, DR instructs patient to laterally bend from side to side. Positive findings is unequal motion indicating possible paraspinal muscular contracture, Ankylosing Spondylitis or antalgic motion.

Braggard's - PT is supine, DR performs SLR to the point of pain and lowers the leg 5 degrees and sharply dorsiflexes the foot. Positive finding is pain, indicating sciatic neuropathy.

Sicard's - PT is supine, DR performs SLR to point of pain and lowers the leg 5 degrees then sharply dorsiflexes the big toe. Positive finding is pain indicating sciatic radiculopathy.

<u>Turyn's</u> - PT is supine, DR sharply dorsiflexes the big toe. Positive finding is pain in the gluteal region (may radiate) indicating sciatic nerve root irritation.

<u>Buckling Sign</u> - PT is supine, DR performs SLR. Positive finding the patient's leg buckets indicating sciatic radiculopathy.

<u>Beery's</u> - PT is standing, PT is asked to sit. Positive finding is when sitting from standing relieves pain indicating tight hamstrings.

<u>Ely's Test (Ely's Sign)</u> - PT is prone, DR brings heel to contralateral buttock. Positive finding is pain radiating to the anterior thigh indicating inflammation of lumbar nerve root.

<u>Yeoman's</u> - PT is prone, DR flexes the leg and extends the thigh. Positive finding is pain in the SI joint indicating sprain/strain of SI joint ligament.

Prone foot to same side butt is Yeoman while prone foot to opposite side butt is Ely's.

<u>Spinal Percussion</u> - PT is sitting or prone. DR taps on spinous processes (SP) in the area of complain and in-between SP. Positive finding is pain. If pain occurs with percussion of SP indicates possible fracture. If pain occurs with percussion between the SP indicates sprain/strain of interspinous ligament.

<u>Goldthwaith's</u> - PT is supine, perform SLR with hand on lumbar SP to feel for "fanning" positive findings is pain, before fanning indicates a SI lesion while pain before fanning indicates a lumbar lesion.

<u>Kemp's</u> - PT is seated/standing, DR induces posterior lateral extension of the lower back. Positive finding is pain. Pain on the side of lateral flexion indicates lateral disc bulge. Pain on the opposite side indicates medial disc bulge.

<u>Lasegue's</u> - PT is supine, DR flexes hip and extends leg. Positive finding is sciatic radiculopathy if pain arrives after leg extension.

Linder's - PT is supine, DR instructs and assists PT to bring their chin to the their chest with thoracolumbar flexion. Positive finding is radiating pain from the lower back indicating sciatic involvement.

Milgram's - PT is supine with legs straight. DR instructs PT to raise both legs off the table together. Positive finding is pain in the lumbar region indicating a possible pathological condition. A lack of pain in the lumbar region rules out a disc lesion.

Minor's Sign - PT is seated, DR instructs PT to stand. Positive finding is when the PT support themselves on the well side and flex the affected leg indicating sciatic radiculopathy.

Neri Bowing - PT is supine, PT flexes at the waist with flexed leg. DR extends let at the knee. Positive finding is pain indicating sciatica.

Straight Leg Raise (SLR) - PT is supine, DR raises a straight leg. Positive finding is pain before 35 degrees that indicates extradural sciatica. Pain from 35 to 70 degrees indicate possible disc lesion, pain beyond 70 degrees indicates lesion of a lumbar joint.

SLR - is the most reliable orthopedic test.

Well Leg Raise (WLR) - PT is supine, DR raises non-symptomatic leg. Positive findings is pain indicating disc lesion.

Fajertanjn's Test - PT is supine, DR performs WLR to point of pain and sharply dorsiflexes the foot. Positive finding is pain on the affected side indicating a medial or central disc protrusion.

Dejerine's Triad - PT position is not important. DR asks PT about pain with coughing, sneezing and/or straining (increases of intrathecal pressure). Positive finding is pain with this activities indicating a space occupying lesion (SOL).

Lumbar Spine Review;
Minor's - sciatica
Braggard's - primary sciatica
Sicard's - primary sciatica
Golodthwait's - lumbar or pelvic lesion
Berry's - tight hamstrings
Belt (supported Adams') - lumbar verse pelvic lesion

Lumbar Disc Review;
Fajersztajn's - contralateral Braggard's
Bowstring - nerve root compression
Bechterew's - disc lesion or primary sciatica
Kemp's - disc herniation
Linder's - nerve root compression
Well Leg Raise - disc protrusion

Upper Extremity Orthopedic Tests:

Painful Arc - Pain with shoulder abduction from 60-120 degrees and no pain throughout the rest of the ROM, indicates supraspinatus tendinitis.

PT cannot maintain the shoulder in 90 degrees of abduction indicates a torn rotator cuff.

Adhesive Capsulitis - characterized by a decrease in ROM with pain in all directions.

Bicipital Tendinitis - pain with resisted supination and pronation.

Anterior Apprehension - PT is seated, DR flexes, abducts and externally rotates PT affected arm. Positive finding is pain (apprehension) indicating chronic shoulder dislocation.

Posterior Apprehension - PT is supine, DR flexes, medially rotates the PT affected arm white applying posterior pressure to the elbow. Positive finding is localized pain indicating chronic shoulder dislocation.

Apley's Scratch - PT is seated, DR instructs PT to place hand behind the head and touch the scapula, then place the hand behind the back and attempt to touch the inferior aspect of the scapula, test is done bilaterally. Evaluate for symmetry. Positive finding is pain, either reproduction or the exacerbation of the complaint and/or asymmetry indicating shoulder dysfunction.

Calloway's Test (sign) - PT is seated, DR measures the girth of of the PT affected shoulder and compares to the unaffected side. Positive finding is increased girth at the acromial process indicating dislocation of the humerus.

Codman's Arm Drop Test - PT is seated, DR instructs PT to abduct arm beyond 90 degrees and lower slowly. Positive finding decent of the arm is unstable, and "drops" indicating a rotator cuff tear.

Dawbarn's Test - PT is seated, DR applies pressure just below the acromial process. If painful Dr abducts the arm past 90 degrees while maintaining pressure. Positive finding is a decrease in pain with abduction indicating subarcromial bursitis.

Dugas's Test - PT is seated, DR instructs PT to touch opposite shoulder and bring the elbow to their chest. Positive finding the PT is unable to touch the opposite shoulder indicating a dislocation of the humeral head from the glenoid cavity.

Yerguson's Test - PT is seated, DR instructs PT to externally rotate and supinate the forearm with DR resistance with palpation of the bicipital groove. Positive finding is pain in the bicipital groove indicating bicipital tendonitis or snapping of the bicipital tendon indicating transverse ligament injury.

Speed's Test - PT is seated, DR resists flexion of the PT supinated and extended forearm. Positive finding is pain in the bicipital groove indicating bicipital tendonitis, superior labral tear.

Push Button Test - PT is seated. DR standing behind the PT applies pressure to the subacromial bursa. Positive finding is pain indicating subacromial bursitis or rotator cuff tear (Subacromial Push-Button Test).

Abbot Saunder's Test - PT is seated, DR abducts, externally rotates and lowers the PT arm while supporting (palpating) the bicipital groove. Positive finding is palpable or audible click in the biceps groove indicating dislocation or biceps tendon injury.

Froment's Test (Paper Sign) - PT is seated. DR places a piece of paper in between the PT thumb and index finger and asks the PT to hold the paper. Positive finding is flexion of the thumb to compensate for paralysis of adductor pollicis. (Take the paper Fro-meets)

Tinel's Sign Wrist - PT is seated, DR taps palmer surface of the wrist with reflex hammer of PT supinated hand. Positive finding is tingling in the hand along the distribution of the median nerve indicating neural compression (carpal tunnel syndrome)

Tinel's Sign Foot (ankle) - PT is prone or supine, DR strikes the posterior tibial nerve behind the medial malleolus. Positive finding is paresthesia radiating to the foot indicating possible tarsal tunnel syndrome (nerve compression).

Phalen's Test - PT is seated, DR instructs the PT to abduct the shoulders, flex the wrists and approximate the hands then hold for 1 minute. Positive finding is tingling of the hand in the distribution of the median nerve indicating neural compression (carpal tunnel syndrome).

Reverse Phalen's - PT is seated, DR instructs PT to abduct shoulders and extend the wrists and approximate the hands and hold for 1 minute. Positive finding is tingling of the hand in the distribution of the media nerve indicating neural compression (carpal tunnel syndrome).

Tourniquet - PT is seated, DR applies blood pressure cuff around the wrist and elevates pressure just above systolic pressure. Positive finding is tingling of the hand in the median nerve distribution indicating neural compression (carpal tunnel syndrome).

Ulnar Tunnel Triad - PT is seated, DR inspects and palpates the ulnar triangle. Positive finding is pain/tenderness and clawing of the ring finger, hypothenar atrophy indicating ulnar nerve ulnar nerve entrapment, compression.

Finkelstein's Test - PT is seated, DR instructs PT to place the thumb across the palmer surface of the hand then make a fist and ulnar deviate the wrist sharply. Positive finding is pain in the wrist indicating deQuiverain's Disease, stenosing tenosynovitis of abductor politic longs and/or extensor policies brevis.

Cozen's Test - PT is seated, DR stabilizes the forearm and instructs PT to make and fist and extend the arm. Positive finding is pain in the elbow indicating lateral epicondylitis (tennis elbow).

Mill's Test - PT is seated, PT pronates and flexes wrist then DR resists supination. Positive finding indicates lateral epicondylitis (tennis elbow).

Golfer's Elbow - PT is seated, DR instructs PT to flex elbow and supinate hand then DR resists extension of the elbow. Positive finding is pain over the medial epicondyle indicating medial epicondylitis (golfer's elbow).

Valgus/Varus Stress Test - PT is seated, DR applies stress to the medial and the lateral collateral ligaments of the elbow. Positive finding is pain, indicating laxity of the painful ligament.

Buerger's Test - PT is supine or sitting, DR elevates PT leg and consecutively dorsiflexes and plantar flexes the foot for more than 2 minutes, lowers the leg and asks the PT to sit up. Positive finding is if it takes more than minute for normal color of the foot to return indicating arterial insufficiency.

Allen's test - PT is seated, DR occlude the radial and ulnar arteries, raises the PT arm and instructs them to open and close a clinched fist for about a minute then DR lowers the PT arm, relieves pressure and observes coloration of the palm. Positive finding is a delay in the return of normal color for more than 10 second indicating arterial insufficiency.

Upper Extremity Review;
Apley's - range of motion
Codman's - rotator cuff
Dugas - chronic dislocation
Apprehension - chronic dislocation
Dawbarn's - sub-acromial bursitis
Yergason's - bicipital tendinitis, transverse humeral ligament
Speed's - bicipital tendinitis
Cozen's - lateral epicondylitis
Mill's - lateral epicondylitis
Tinel's - carpal tunnel
Phalen's carpal tunnel
Finklestein's - DeQuervain's stenosing tenosynovitis

Lower Extremity Orthopedic Tests

Thomas' Test - PT is supine. DR instructs PT to pull each knee to the chest one at a time. Positive finding is involuntary flection of the opposite knee indicating possible hip flexor contracture.

Ober's Test - PT is side lying, DR abducts PT leg and releases it. Positive finding is failure of the leg to defend smoothly indicating possible iliotibial band contracture.

Dreyer's Test - PT is supine, DR instructs PT to raise their leg. IF unstable, DR stabilizes the patellar tendon just above the knee and PT tries again. Positive finding is the PT ability to raise the leg with tendon stabilization indicating patella fracture.

Patellar Apprehension - PT is supine, DR laterals displaces patella. Positive finding is look of apprehension indicating chronic lateral patellar displacement.

Patellar Ballottment - PT is supine, DR applies inferior traction to the patella while tapping the patella toward the femur. Positive finding is a sensation of the patella floating indicating retropatellar swelling.

Patellar Grinding - PT is supine, DR applies pressure to the patella and moves is medial and lateral. Positive finding is pain indicating chondromalcia patella or retropatellar arthritis.

Abduction Stress Test (Valgus Stress Test) - PT is supine, DR stabilizes the medial thigh while applying lateral pressure (pulling) to the leg. Performed at full extension and 20-30 degrees of flexion. Positive findings are pain; with extension indicates possible medial collateral ligament, cruciate ligaments or posterior lateral capsule injury. Pain with flexion indicates possible medial collateral ligament, Iliotibial band or posterior lateral capsule injury.

Adduction Stress Test (Varus Stress Test) - PT is supine, DR stabilizes medial thigh while applying medial pressure to the leg Performed with the leg in full extension and with 20-30 degrees of flexion. Positive findings are pain; with extension indicates possible cruciate ligament, lateral collateral ligament or posterior medial capsule injury. Pain with flexion indicates possible lateral collateral, PCL or posterior mensicofemoral ligament injury.

Apley's Compression - PT is prone, DR flexes PT leg to 90 degrees, DR stabilizes the PT's thigh with their knee and places downward force to the PT heel with internal and external rotation of the leg. Positive finding is pain indicating meniscus tear on the side of pain.

Apley's Distraction - PT is prone, PT flexes leg to 90 degrees, DR stabilizes the thigh and applies traction to the foot while internally and externally rotating the leg. Positive finding is pain in the knee indicating collateral ligament instability on the side of pain.

Bounce Home Test - PT is supine, DR instructs PT to flex the leg. DR supports the foot and allows the leg to fall back into extension. Positive finding is an inability to fully extend the knee indicating a mescal injury.

Drawer Sign - PT is supine, DR flexes PT leg and placed foot on the table and grasps the tibia applying pushing and pulling pressure. Positive findings are anterior slide of the tibia indicating ACL injury and posterior slide indicating PCL injury.

Drawer Sign of the Foot - PT is supine. DR grasps and supports the foot and applies pushing and pulling pressure. Positive findings is gapping of the ankle. Gapping with pushing indicates possible anterior talofibular ligament tear or injury. Gapping with pulling indicates possible posterior talofibular ligament tear (injury).

Lachman's Test - PT is supine, DR pulls the tibia anterior with the knee flexed to 30 degrees. Positive finding is pain (soft end feel) indicating ACL tear.

Slocum's Test - PT is prone, DR performs Drawer Test with external rotation positive findings include pain and anterior or posterior translation indicating ligamentous injury.

McMurray's Test - PT is supine, DR flexes PT leg then internal and externally rotes the leg while extending it. Positive finding is palpable or audible click in the knee indicating a meniscus tear.

Lateral Stability Test - PT is supine, DR grasps and supports the foot and performs passive inversion of the foot. Positive findings is gapping indicating the possible tear of the anterior talofibular ligament and/or calcaneofibular ligament.

Medial Stability Test - PT is supine, DR grasps and supports the foot and performs passive eversion of the foot. Positive finding is gapping indicating possible deltoid ligament tear.

Thompson's (Simmond's) Test - PT is prone, DR sharply squeezes the calf, Positive finding is failure of the foot to plantar-flex indicating achilles tendon tear.

Slouch Test (Slump Test) - PT is sitting, DR instructs PT to place hands together behind their back and flex their spine (slump or slouch) and then flex their neck. DR places a hand on top of the PT head and instructs PT to extend the knee and dorsiflex the foot and return to normal (neutral) position. Positive finding is an increase in pain (symptoms) in the slumped position that decreases with neck flexion indicating lumbar disc pathology.

Unhappy Triad - damage to the medial collateral ligament, medial meniscus and anterior cruciate ligaments.

Neurologic levels in the lower extremity:
Motor:
L3 – quadriceps.
L4 – tibialis anterior.
L5 – toe extensors.
S1 – peroneal.

Sensation/Dermatomes:
T12 – Lower abdomen proximal to inguinal ligament.
L1 – upper thigh distal to inguinal ligament.
L2 – mid thigh.
L3 – low thigh.
L4 – medial leg and foot.
L5 – lateral leg and dorsum foot.
S1 – lateral foot.
S2 – longitudinal strip posterior thigh.

Deep Tendon Reflex (DTR):
L4 – patella.
L5 – tibialis posterior (difficult to elicit).
S1 – Achilles.

Lower Extremity Review:
Patrick's - hip joint pathology
Trendeleburg's - contralateral hip abductors
Ober's - tensor fascia lata contracture (one leg ober the other)
Thomas' - hip flexor contracture
Lageurre's - anterior hip joint
Ortolani's - congenital hip dislocation
Drawer Sign - cruciate ligament stress test
Apley's Compression - meniscus or collateral ligaments
McMurray's - medial meniscus
Homan's deep vein thrombophlebitis
Allis' - anatomical short leg.
Thompson's (Simmond's) - ruptured achilles tendon

Organic Disease Orthopedic Tests

<u>Schober's Test</u> - PT is standing, DR marks the PT at the L5 SP, 5 cm below and 10 cm above. DR instructs PT to bend forward and touch their toes. Positive finding is failure of the space between the superior and inferior marks to increase by 5 cm or more indicating Ankylosing Spondylitis (AS).

<u>Brudzinski's Test</u> - PT is supine, DR slowly elevates the head and passively brings PT's chin to their chest. Positive finding is buckling of the PT knees indicating meningeal irritation.

<u>Kernig's Test</u> - PT is supine, DR flexes thigh to 90 degree and attempts to extend the leg. Positive finding is if the PT resists extending the leg or (kicks out leg) indicating meningeal irritation. "Kernig's kicking"

<u>Swallowing Test</u> - PT is sitting, DR asks PT to swallow. Positive finding is pain with swallowing indicating Ankylosing Spondylitis (AS).

<u>Lewin Supine</u> - PT is supine, DR holds the PT thighs down and asks PT to sit up. Positive finding is the inability to sit up indicating AS.

<u>Lewin Standing</u> - PT is standing, DR pulls posterior on the knee while supporting the PT. Positive finding is buckling of the knee indicating tight hamstrings.

<u>Gower's Sign</u> - PT is supine, DR instructs PT to rise. Positive finding is when the PT is arising from the supine position they first turn to the prone position and then "climbs up themselves" to rise indicating muscular dystrophy.

<u>Lhermitte's</u> - PT is supine, DR instructs PT to bring their chin to the their chest. Positive finding is an electric shock sensation down the spine and arms indicating Multiple Sclerosis (MS) or other demyelinating lesion.

<u>Homan's Sign</u> - PT is supine, DR elevates the leg and dorsiflex the foot and squeeze the calf. Positive finding is deep pain in the posterior leg (calf) indicating venous thrombophlebitis.

Libman's Test - PT is seated, DR applies pressure bilaterally to the mastoid processes. Positive finding is pain indicating a patient with low pain threshold or malingering. Pressing directly on hard bone is typically not painful.

Rust Sign - PT is recumbent (supine), DR asks PT to rise. Positive finding i when the PT grasps the head/neck with both hands before rising indicting neck fracture or instability.

Shepelmann's - PT is seated, DR instructs PT is laterally bend from side to side. Positive finding is chest pain. Pain on the side of concavity indicates neuritis (intercostal neuralgia), pain on the side of convexity indicates myofascitis or Dry Pleurisy.

Sternal Compression Test - PT is supine. DR applies downward pressure on the sternum. Positive finding is pain on the lateral border of the rib cage indicating potential fracture.

Thomas' Sign - PT is standing, DR pinches the trapezius muscle. Positive finding loose flesh, flaccid muscle, indicating spinal cord lesion.

Beevor's Sign - PT is supine, DR instructs PT to perform a crunch (partial sit-up). Positive finding is lateral deviation of the umbilicus (belly button) indicating a nerve root lesion.

Chest Expansion Test - PT is seated or standing, DR measures chest circumference at the nipple line and instructs the PT to inhale fulling. Positive finding chest expansion is less than 2 inches in males or less than 1.5 inches in females indicating ankylosing spondylosis (AS).

Valsalva Test - PT is instructed to take a deep breath and bear down, exerting an inward pressure as if having a bowel movement, increasing the intrathecal pressure. Positive finding is radicular pain indicating a space occupying lesion.

Malingering Orthopedic Tests

Burn's Bench Test - PT is kneeling, DR supports the back of the legs and instructs the PT to flex forward. Positive finding the PT will claim they cannot perform the test indicating that they are malingering.

Hoover's Sign - PT is supine, DR place a hand under the well leg (unaffected) and instructs the PT to raise the affected leg. Positive finding is if the DR does not feel any pressure on their hand under the well leg indicating the PT is malingering (not trying, being dishonest).

Lasegue Sitting Test - PT is seated, DR instructs PT to extend one leg at a time. Positive finding is the PT is able to perform the test without tripod sign indicating malingering if sciatica is the the PT chief complaint.

Tripod sign - PT is seated and supports themselves with an arm behind them to assist with motions such as rising or extending the leg as described above and Bechterew's Test.

Magnusson's Test - PT is seated, DR ask PT to point to the pain then distracts the patient and asks them to point to the pain again later. Positive finding is the patient does not point at the same place twice indicating that they are malingering.

Mannkopf's Test - PT is in any position, DR establishes radial pulse and monitors throughout test of changes. DR then applies pressure to the site of PT complaint (area of pain) positive finding is no change in pulse indicating malingering. If the PT is not malingering DR would expect radial pulse to increase by 10 beats per minute.

McBride's Test - PT is standing, DR instructs PT to bring their foot toward their mouth. Positive finding PT refuses to attempt the test indicating that they are malingering.

Rotator Cuff Muscles (4): **SITS**
Supraspinatus - Abduction, inn. Suprascapular n., Greater Tubercle.
Infraspinatus - External Rotation, inn. Suprascapular n., Greater Tubercle.
Teres Minor - External Rotation, inn. Axillary n., Greater Tubercle.
Subscapularis - Internal Rotation, inn. Subscapular n., Lesser Tubercle.

Scapular Motions (3)
Elevation (shrug) - Trapeziua and Levator Scapula mm.
Retraction (approximate) - Rhomboid Major and Minor mm.
Protraction (separate) - Serratus Anterior.

Shoulder Abduction;
0-20 degrees at Glenohumeral (GH) joint only
20-120 degrees at the GH and Scapulothoracic Junction (2:1 ratio)
120-150 degrees at AC, GH and Scapulothoracic Junction.
150-180 degrees at SC, AC, GH and Scapulothoracic Junction.

Frozen Shoulder - when the ratio of GH to scapulothoracic junction motion drops to 1:1.

Femoral Angle - The angle formed by the intersection of the femoral neck and the medial aspect of the femoral shaft on AP Pelvis x-ray also known as the angle of inclination. Normal angle is 120 to 130 degrees. A decreased angle below 120 degrees is called Gene Vara or knock kneed (Mickulicz's angle) while an increased angle of more than 130 degrees is called Genu Valga or bow legged.

Q angle - the angle formed by a line representing the force of the quadriceps from the ASIS to the center of the patella and another line from the center of the patella to the tibial tubercle. Normal for men is 13 to 15 degrees while the normal rang for women is 15 to 17 degrees.

Pes Planus - Commonly called flat feet, the talar head displaces medially and inferior (plantward). This condition is commonly associated with stress fractures.

Pes Cavus - Commonly called high arches, there is fixed plantar flexion of the foot. Considered the opposite of flat feet.

Ankle Sprains (3 Grades)

Grade 1 - mild to minimal, no ligament tear with tenderness and swelling treated with R.I.C.E.

Grade 2 - moderate, incomplete or partial tear (rupture) of ligament(s) with obvious welling, bruising (ecchymosis) and difficulty walking. Usually treated with a walking cast.

Grade 3 - severe, complete future of ligament(s) with swelling, bruising, ankle instability and inability to walk. Commonly requires surgery to repair ligament rupture.

Stability Test of the Ankle;
Medial (Valgus) stress, positive with gapping/pain indicates detoid ligament involvement from eversion sprain.
Lateral (Varus) stress, positive with gapping/pain indicates Anterior Talobfibual ligament involvement from inversion sprain.

Facet Joint Pathology - scleratogenous pain exacerbated by extension. Positive Kemp's test, confirmed with x-rays (facet joints best visualized on lateral and oblique lumbar films).

Disc Pathology - antalgic pain, positive SLR, Bechterew's and Linder's confirmed with MRI.

Sub-Rhizal Disc (intermediate disc) - presents with unilateral sciatica, forward antalgia and positive Kemp's test bilaterally.

Central Disc - presents with bilateral sciatica, forward antalgia and positive Kemp's test bilaterally.

IVF Pathology (Encroachment) - pain and/or paraesthesia exacerbated by motion, positive compression and distraction tests, positive Bakody and/or reverse Bakody test, confirm with oblique X-ray, CT scan.

Spinal Tumor - deep boring pain that is unrelenting worse at night, positive SOL orthopedic tests confirmed with MRI.

Disturbances in sensation: Neurological findings.

Agraphesthesia - inability to recognize traced or written letters/numbers/outlines on the skin.

Aphonia - inability to produce sound.

Astereognosis - inability to recognize familiar objects by sense of touch.

Barognosis - inability to distinguish between two different weights.

Hyperpathia - painful stimuli produces exaggerated pain in the PT.

Allodynia - non-painful stimuli produces pain in the PT.

Anesthesia - no response to stimuli.

Hypoesthesia - decreased response to stimuli.

Pallesthesia - vibratory sensation felt on the skin or bone.

Akinesthesia - loss of sense of motion: extent, direction and weight.

Dysesthesia - Abnormal sensations on the skin. Numbness, tingling, burning or cutting pain. Tested with pin wheel. Impaired or abnormal interpretation of normal stimuli.

Dysarthria - altered speech due to loss of motor control.

Dyskinesia - any impairment of voluntary movement.

Paresthesia - abnormal sensations on the skin. Numbness, prickling, tingling, increased sensitivity.

Agnosia - loss of comprehension of auditory, visual or other sensations with sensory spheres intact.

Aphasia - loss of ability to communicate through speech, writing, or signs.

Phasia - the conceptual skill of speech.

Anosmia - loss of sense of smell.

Stereognosis - the ability to identify an object by touch only.

Akinesia - loss of muscle movement.

Apraxia - decreased voluntary motor function, cerebrum.

Causalgia - First sign burning pain long a peripheral nerve distribution.

Neuralgia - Pain along the course of a nerve.

Neuritis - Inflammation of nerve with pain, paresthesia or anesthesia, paralysis, diminished reflexes.

Radiculitis - Inflammation of a spinal nerve root. Dermatomal and sharp pain.

Nerve Injuries;

Type I - Neurapraxia, a local nerve block with no physical disruption of the axon. May present with transient paralysis, minor sensory changes and no degeneration. Recovery in hours to days.

Type II - Axonotmesis, a physical disruption of the axon (Wallerian degeneration) that results in temporary paralysis and sensory changes. If the Schwann cell sheath is intact recover is possible in weeks to months.

Type III - Neurotmesis, is a partial or complete tear (severance) of the nerve with full degeneration and no recovery is possible.

Reflex - involuntary motor responses to stimuli.

Wexler Reflex scale:
0 = no reflex
1 = hyporeflexic
2 = normal
4 = hyperreflexic with transient clonus
5 = hyperreflexic with sustained clonus.

A decreased reflex indicates a **L**ower **M**otor **N**euron **L**esion (**LMNL**) and an increased response indicates an **U**pper **M**otor **N**euron **L**esion (**UMNL**).

Deep Tendon Reflexes; (DTR) illicit by striking the tendon with a reflex hammer. All relaxes should be tested bilaterally and compared.

Biceps - tests C5, the musculocutaneous nerve.

Brachioradialis - test C6, the radial nerve.

Triceps - tests C7, the radial nerve.

Pectoralis - place thumb on the tendon in the axilla and strike with hammer, test C5-T1, the anterior thoracic nerve.

Patellar - (Quadricepts Knee Jerk Reflex) test L2 - L4, the femoral nerve.

Achilles - (ankle jerk) test S1, tibial nerve.

In theory any muscle tendon that can be palpated can illicit a reflex testing the nerve that innervates that muscle. These are the most common DTR used during the neurological examination.

Jendrassik maneuver - techniques used to distract the patient that help illicit the reflexive response.

Carpopedal - Spasmodic contraction of the hands or feet, especially the wrist and/or ankle indicates tetany.

Trousseau's Sign - Compression of the brachial artery causes carpopedal (wrist spasm) indicates tetany.

Chvostecks Sign - Tapping over facial nerve (TMJ) causes ipsilateral spasmodic facial contraction indicating tetany.

Erb's Sign - increased electrical excitability of the peripheral nerves to the galvanic current indicated tetany.

Erb's Paralysis - Injury to the upper brachial plexus (C5/C6) resulting in paralysis of the upper arm. Associated with "waiter's tip hand."

Jaw jerk sign (aka the masseter reflex) place thumb on an open jaw and strike it with a reflex hammer. The reflex is normally absent or slight, strong reflex indicates CN V lesion.

Westphal's sign (aka Erb-Westphal sign) is a decrease or loss of Deep Tendon Reflex (DTR) especially the patellar reflex (knee jerk) indicates a lower motor neuron lesion (LMNL).

Pathological Reflexes;

Babinski - Firm stroke from the lateral aspect of the plantar surface across the foot to the big toe. Positive if patient has Babinski response.

Babinski Pronation - Tap the dorsum of a supinated hand. Positive if patient involuntary pronates hand.

Babinski response - dorsiflexion of big toe with fanning of the other four toes.

Chaddock - Stroke the lateral malleolus to the small toe. Positive with Babinski response. "C" shape stroke around lateral malleolus to small toe.

Chaddock's Wrist - Stroke distal ulnar aspect of the forearm near the wrist. Positive with involuntary flexion of the wrist with extension and fanning of the fingers.

Oppenhein - Stroke dow the tibial crest to ankle. Positive with Babinski response.

Gordon's - Squeeze the gastric muscle (calf). Positive with Babinski response.

Gordon's Finger - Stroke the pisiform. Positive with flection of the wrist and fingers.

Schafer's - Firmly squeeze the achilles. Positive with Babinski response.

Rossolimo - tap the ball of the foot. Positive with plantar flexion of the big toe and curling of the other toes.

Gonda - depress the 4th toe and release with snap, flick. Positive with involuntary dorsiflexion of the big toe.

Hoffman - extend the patient's middle finger and flick the tip down. Positive with flexion and adduction of the thumb and flexion of the other fingers.

Tromner - sharply tap the middle 3 fingers. Positive with flexion of all the fingers including the thumb.

Glabella - sharply tap the patient between the eye brows with index finger. Positive finding is tonic spasm of the orbiculares muscle.

Snout - sharply tap the nose or center of the upper lip. Positive with involuntary and exaggerated contraction of the lips.

Superficial reflexes - Lost with both UMN and LMN lesions.

Ciliospinal reflex - Pupil dilation following painful stimulation to skin of the neck. Autonomic modulation.

Corneal reflex - CN V afferent, CN VII efferent.

Oculocardiac Reflex - decrease in pulse with pressure applied to the eyeball or traction of the extra-ocular muscles. Visceral/Organic reflex of the afferent CN V and the efferent CN X.

Ciliospinal Reflex - dilation of the eyes with pinching of the neck. Visceral/Organic reflex of the cervical sympathetics.

Carotid Reflex - (carotid sinus reflex) manual stimulation of the carotid sinus decreases pulse. Never perform bilaterally, can result in dangerous drop in blood pressure or cardia arrest. Visceral/Organic reflex.

Corneal Reflex - (blink reflex) involuntary blinking with stimulation of the cornea, such as touching with a piece of cotton. CN V is the afferent while CN VII is the efferent parts of this superficial reflex.

Abdominal Reflex - superficial reflex performed by stroking the 4 quadrants with the reflex hammer. The umbilicus should deviate toward the stimulation. Tests T7-T12 corresponding spinal levels.

Cremasteric Reflex - stroke up the inner thigh of a male and the ipsilateral testes will rise. Afferent femoral nerve, efferent genitofemoral nerve. Somatosomatic superficial reflex.

Giegel's Refelx - stoke up the inner thigh of a female and the poupart's (inguinal) ligament contracts. Tests afferent femoral nerve and efferent genitofemoral nerve. Somatosomatic superficial reflex.

Plantar reflex - normal Babinski reflex, superficial reflex, stroke up the bottom of the foot expect curling of the toes and pulling the foot away. Test the tibial nerve.

Gag Reflex - (pharyngeal reflex) a laryngeal spasm caused my mechanical stimulation of the posterior mouth around the tonsils or back of the throat. Afferent CN IX, Efferent CN X. Superficial reflex.

Uvular Refelx - Say AHHH! the uvula should raise equally if it deviates to one side indicates a motor lesson on opposite side of deviation. This is part of the gag reflex.

Carpal Tunnel - compression of the medial nerve (C5, C6, C7, C8, T1) presents with numbness and pain in the distal forearm or wrist radiating into the palmar aspect of the first three digits of the hand that is worse at night. Tests; Tinel's and Phalen's

Elbow Tunnel compression of the ulnar nerve (C8, T1) presents with numbness and pain in the medial aspect of the wrist and the little finger. Test; Tinel's (tapping the medial epicondyle).

Wartenberg's syndrome - compression of the superficial radial nerve (C6) presents with pain along the lateral aspect of the distal third of the forearm.

Anterior Interosseous Nerve syndrome - the compression of a branch of median nerve presents with weakness of the pinch grip between the thumb and index finger.

Guyon's Canal syndrome [ulnar nerve-C8,T1]: Pain or paresthesia along the little finger and medial half of ring finger. Test; Froment's

Meralgia paresthica - compression of the lateral femoral cutaneous nerve (L2, L3) presents with pain and paresthesia along the antero-lateral aspect of the thigh.

Piriformis syndrome - compression of the sciatic nerve (L4,5 S1,2,3) presents with pain in the buttock radiating into the back of the thigh and leg. Test; Freiberg's

Anterior compartment syndrome - compression of the common fibular nerve (L4,5, S1) presents with pain and paresthesia along the anterolateral leg and dorsum of the foot.

Tarsal Tunnel Syndrome - compression of the posterior tibial nerve (L4, L5, S1, S2) presents with pain in the plantar aspect of the foot.

Lower Motor Neuron (LMN) - Nerve to myoneural junction (muscle), ventral horn cell, anterior horn cell.

Upper Motor Neuron (UMN) - Brain and spinal cord, not including the ventral horn.

UMN lesion (UMNL)	LMN lesion (LMNL)
Increased DTR's	Decreased DTR's
Spastic paralysis	Flaccid paralysis
Increased muscle tone	Decreased muscle tone
Pathological reflexes	No pathological reflexes
Clonus	No Clonus
Hypertonic	Hypotonic
No Atrophy	Atrophy
No Fasciculations	Fasciculations
Absent Superficial Reflexes	Absent Superficial Reflexes

UMLN Conditions - Multiple Sclerosis (MS), Cerebral Palsy (CP), Stroke (CVA), Brain Tumor, Amyotrophic Lateral Sclerosis (ALS) and more.

LMNL Conditions - Subluxation, Disc Herniation, Polio, Bell's Palsy, ALS, and more.

Cerebellar Sign and Symptoms;
Ataxia - staggering, uncoordinated reeling or drunken gait.

Adiadochokinesia - inability to perform rapidly alternating movements.

Dysmetria - overshooting the intended mark, or past pointing.

Dyssynergia - general lack or loss of motor coordination, an aspect of ataxia.

Rebound Phenomenon of Stuart-Holmes - the inability to check a movement when resistance is removed.

Amyotrophic lateral sclerosis (ALS)- AKA Lou Gehrig Disease motor neuron disease causing LMN signs in upper extremities, and UMN signs in lower extremities.

Myasthenia gravis - sporadic muscular weakness that improves with rest that is caused by antibodies to Acetylcholine receptors at the neuromuscular junction.

Tabes dorsalis - ataxia due to loss of proprioceptive paths.

Wallenberg's Syndrome - thrombosis (occlusion) of posterior inferior cerebellar artery causing vertigo, ataxia, nausea, Horner's syndrome, contralateral hemiparesis, loss of the pain and temperature ipsilaterally of the face/head and contra-laterally in the trunk and extremities with loss of hearing and tinnitus.

Barre Lieou - vertigo, tinnitus, nausea associated with vertebral artery disturbance.

Guillain Barre Syndrome - acute polyneuropathy with muscular weakness and some sensory loss, usually preceded by a nonspecific febrile (usually viral) illness one to three weeks prior. Paralysis begins distally affecting the lower leg(s) and may progress toward the trunk threatening respiration (ascending paralysis).

Syringomyelia - chronic disease with fluid filled cavities in the spinal cord that result in loss of pain & temp (painless burns) with a shawl like distribution. Touch and pressure sensation are OK.

Carpal tunnel syndrome - Median nerve compression, can be caused by lunate subluxation.

Meralgia paresthetica - compression of the lateral femoral cutaneous nerve (L2-L3 nerve roots) producing anterior lateral thigh pain.

Horner's syndrome - Interruption of the C/S sympathetic chain. Ptosis, myosis, anhydrosis.

Tic Douloureax - aka Trigeminal neuralgia 5th cranial nerve involvement, bouts of severe lancing pain along distribution of the trigeminal nerve.

Complex Regional Pain Syndrome - Chronic pain in the arm or leg that develops after a traumatic injury, surgery, stroke or heart attack. The cause is unknown. Pain that is longer lasting and greater than expected is characteristic of this condition. AKA Reflex Sympathetic Dystrophy (RDS).

Reflex Sympathetic Dystrophy Syndrome (RSDS) - Persistent arteriole vasospasm due to irritation of the local sympathetic fibers. Irritation is typically a minor trauma. RSDS is characterized as excessive pain, causalgia (burning pain), swelling, edema, cyanotic moist glossy skin, spotty osteoporosis, decreased ROM and possible joint fibrosis. (Sudeck's Atrophy)

Sudeck's Atrophy - a boney version of RSDS (spotty osteoporosis), patient typically over 50 YOA, most common sites are the shoulder and hand with pain, swelling, stiffness and distal atrophy.

Shoulder-Hand Syndrome - a form of RSDS causing excessive pain, stiffness, decreased ROM, edema, cyanosis or the shoulder and hand but not the elbow. Thickening of the palmer fascia and atrophy may occur. Most common after trauma of the cervical or shoulder region or after a myocardial infarction.

Bell's palsy - 7th cranial nerve involvement, unilateral facial nerve paralysis with sudden onset.

Erb's palsy -UMN lesion, paralysis of the muscles of the shoulder and upper arm, C5and C6 roots.

Klumpke's palsy - LMN lesion, atrophic paralysis of the forearm, C8 and T1 roots. Injury to the lower brachial plexus (C8/T1) causes paralysis of the intrinsic muscles of the hand and the flexors of the wrist. Associated with "Claw Hand" appearance.

Myerson's sign - tonic spasm of the eyelid with tapping on the forehead.

Homan's sign- diffuse calf pain or behind knee upon forced dorsiflexion of the foot, indicates thrombophlebitis. (DVT Deep Vein Thrombosis)

<u>Minor's sign</u> - patient arises from seated position with affected leg bent, balancing on healthy side, hand on chair.

<u>Gower's Sign (maneuver)</u> - Pt "climbs up on themselves", weak extensor muscles similar to miner's sign.   Seen with Muscular Dystrophy.

<u>Stretch reflex</u> - Involves 1 interneuron that synapses with input sensory nerve to output LMN.

<u>Dorsal Root Ganglion</u> (DRG) - Origination of most of the primary neurons of the sensory nerves.

<u>Crainal Nerve tests</u>; sensory (S), motor (M), both (B)

I. <u>Olfactory</u> - (**S**) ask patient to identify a failure odor, coffee.

II. <u>Optic</u> - (**S**) Snellen Eye Chart, Accommodation

III. <u>Ocumlomotor</u> - (**M**) Levalro Palpebrae

IV. <u>Trochlear</u> - (**M**) Superior Oblique

V. <u>Trigeminal</u> - (**B**) Corneal Reflex, Cotton Wisp Test, Occulocardiac Reflex

VI. <u>Abducens</u> - (**M**) lateral rectus

VII. <u>Facial</u> - (**B**) Taste anterior 2/3 of Tongue, Muscle of facial expression

VIII. <u>Vestibulochochlear</u> - (**S**) Mittlemeyer Test, Webers, Rhinne's, Whisper

IX. <u>Glossopharyngeal</u> - (**B**) Taste Posterior 1/3 tongue. Carotid Reflex, Gag reflex, Uvular Reflex.

X. <u>Vagus</u> - (**B**) Swallowing test,

XI. <u>Spinal Accessory</u> - (**M**) Muscle test SCM and Traps.

XII. <u>Hypoglossal</u> - (**M**) stick out tongue.

OOOTTAFVGVSH
Oh, **O**h, **O**h, **T**o **T**ouch **A**nd **F**eel **V**ery **G**ood **V**ag, **S**o **H**appy

SSMMBMBSBBMM
Some **S**ay **M**arry **M**oney **B**ut **M**y **B**rother **S**ays **B**ig **B**oobs **M**atter **M**ost.

<u>SO4-LR6/3</u> - **S**uperior **O**blique CN**4**, **L**ateral **R**ectus CN**6**, all other Eye Muscles are CN **3**. (SO4-LR6 over 3)

<u>Myelopathy</u> - Spinal cord compression, which can come from tumor, herniated disc or any space occupying lesion that presents with bi-lateral symptoms which include sharp shooting pain and uncoordinated use of the hands or walking.

<u>Multiple Myeloma</u> - Malignant disease of proliferating neoplastic plasma cells that replace or crowd out bone marrow limiting healthy cells which can result in osteoporosis, hypercalcemia, anemia, renal disease, & infection. PT is typically over 50 YOA with persistent back pain that is unrelieved by rest that is worse at night with fatigue and recurrent infections. Lab findings include Bence-Jones protein in the urine (proteinuria) and increased IgG in the blood.

<u>4 Types of Torticollis</u>; literally translates to "twisted neck" is a condition in which the neck muscles contract causing the head to twist to one side. AKA Wry Neck, and Loxia

<u>Congenital Torticollis</u> - present at birth this form of torticollis maybe due to a fibrous tumor, hematoma or other pathology results in the unilateral contraction of the SCM muscle pulling the head to one side. It is possible the SCM on one side is simply too short.

<u>Acquired (Acute) Torticollis</u> - presents with sudden onset, transient spasm of the SCM maybe due to disease process of the cervical spine, upper respiratory infection (pharyngitis), rheumatism, cerebellar tumor or more. This self limiting condition the occurs spontaneously.

<u>Spasmodic Torticollis</u> - painful, persistent intermittent unilateral contraction of the SCM. AKA; Intermittent torticollis, cervical dystonia, idiopathic cervical dystonia.

Trochlear Torticollis - in not related to the SCM but damage to the trochlear nerve (CN4) that innervates the superior oblique muscle of the eye that is responsible for depression, abduction and intorsion of the eye. Damage to CN4 results in the eye becoming extorted leading to vision problems that are resolved with turning the head away from the affected side balancing the eyes. This condition can be diagnosed with Bielschowsky head tilt test where the head is turned toward the affected side. Positive finding is the affected eye elevates, appearing to float upward indicating involvement of the trochlear nerve (CN4).

Torticollis can also be described using the position of the head and neck.

Laterocollis - the head is tipped toward the shoulder.
Anterocollis - the head and neck are flexed forward.
Retrocollis - the tea and neck are in hyper extension.
Rotational Torticollis - the head rotates in along the longitudinal axis.

Charcot-Marie-Tooth - a genetic disease associated with perineal nerve atrophy resulting in foot drop, stoppage gait and sensory loss along the distribution of the nerve.

Amylotrphic Lateral Sclerosis - a chronic progressive neurological disease of both upper and lower motor neurons. Typically begins as weakness and atrophy in the hands with spasticity and hyperreflexia in the legs without any sensory disturbances.

Chiropractic Principles

Spinal Manipulation dates back to around 2700 BC when Kong-Fou made the first known written account of it being practiced. Spinal Manipulation has been practiced in ancient civilizations from Babylonia to Tibet and central America. Hippocrates, the father of medicine, likely used manipulative therapies. It was Galen that taught his students, "look to the nervous system as the key to maximum health."

<u>Spinal Irritation</u> - Thomas Brown coined the term in 1828. The American Journal of Medical Science printed news about spinal irritation in 1832. J. Evans Riadore wrote 'Irritation of the Spinal Nerves' in 1843 and became the contemporary father of the nerve compression hypothesis.

<u>Propioceptive insult hypothesis</u> - gamma motor gain. Excessive sensory information effects normal function.

<u>Reverberating impulses</u> - Impulse spreads through synapses in self perpetuating cycles.

<u>Histeresis</u> - Deformation caused by rapidly changing forces.

<u>Creep</u> - Deformation caused by continuous forces.

<u>Neuropraxia</u> - a type of peripheral nerve injury, and is known as the mildest form of nerve injury. It is classified as a transient conduction block of motor or sensory function without nerve degeneration, although loss of motor function is the most common finding.

<u>Wallerian Degeneration</u> - is an active process of degeneration that results when a nerve fiber is cut or crushed and the part of the axon distal to the injury degenerates, typically considered permanent.

<u>Bell-Magendie Law</u> - the anterior spinal nerve roots contain motor fibers and the posterior roots contain sensory fibers and both are conducted in only one direction.

<u>Aberrant Motion</u> - includes chaining the axis of motion that results in hypo mobility is some direction and hyper mobility in other directions. Aberrant motion can be described as a segment that is both hypo and hyper-mobile.

Neuropathophysiology - the negative neurological effects of subluxation.

Kinesiopathophysiology - the negative effects of subluxation on motion. The 3 types are hypo-mobility, hyper-mobility and aberrant motion. These effects are directly affected by the chiropractic adjustment.

Myopathology - the negative effects of subluxation on muscle, namely spasm (acute) and atrophy (chronic).

Histopathology - the negative effects of subluxation on cells.

Inflammation - 5 cardinal signs of inflammation; redness, heat, swelling, pain, and loss of function (histopathology). A universal response of the body to protect itself from infection, illness or injury.

Biochemical irritation - subluxation can result in the release of substances the can result from tissue damage; histamines, prostaglandins and kinins.

Pathophysiology - long term negative effects of subluxation on the body (spine) and body systems.

Nerve Tracing - a method used by D.D. Palmer that used palpation from the point of pain to the spine where he would then adjust.

Important People:

Carver - structural model of subluxation and altered biomechanics, pelvic distortion model. The spine adapts to structural stress.

Dejarnette - SOT, CSF flow through the pumping action of the sacrum, pelvic blocking.

Gillet - Fixation Theory of Subluxation, hypomobility and hypermobility, spinal biomechanics, motion palpation.

Gonstead - all subluxations start posterior, disc wedging, hypomobility. Disc theory and seated cervical adjustments.

Hahnemann - father of Homeopathy, treat like with like (disproven).

Hippocrates - father of modern medicine.

Kirkaldi and Willis - nerve root entrapment syndromes.

Illi - (illium) biomechanics of the pelvis, hypermobility, SI joint motion.

Janse - President of National from 1940-1990.

Korr - Segmental Facilitation Theory

Logan - Basic Technique, sacrum is the keystone of the spine. Sacrotuberous ligament.

McMannus - flexion distraction table

Cox - Flexion distraction technique.

B.J. Palmer - The developer of chiropractic, known for the HIO technique and philosophy that focus on adjustments of atlas and axis only based on cord compression theory. Metic Chart, Nerve Tracing, Research

D.D. Palmer - Founder, Discoverer of Chiropractic in 1895 was the first to make short lever adjustments of the spine. Proposed subluxation caused increase/decrease in tone that resulted in disease is the foundation that chiropractic was founded upon (nerve compression theory). Characterized the causes of subluxation as chemical, physical, and emotional.

Hans Selye - General Adaptation Syndrome (GAS) described the body's response to stress in phases alarm, resistance, adaptation, exhaustion. Neuro-immuno-modulation (neurodystrophy).

Dr. C.H Suh - proved the susceptibility of never roots to compression at the University of Boulder Colorado.

Andres Still - founder of osteopath, emphasis on circulatory system, osteopathic lesion.

Junghann - coined the term functional spinal unit as the shortest segment of the spine with will still demonstrate spinal motion(s).

<u>Triano and Luttges et al.</u> - demonstrated that compression (irritation) of spinal nerves in test animals can alter protein composition proximally and distally to the compression.

<u>Sam Weed</u> - named chiropractic.

<u>Langworthy & Smith</u> - wrote the first chiropractic text book.

<u>John Faye</u> - Vertebral Subluxation Complex.

<u>Principles of Chiropractic</u>;

<u>The Major Premise</u> - A universal intelligence exists in all matter continually giving to it all of its properties and actions, thus maintaining it in existence.

<u>The Chiropractor Meaning of Life</u> - the expression of intelligence in matter.

<u>The Triune of Life</u> - Life is trinity of intelligence, force and matter.

<u>The Perfection of the Triune</u> - In order for there to be 100% life, there must be 100% intelligence, 100% force and 100% matter.

<u>Intelligence in Matter</u> - the amount of intelligence for any given amount of matter is 100% and proportional to its requirements.

<u>Function of Intelligence</u> is to create force.

The amount of force created by intelligence is that which unites intelligence and matter.

<u>Function of Force</u> - unite intelligence and matter.

<u>Universal Forces</u> - the forces of universal intelligence are manifested by physical laws. They are unswerving and unadaptive and have no solicitude for the structures (matter?) in which they work.

There can be interference with the transmission of universal forces.

The function of matter is to express force.

Universes Life - Force is manifested by motion in matter, all matter has motion, therefore there is inverses life in all matter.

No motion with the effort of force - Matter can have no motion without the application of force by intelligence.

Intelligence in both Organic and Inorganic Matter - Universal Intelligence gives force to both organic and inorganic matter.

Cause and Effect - Every effect has a cause and every cause an effect.

Evidence of Life - the signs of life are evidence of the intelligence of life.

Organic Matter - the material of the body, of a living thing, is organized matter.

Innate Intelligence - a living this has an inborn intelligence within its body called innate intelligence.

The Mission of Innate Intelligence - To maintain the material of the body of a living thing to active organization.

The Amount of Innate Intelligence - This is 100% of innate intelligence in every living thing, the requisite amount of proportional to its organization.

The Function of Innate Intelligence - To adapt universal forces and matter for use in the body so that all parts of the body will have coordinated action for mutual benefit.

Limits of Adaptation - Innate intelligence adapts forces and matter for the body as long as it can do so without breaking a universal law, or (in other words) innate intelligence is limited by the limitation of matter.

The Character of Innate Forces - the forces of innate intelligence never injure or destroy the structures in which they work.

Comparison of Universal and Innate Forces - in order to carry on the universal cycle of life, universal forces are destructive and innate forces are construction in regards to matter.

Normality of Innate Forces - Innate intelligence is always normal and it its function is always normal.

The Conductors of Innate Influences - the forces of innate intelligence operate through or over the nervous system in animal bodies.

Interference with Innate Forces - There can be interference with the transmission of innate forces.

The Cause of Disease - Interference with the transmission of innate forces causes the incoordination of disease.

Subluxation - interferences with the transmission of information in the body is always directly or indirectly due to subluxation in the spinal column.

The Principle of Coordination - the harmonious action of all the parts of an organism in fulfilling their purpose.

The Law of Demand and Supply - exists in the body in its ideal state, wherein the clearing house is the brain, innate is virtuous banker, brain cells the clerks and the nerve sells the messengers.

Hole in One - proposed by B.J. Palmer, the hypothesis that subluxation and occlusion of a foramen could only occur at atlas or axis. The criteria for his definition of subluxation had 4 elements. (1) misalignment of the vertebra in relationship to adjacent segments. (2) Occlusion of a Foramen. (3) Pressure upon a nerve. (4) Interference with the transmission of the metal impulse.

Axis of Motion - Smith wrote that subluxation alters the axis of motion of a vertebra that results in changes in shape of the spinal canal and IVFs.

Phases of Subluxation Degeneration (3):

1. Segmental Dysfunction - no radiographic signs of degeneration. Decreased range of motion and MRI my show early IVD dehydration.
2. Instability - loss of joint space from articular cartilage degeneration./
3. Stabilization - late state DDD results in ankylosis of the joint(s)

Dentate Ligament Distortion Hypothesis - The dentate ligament connects the spinal cord to the dura mater in such a way to prevent the spinal cord from changing shape in the lateral dimension. The dentate ligament arises out of the pia mater and connects it to the dura mater. CNS irritation is caused by rotation of the vertebral bodies. The average misalignment between the atlas and occiput is 3 degrees putting stress on the dentate ligament causing mechanical tension on the spinal cord. The Spinocerebellar tracts are located at the attachments of the dentate ligaments. Mechanical irritation of the spinocerebellar tracts can cause sharp pain in the pelvic, this is on possible explanation for how an upper-cervical subluxation can produce blowback pain.

Reflex muscle spasm - the result of proprioceptive irritation mediated by motor neurons.

Segmental Facilitation Theory also known as (AKA) Fixation Theory, Segmental Reflex Facilitation, Model of Subluxation Facilitation is characterized as chronic neural dysfunction due to prolonged segmental dysfunction resulting in lowered firing threshold leading to aberrant neural reflexes. Hypomobility of a motor unit in the spine results in hyper mobility of the motor unit above and below hence Segmental Facilitation, excessive sensory input into the cord at the level of involvement from the posterior horn to the lateral horn resulting in hypersympathetic responses (reflexes). Basically a dysfunction motion segment (subluxation) becomes hyper sensitive resulting in an increase of sympathetic activity. Facilitation, irritation, stimulation, excitation, hypertonicity, all mean essentially the same thing in this case. Korr, Gillet, Junghanns,

Key words that indicate Segmental Facilitation Theory; decreased skin resistance, gamma motor gain, Irwin Korr (osteopath), Gillet, aberrant neural or abnormal reflexes, central excitatory state.

Nerve Compression Theory: Decreased action potentials (nerve transmission) due to the compression of a nerve. Subluxation, DJD, Disc, osteophytes and the like can compress a nerve. Direct compression (subluxation) of a nerve alters axoplasmic flow, affecting tone stretching the nerve root and ultimately results in degeneration, or trophic changes in the both the nerve and the muscle it supplies. This is in direct relationship to axoplasmic aberration. The nerve root stretching or compression is important because the nerve root lacks the same protective perineurium that is present in peripheral nerves. If chronic Wallerian Degeneration is possible. Acute signs and symptoms excitation, hyperesthesia, spasm hypersympathetic and hypoparasymathetic. Chronic nerve compression signs and symptoms are basically the opposite; hypesthesia, hyperparasympathetic, hyposympathetic, atonia, paresis.

Key words that indicate Nerve Compression Theory; trophic changes, amplitude of action potentials, axoplasmic aberration, 1st concept of subluxation, Neuropraxin, Wallerian Degeneration, D.D. Palmer.

<u>Cord Compression Theory</u>: Spinal Cord Compression maybe due to ligamentous laxity from conditions such as Rheumatoid Arthritis, Ankylosing Spondylitis, Down's Syndrome or trauma to the upper cervical spine. The upper cervical region is compromised. This theory led to B.J Palmer's development of the HIO technique.

Key word indicating Cord Compression Theory; C1-C2, upper cervical relieves low back pain, central canal stenosis, B.J. Palmer.

<u>Vertebral Subluxation Complex</u>; segmental dysfunction due to postural habits, trauma, infection, degeneration, arthritis, congenital deformity. Dysfunction of the motion segment leads to hyper or hypo mobility resulting in aberrant motion.

<u>Axoplasmic Aberration Theory</u>: Irritation of the nerve root due to subluxation decreases axoplasmic transport of nutrients that result in decreased reflexes and other trophic changes. Caused by compression of the nerve or plexus. This is very similar to Fixation theory. Disrupted active transport of proteins and glycoproteins from the nerve cell body to the synaptic membrane is an example of axoplasmic aberration. Axoplasmic Aberration must include trophic changes. The flow is slow theory.

<u>Vertebrobasilar Artery Insufficiency Theory of Subluxation;</u>
A cervical subluxation compresses the vertebral arteries that cause symptoms to appear when the cervical spine is in extension, extension with rotation or extension with lateral flexion. George's test is used for screening. Symptoms include, vertigo, dizziness, ataxia, nystagmus.

Neurodystrophy Theory; AKA Neuroimmunomodulation:
Nervous System dysfunction results in stress on the body, viscera and related structures. Increased or decreased energy lowers tissue resistance and decreased the immune response.

Key Words for Neurodystrophy; immune system, allergy, lowered or decreased resistance, stress, Selye.

4 Types of Fixations (Gillet)

Type I Muscular - due to chronic involuntary hypertonicity of the muscles. Palpation reveals deep, tight and tender fibers, ROM is restricted with rubbery end block.

Type II Ligamentous - chronically fixated segment with ligamentous shortening. Palpation reveals abrupt hard block end feel with no joint play within a normal range of motion.

Type III Articular (capsular) - A major (primary) fixation due to an intra-articular adhesion. The joint is immobile in all directions and my eventually may become ankylosed.

Type IV Bony - due to exostosis. Palpation reveals free motion to a point with abrupt complete hard arrest, bone to bone, as two hard surfaces meet.

Types of Subluxations (7);

Functional - a minor malposition and/or fixation of joint with normal articular integrity.

Pathological - a malposition and fixation of a joint with deformity caused by degeneration.

Traumatic - external mechanical force caused subluxation.

Reflex - abnormal visceral or somatic reflexes causing abnormal or asymmetrical muscle contraction that results in malposition/fixation.

Defect - congenital anomaly or defect of the spinal or pelvic structures.

Fixation - a hypo-mobile segment that does not contribute to normal motion.

Hyper-mobile - compromised anatomical integrity of a joint as a result of trauma or articular degeneration that results in excessive mobility of a motion segment.

Etiology of Subluxation

Acute Trauma - muscle/tissue damage releases excitatory substances to palms receptors and initiate an inflammatory reaction.

Micro-Trauma - longer duration of repeated traumas of less magnitude or severity that produce alterations of the spinal musculature that are similar to acute trauma.

Postural Compensation - adaptation to minor mechanical faults of support lead to minor dyskinesia and the ranges of motion and minor instability of asymmetry of position may produce spinal muscular effort to self-correct posture. The Proprioceptive sensory awareness to minor structural faults of sectional (segmental) deviation promos para-spinal activity in and attempt to correct the perceived fault.

Biomechanics - alterations in the biomechanics structure can alter muscular efforts (function/action) of the spine that are required for normal spinal function.

Psychological - Mental or emotional stress change the tone of the body and para-spinal musculature.

Neuromuscular Disease - Muscular imbalance, deviations in tone or strength and the proprioceptive alterations of the disease process may alter vertebral position and the quality of motion at that vertebral level initiating pathological reflexes

Secondary Motor Reaction - stimuli or irritation may result in abnormal function of the spinal muscles.

Terms;

<u>Chiropractic Adjustment</u> - The purpose of the chiropractic adjustment is to correct the vertebral subluxation.

<u>Manipulation (Manual Therapy)</u> - attempt to correct or restore motion in a joint and use adjunctive procedures to reduce inflammation.

<u>Vertebral Subluxation Complex (VSC)</u> - the concept that a subluxation is a complex consisting of; kinesiopathology, neuropathophysioilogy, myopathology and histopathology.

<u>Kinesiopathology</u> - disorder or derangement in the normal motion of a joint, articular adhesions. (aberrant motion, hypo/hyper-mobility)

<u>Neuropathophysiology</u> - neural irritation (facilitation) and/or neural inhibition reduce the normal function of neural tissue.

<u>Myopathology</u> - abnormal muscular function as the result of subluxation such as spasm in the acute phase and atrophy if allowed to become chronic.

<u>Histopathology</u> - abnormal motion of joint and irritation or the inhibition of neuronal tissues that can lead to inflammation. Cell damage results in the release of histamines, prostaglandins and kinins that initiate inflammation. This decreases the amount oxygen available to the tissues (hypoxia) that can result in anoxia and finally ischemia.

<u>Nerve Traction</u> - results in conduction block, interference with transmission.

<u>Acute Nerve Compression</u> - irritation results in facilitation, increased excitation.

<u>Chronic Nerve Compression</u> - characterized by inhibition and degeneration.

<u>Posterior Horn (sensory)</u> - is hyper reflexive with acute compression and inhibited with chronic compression. (hyperesthesia, anesthesia)

<u>Anterior Horn (motor)</u> - is hyper reflexive with acute compression (spasm) and inhibited with chronic compression (flaccidity).

<u>Lateral Horn (sympathetics)</u> - is hyper reflexive with acute compression (vaso/bronchodilation) and inhibited with chronic compression (vaso/brochodiliation).

<u>Referred Pain Patterns</u>:
Esophagus - upper back
Heart - can produce left should, arm, hand pain or pressure.
Liver - can produce right neck/shoulder pain.
Duodenum - RUQ and back
Diaphragm - Right Shoulder
Pancreas - in LUQ, produces back pain into the right shoulder.
Appendix - in RLQ, can produce umbilical or epigastric pain.
Kidneys - produces back pain radiating to back or gut.
Colon - RLQ, LLQ, lower back.
Small Intestine - in RLQ produces lower back or peri-umbilical pain.
Spleen - produces pain the left shoulder made worse with breathing.
Gall Bladder - located in RUQ produces pain in Right shoulder (blade).
Ureter - in males ureter pain is referred to the testis.
Bladder - can produce peri-anal and/or inner thigh pain.

<u>Subluxation</u> - is a process not a lesion.

<u>Morphogenic Influence</u> - spinal manipulative therapy (SMT) improves transport and affects end organ health.

<u>Fixation by Adhesion</u> - is a type of fixation (subluxation) that is caused by trauma and/or immobilization.

<u>Fixation by Meniscoid</u> - a type of fixation that is caused by intra-articular tabs of synovium getting trapped inside the joint surfaces.

<u>Nuclear Fixation (Fixation by Nuclear Fragments)</u> - a type of fixation that is caused by the prolapsing of a disc (herniation) with annular fibers that restrict endplate motion.

Mechanical Stress increases intracellular protein metabolism.

Hypersympatheticotonia - the facilitation of the muscle spindles based on the theory of strain and counter strain.

Migraine - a type of headache that produces moderate to sever pain in typically throbbing one side of the head and associated with nausea, weakness, sensitivity to light and/or sound.

Classic Migraine - reoccurring headaches that strike after or at the same time as a sensory disturbance called an aura that indicate to the patient a migraine is either occurring or about to occur. The aura could be visual, tactile or visceral.

Cluster Headaches (histamine headaches) - a series of short but extremely painful headaches every day for weeks or months at a time usually during the spring or fall. These headaches are exacerbated by alcohol. Other AKA include; red migraine, Horton's headache, Cephalalgia, Sphenopalatine Neuralgia.

Brain Tumor - very gradual onset of head pain that is always progressive (getting worse). Other signs of any increased intracranial pressure are possible; papilledema, bradycardia, confusion and disorientation. Motor and sensory changes.

Tension Headache - the most common type of headaches in adults the pain is typically dull, tightness or pressure around the forehead or the back of the head and neck, in a hatband distribution, giving this type of head ache the AKA Hatband Headaches.

Sinus Headache - Infection or inflammation of the sinus(es) produces facial pain between the eyes, under the eyes, in the upper jaw or teeth. Bending forward moves the fluid that has accumulated in the sinus and increases pain. These headaches can last from several hours to a few days.

Sub-Arachnoid Hemorrhage - sudden onset of extreme pain often described as the worst headache ever that is progressive. Stiff neck, increased blood pressure, motor and sensory changes (neurological) vomiting and possible loss of consciousness.

Functional Subluxation - a slight malposition or fixation with normal articular integrity.

Pathological Subluxation - a malposition of a joint where the anatomical structures are deformed by degeneration or disease process.

Traumatic Subluxation - a malposition of a joint due to either external or internal mechanical forces and muscle spasm.

Reflexive Subluxation - an abnormal visceral or somatic reflex causes an abnormal muscle contraction that results in a malposition (fixation).

Fixation - a spinal or pelvic segment who's normal motion is restricted or affects motion of the region.

Defect Subluxation - is due to congenital defects.

Hyper Mobile Subluxation - increased motion of the segment/joint results in malposition of the structures that the join is composed of.

Intervertebral Encroachment Theory - IVF encroachment of the dorsal root ganglia (DRG) results in the release of substance P destroying the disc.

Substance P - a compound that is thought to be involved with synaptic transmission of pain, it is a polypeptide with eleven amino acid residues. That means it is acidic (11 amino ACIDS) and contributes to degeneration of the disc. Substance P will inhibit pain the CNS and stimulate pain in the PNS.

Doral Root Ganglia (DRG) - the neurological structure that is the most sensitive too compression. AKA, spinal ganglion, posterior root ganglion is a cluster of cluster of cell bodies of first order sensory neurons.

Bone Pain - deep boring pain that is localized and constant and unrelated to rest or activity that maybe worse at night.

Muscle (Somatic) Pain - often described as dull, achey, diffuse pain that is difficult to localize and can be aggravated with activity and relieved by rest.

Nerve Root Pain - sharp, shoot, sever pain that radiates and follows the distribution of a nerve or dermatome.

Radiculo - involving the nerve root, radiculopathy.

Radiating - pain along a nerve.

Vascular Pain - diffuse, poorly defined ashiness that is throbbing and may feel like a heaviness.

Causealgia - sever burning pain in a limb cased by injury to a peripheral nerve.

Thalamic Pain (Dejenrine Roussy Syndrome) - a vague unpleasant feeling that can persist after a stroke on the contralateral side of the lesion that can be aggravated by mental stress.

Visceral Pain - diffuse poorly defined pain that maybe described as cutting or burning visceral pain is commonly referred from the organ to an anatomical structure innervated by the same nerve. Visceral pain is often associated with additional symptoms such as nausea or pallor.

Arthritic Pain - is deep pain that increased with activity or position and decreases with rest and/or changing position.

Sclerotogenous (Sclerotomal) Pain - musculoskeletal injury that does not involve a nerve will be dull, achy, poorly defined but arising from deep structures of the body.

Spinous Process (SP) Movement;

Cervical - the SP moves away from the side of rotation and toward the convexity with lateral flection.

Lumbar - the SP moves toward the side of rotation and into the convexity with lateral flexion.

Cervical Muscles - move the head and neck, suspend the shoulder girdle, suspend, fix and elevate the thoracic outlet.

Afferent - sensory information (impulses) from the periphery to the posterior form of the spinal cord. (posterior horn)

Efferent - motor information that emanates from the anterior horn of the spinal cord to the periphery.

Bone - protect and support the frame of the body.
Muscle - voluntarily and involuntarily moves the joints.

Ligaments - hold bones (vertebrae) together.

Facet Joints - guide motion in regions of the spine.

Cervical Facet Joints - 45 degree angle to eat horizontal plane, and 0 degrees to the coronal plane allows flexion, extension, lateral flexion and rotation of the cervical spine.

Thoracic Facet Joints - 60 degrees to the horizontal plane and 20 degree to the coronal place allows flexion and extension of the spine but restricts intersegmental flexion, extension and rotation.

Lumbar Facet Joints - Perpendicular to the horizontal plane and at a 45 degree angle to the coronal plane allow for flexion and extension but limits intersegmental flexion, extension and rotations.

Intervertebral Disc (IVD) - acts as a fulcrum of motion for the function spinal unit and function as a shock absorber for the rest of the spine. Form a symphysis joint and are avascular. The IVD taken in nutrients and removes waste by a process of nutritive imbibition (drinking). Healthy adolescent dis is approximately 80% water.

Circumferential Tears - damage to the outer layer of a IVD are often the first stage of the degeneration of a disc.

Radial Tears - damage though the outer fibers of the IDVt hat allow the nucleus to protrude or escape from the annulus fibers.

Nerve Root (spinal) - nerve fiber bundles that come off the cord and exit at each corresponding spinal segment to all parts of the body. Nerve roots are covered by dura mater and susceptible to the effects of compression. A peripheral nerve (outside the IVF) is covered by epineurium and perineurium and not susceptible to compression.

10 mm Hg pressure applied to 2.5 mm of nerve root results in a number of fibers becoming non-conductive (blocked). After 15 minutes there is a 25% decrease in nerve conduction and after 30 minutes a 50% decrease.

Causalgia - Pain along distribution of a peripheral nerve.

Recurrent Meningeal Nerve (Sinuvertebral Nerve) - does NOT innervate the ALL and is the meningeal branch of a spinal nerve that innervate the facet joints, the annulus fibers of the IVD and the ligaments and periosteum of the spinal canal. AKA Recurrent nerves of Luschka.

Creep - viscoelastic material deforms with time as it is subjected to constant, suddenly applied lead, such as weight lifting.

Lesion - Osteopathic equivalent of the subluxation.

Nutation and counter-nutation - are the motions of the sacrum. As one side nutates (moves anterior and inferior) the other side counter-nutates (moves posterior and superior).

Ankylosis - the fusion of bones across a joint,

Neuralgia - Pain along the course of a nerve.

Neuropraxia - the mildest form of nerve injury, typically occurs in the PNS as a result of blunt force trauma that results in transient loss of conduction without degeneration. Temporary loss of function is the most common finding.

Neuritis - Inflammation of nerve with pain, paresthesia or anesthesia, paralysis, diminished reflexes.

Radiculitis - Inflammation of a spinal nerve root, dermatomal, sharp pain.

Facilitation - increased afferent stimulation decreases synaptic threshold leading to a hyperactive response.

Postural Muscles - are involuntary muscle.

Vertebral Artery - Transmits the transverse foramen from C2 to C6.

Axis (C2) - has 7 ossification centers, 5 primary and 2 secondary.

Alar Ligament - restricts rotation and lateral bending
Apical Ligament - Top of the dens.

Cruciate Ligament - formed by the apical and transverse ligament combining.

Transverse Ligament - limits flexion and extension in the upper cervical region.

The upper cervical joint complex has no disc to limit motion or act as a fulcrum and there is little in the way of a boney locking mechanism to prevent motion.

50% of cervical spine rotation occurs at between atlas and axis.

Flava Ligament, Ligamentum Flava - yellow elastic tissue, less elastin compared to other ligaments.

Motion Segment - any two vertebrae and the intervertebral disc that connects them and related anatomy is the function unit of the spine.

Anterior Motion Segment - the vertebral bodies and disc that are responsible for weight bearing.

Posterior Motion Segment - the articular facets, mechanoreceptors and nociceptors that guide directional motion.

Borders of the Intereveretebral Foramen (IVF) - Posterior boarder is the facet joint. The anterior boarder is the intervertebral disc (IVD) and the posterior aspect of the vertebral body. The normal shape of the IVF is elliptical (bean) shaped.

The normal motions lateral flexion, extension, and rotation will decrease the size of the IVF by up to 33% in the cervical & lumbar regions of the spine.

Contents of the IVF – 30-50% is the nerve root. The rest is lymphatic channels, the spinal segmental artery and vein, adipose tissue and transforaminal ligaments that prevent the nerve root from moving freely in IVF.

Facets - interlocking joints that guide directional motion.

Ligaments - limit the amount of motion.

Steele's Rule of Thirds - The spinal canal at C1 is 1/3 odontoid, 1/3 spinal cord and 1/3 protective fat or fluid (CSF).

Visual Analog Scale - used to quantify the pain of subluxation.

Sclerotogenous Pain - results from injury to the facet or SI joints is usually dull in natural and poorly localized.

Trophic - related to nutrition or growth.

Somatic - referring to the body (soma) skin, bone, nerve and muscle.

Viscera or visceral - related to the organs, blood or lymph.

Dermatogenous Pain - results from nerve root compression or irritation the pain is usually sharp or burning and follows the course of a dermatome, radicular pain.

Bradykinin - released from damaged muscle sensitizing nociceptors. (inflammation)

C Fibers - small, slow non-myelinated nerves that carry the pain message.

Hysteresis - tissue changes (deformity) and the loss of energy to heat during a *cycle of loading and unloading.*

Hyperemia - excess blood in vessels supplying a region of the body.

Meniscoid - intra-articular synovial tabs that may prevent full range of motion in the joint.

Normal thoracic Kyphotic curve is due to slight wedging of the Thoracic vertebral bodies.

Typical thoracic vertebra has <u>ten synovial articular surfaces</u>.

Chief function of the anterior portion of the motion segment is <u>weight bearing</u> (vertebral body).
The weakest aspect of the vertebral motion segment during axial compression is the end plate.

C7 nerve root involved in both flexion of the wrist and extension of the elbow. (7 Carat ring, a woman will flex her wrist and extend her elbow to show off her 7 carat ring)

<u>Uncinate process</u> - are found in the Mid cervical region. (C3/C7)

C5 - C6 Segment has the steepest disc plane angle.

<u>Posterior Longitudinal Ligament (PLL)</u> - is least resistance to tensile strength because it is "stretchy."

<u>Anterior Longitudinal Ligament (ALL)</u> - the thickest, strongest spinal ligament that is the most restrictive to motion as it limits extension, rotation and lateral flexion of the spine.

Dorsal Colum lesion produces akinesthesia of a lower extremity.

Dorsal Scapular Nerve innervates the rhomboids.

Gag Reflex Tests Cranial Nerve X (10)

<u>S</u>erratus <u>A</u>nerior is innervated by the <u>L</u>ong <u>T</u>horacic Nerve (SALT).

Greater occipital neuralgia associated with spasm of splenius capitus muscle(s).

Waddling gait indicates Duchenne's Muscular Dystrophy.

ALS (Lou Gehrig's Dx) first presents in the hands.

Golgi Tendon Organ (GTO) - muscle receptor stimulated by tension or passive stretch of the muscle tendon. Afferent supply from large type A nerve fibers.

Nociceptor - Pain receptor.

Proprioceptor - kinesthetic receptors near the facets that indicate the position of the joints in the spine. Receptor types include; complex nerve endings and free nerve endings.

Free Nerve Endings - unspecialized afferent nerve fiber that synapses with a sensory neuron most commonly cutaneous nociceptors.

Pacinian corpuscles - mechanoreceptor responsible for detection of pressure and vibration.

Ruffini endings - mechanoreceptor detects touch, pressure, vibration and the sensation fo stretch in the skin, sustained pressure on the skin and heat. The temperature receptor.

Muscle Spindle - stretch receptor in muscle supplied by large type A afferent nerve fibers.

Myelopathy - injury to the spinal cord due to compression.

Parasympathetics - CN's 3,7,9,10 and Sacral nerves S2,S3 and S4.

Autonomic Nervous System - is composed of both the sympathetic and parasympathetic nervous systems.

Sympathetic Nervous System - is located in the lateral form of the spinal cord from T1-L1(L2) giving it the name Thoracolumbar Nervous System. AKA the Fight or Flight response which includes; bronchodilation, vasoconstriction, pale skin, tachycardia, and increased sweating.

Parasympathetic Nervous System - is located in or composed of cranial nerves 3,7,9 and 10 as well as Sacral nerves, 2,3 and 4 giving it the name CraniaSacral Nervous System, AKA the Feed and Breed response. Actions include, urination, defecation, eating, sexual activity, increased peristalsis, bradycardia and increased blood flow to organs.

Axoplasmic Flow - can move toward the cell body, retrograde or away from the cell body or anterograde.

Anterograde axoplasmic flow moves forward from the cell body to the terminal. This is the most common and fastest type of axoplasmic flow involved with nerve growth and other trophic mechanisms.

Retrograde axoplasmic flow moves from the terminal toward the cell body, is less common and slower than anterograde.

Goals of the Chiropractic Adjustment is to break up adhesions, increase mobility (motion), increase mechanoreceptor stimulation closing the pain gate and restoring optimum neurological function and inhibit Alpha Motor Neurons.

Alpha Motor Neuron - large multipolar lower motor neurons of the brainstem and spinal cord that innervate extrafusal muscle fibers.

Plum Line Analysis aka Lateral Plum Line analysis - imaginary line that is expected to fall from the external auditory meatus centrally through the shoulder, center of the hip, just posterior of the patella and anterior to the lateral malleolus. Some sources include the plum line passing through the anterior body of C7 and the anterior third of the sacral base.

Physiological Laws;

Wolff's Law - bone grows and remodels according to the stress placed up that bone.

Hilton's Law - The nerve root that supplies a joint will also supply the muscle acting on that joint and the skin surrounding it.

Heuter-Volkmann Law - increased epiphyseal pressure lead to decreased growth and decreased pressure increases growth.

Starling's Law - the stroke volume of the hearty increases in response to the increase in the volume of blood in the ventricles before contraction while other factors remain constant.

<u>Bell-Magendie Law</u> - Anterior horn is motor, posterior horn is sensory.

<u>LaPlace's Law</u> - the larger radius of a vessel the larger the wall tension required to withstand the internal pressure of the fluid it transmits.

<u>Landmarks</u>

<u>C1 (Atlas) Transverse Process</u> - Anterior and inferior to the mastoid process.

<u>Styloid Process</u> - Deeper and anterior to the atlas transverse process.

<u>C2 (Axis)</u> - The first palpable spinous process.

<u>C3</u> - Hyoid Bone

<u>C4/C5</u> - Thyroid

<u>C6</u> - Cricoid, Carotid Tubercle, Last moveable spinous

<u>C7</u> - Vertebral Prominens

<u>T3</u> - Scapular Spine

<u>T5</u> - Sternal Angle

<u>T6</u> - Inferior Scapular Angle recumbent

<u>T7</u> - Inferior Scapular Angle erect (7 up)

<u>L4</u> - Iliac Crest

<u>S2</u> - Posterior Superior Iliac Spine (PSIS)

<u>S4</u> - Posterior Inferior Iliac Spine (PIIS)

Basic Metic Chart:

C1 - global effects

C2/3 - Tonsils, optic nerve, tongue, outer ear, teeth

C4 - eustachian tube, mouth, nose, lips.

C5 - pharynx, larynx, vocal cords

C6 - muscles of the neck and shoulders

C7 - Thyroid gland

T1-4 - Heart and Lungs

T4 - Gallbladder

T5-9 - Stomach

T6-10 - Liver and Pancreas

T9 - Adrenal glands

T10-12 - Kidneys

L1 - Colon

L1/2 - Colon, Ovaries

L3 - Sex organs, Urinary bladder

L4 - Prostate, Sciatic nerve.

L5 - lower leg, ankles, feet and toes.

Sacrum - Uterus, Colon.

Coccyx - rectum, anus

Pilomotor Responce (reflex) - involuntary erection of the hairs on the neck and/or arms that can be caused by cold, excitement or fear.

Sudomotor Responce (reflex) - stimulation of the sweat glands by sympathetic nerve system by activation of muscarinic acetylcholine receptors.

Pelvic Splanchnic Nerves -

Preganglionic fibers (Sympathetics) - white rami communicans, run from anterior nerve root to the sympathetic ganglionic chain located laterally to the vertebral body from the skull to the coccyx. They are cholinergic myelinated fibers.

Preganglionic fibers (Parasympathetics) - run from the CNS to ganglia located on or near the organs they supply. They are cholinergic myelinated fibers.

Cholinergic - acetylcholine is their neurotransmitter.

Postganglionic fibers (Sympathetics) - gray rami communicans, from the sympathetic chain ganglia to the organs they supply. They are unmyelinated and adrenergic.

Adrenergic (noradrenalin) - norepinephrine is their neurotransmitter.

Postganglionic fibers (Parasympathetics) - from the parasympathetic or autonomic ganglia to the organ and are cholinergic.

Planes of motion: Sagittal = flexion/extension, Transverse = rotation, Coronal = lateral flexion

Axis of motion:
X axis = flexion/extension	+X = flexion	-X = extension
Y-axis = rotation	+Y = left rotation	-Y = right rotation
Z-axis = lateral flexion	+Z = right lat. flexion	-Z = left lat. flexion

Spinous (body) motion - Cervical and upper Thoracic spinous processes rotate to the convexity and the body to concavity. The lower thoracic and lumbar spinous processes rotates to concavity and the body to convexity.

Motor evaluation - Grade motor strength (0-5)
- 5 = full ROM with resistance, normal
- 4 = full ROM with some resistance, good
- 3 = full ROM with gravity, fair
- 2 = ROM present without gravity
- 1 = no ROM, traceable, palpable contraction
- 0 = no ROM, no traceable, palpable contraction, no joint motion

Grade reflexes (0-5)
- 0 - absent
- 1+ - hypoactive
- 2+ - normal
- 3+ - hyperactive
- 4+ - hyperactive with transient clonus
- 5+ - hyperactive with sustained clonus

Reflexes; Achilles (S1), Patellar (L4), Brachioradialis (C6), Triceps (C7), Biceps C5-C6.

Babinski's
- pathological reflex indicating UMNL presents with Ankle clonus and dorsiflex of the ankle.

Dermatomes

Cervical spine;
- C1 - none
- C2 - above occiput
- C3 - below occiput
- C4 - nape of neck
- C5 - lateral brachium
- C6 - lateral antebrachium, thumb, 1st finger
- C7 - middle finger
- C8 - medial antebrachium, 4th & 5th fingers

<u>Thoracic spine</u>;
T1 - medial brachium
T4 - nipple
T7 - xiphoid process
T10 - umbilicus
T12 - above inguinal crease

<u>Lumbar spine</u>:
L1 - below inguinal crease
L4 - medial leg to foot and big toe
L5 - dorsum of foot
S1 - lateral leg and foot

You got this. It is just a test. One that if need be you can take again. Breath, relax and enjoy the experience. The people you are surrounded by now will mean more to you than the answer to any board question. Life is a journey not a destination and right now you are surrounded by traveling companions that have shared this wonderful moment in your each others lives. Soon your paths will diverge but your journey will remain remarkably similar making these relationship particularly meaningful. Taking board exams can be stressful. You have put in the work, gone the extra mile and you will pass. Now take a moment to enjoy the people and experience of being a chiropractic student. Before you know it school and this moment of your life will be in the past. Good luck.

Made in the USA
Monee, IL
10 November 2024

69794187R00142